THE BIG BOOK OF BASEBALL STORIES

THE BIG BOOK OF BASEBALL STORIES

Timeless and Compelling Tales of Our National Game

EDITED AND WITH AN INTRODUCTION BY

JEFF SILVERMAN

LYONS
PRESS

Essex, Connecticut

An imprint of The Globe Pequot Publishing Group, Inc.
64 South Main Street
Essex, CT 06426
www.globepequot.com

Distributed by NATIONAL BOOK NETWORK

British Library Cataloguing in Publication Information available

Library of Congress Cataloging-in-Publication Data
Names: Silverman, Jeff, 1950– editor.
Title: The big book of baseball stories : timeless and compelling tales of our national game / edited by Jeff Silverman.
Description: Essex, Connecticut : Lyons Press, [2024] | Series: Jumbo story collections
Identifiers: LCCN 2024006430 (print) | LCCN 2024006431 (ebook) | ISBN 9781493086207 (trade paperback ; acid-free paper) | ISBN 9781493086214 (epub)
Subjects: LCSH: Baseball stories, American. | Baseball—United States—Anecdotes.
Classification: LCC PS648.B37 B38 2024 (print) | LCC PS648.B37 (ebook) | DDC 813/.0108355—dc23/eng/20240520
LC record available at https://lccn.loc.gov/2024006430
LC ebook record available at https://lccn.loc.gov/2024006431

Baseball . . . well—it's our game: that's the chief fact in connection with it: America's game: has the snap, go, fling, of the American atmosphere—belongs as much to our institutions, fits into them as significantly, as our constitutions, laws: is just as important in the sum total of our historic life.

—WALT WHITMAN

I enjoy a good game of baseball.

—MARK TWAIN

I know of no subject, save perhaps baseball, on which the average American newspaper, even in the larger cities, discourses with unfailing sense and understanding.

—H. L. MENCKEN

Contents

CONTENTS

INTRODUCTION

So what's the essential quality that gives long life to a baseball story? Let's touch base for a moment with America's *other* national pastime: the movies.

Every year, the American Film Institute hands out a Life Achievement Award to an honoree whose work—so the AFI's solons assure us—has stood or will stand the test of time. What a nice sound—the test of time—and what an exacting criterion. To satisfy it, the work must certainly have legs, like Cobb and Brock and Ricky Henderson; personality, like Ruth and Stengel and Griffey Jr.; power, like Pujols and the Big Train; craft, like Koufax and Mathewson; grace, like DiMaggio, Williams, and Mays; courage, like Robinson and Aaron; durability, like Ripken and Ryan; and character, like Clemente, Gehrig, Jeter, and Gwynn. As commendable, individually, as these qualities certainly are, they need more than themselves alone to pass the test; each needs at least a touch of the other. To survive and be remembered is, in short, a tall order.

Each of the tales—the fictions and the facts—that makes up *The Big Book of Baseball Stories* has, minus the finale, stood this test of time. They satisfy the most readily measured threshold—legs—with ease. Each—except the last—is at least a century old. They gave voice to a game before the movies realized they had any voice at all. They come from a time when Cobb and Speaker were hitting .400; when Johnson and Matty were mowing 'em down; and when artists such as Chaplin and Keaton were taking cuts and making cuts, inventing, as they went along, the grammar of the movies frame by frame.

It was a good time for invention, those days, and in their own way, writers such as Ring Lardner, Damon Runyon, Grantland Rice, Zane

Grey (yes, *that* Zane Grey, a helluva college outfielder, by the way), Charles Van Loan, Gerald Beaumont, Charley Dryden, John Kieran, Hugh Fullerton, Fred Lieb, and even P. G. Wodehouse (more associated with a golf ball than one of horsehide stitched together) were, as well, busy making up the language and syntax of the baseball story as they went along. With their pens and typewriters, they would teach us a new way of seeing and experiencing America's game; reaching into its heart, they pulled out what would become the ever more sophisticated language of baseball on the page.

There's wizardry in that accomplishment to be sure, and the best way to fall under its spell is to continue reading what they batted out. Granted, some of their words and phrases and idioms feel dated—what *doesn't* after a hundred years or so of service—but that hardly matters because what they discovered about the game and its hold over us—fans and players alike—is as fresh and excited as a busher's face the first time he puts his major league flannels on. Keaton and Chaplin are still funny; so are Lardner and Wodehouse. They're old, sure, but their bones don't creak. What they've set down remains energetic and bright, keenly observed and keenly wrought. All these decades later, the words continue to tingle.

Of course, when you understand human nature and baseball nature—as these writers did—the work doesn't really age, just the paper it's printed on. New generations may find more dazzling or sophisticated ways to say things, as new generations of filmmakers keep upping the ante on their special effects, but is what they're revealing to us about who we are any sharper, clearer, more incisive or passionate? A home run is a home run whenever it's hit.

Let me suggest one more connection that ties the early days of baseball writing to the early days of motion pictures: there's a history, memory, and sheer enjoyment that's lost when we fail to preserve and keep contact with the legacy handed down to us.

Half a lifetime ago, when I had jumped ship from the newspaper game to become a rookie screenwriter working in Hollywood, I became friends with an older writer–director named Richard Brooks. In the late 1950s, he created one of the most memorable on-screen fires in his

Oscar-winning adaptation of *Elmer Gantry*. Since the blazing tabernacle scene climaxing the movie would be shot indoors on a soundstage, every inch of the set had been treated with heavy fire retardant before the cameras rolled. Starting a fire twenty thousand leagues under the sea would have been a snap by comparison.

Naturally, Brooks's crew couldn't get the flames to go, so Brooks asked the fire marshal on set what to do. The answer stunned the filmmaker. The fire marshal told Brooks to raid the studio vault, pull out as many old cans of the silent movies stored inside as he could, then coat the set with their contents. "Are you mad?" Brooks, a noted rager, raged. "That's the heritage of our craft." The fire marshal shook his head sadly. He knew that. But he also knew that no one had put much thought into how best to preserve it. When Brooks opened those precious cans of ancient history, what he mostly found was highly combustible silver nitrate powder; the old film had decomposed as badly as a forgotten corpse. Brooks spread it around the set, and as the past exploded around him, a remarkable movie moment rose from its ash. Still, what was lost in those cans remains lost forever, and no one could have saved it.

Thankfully, baseball's past has been better preserved in archives and libraries from coast to coast. But preserving the past isn't enough. These stories aren't just museum pieces; they live with the spirits of their creators and the spirit of the game. Now and again, they need to come out, stretch their muscles, and show off just how good they are. For them. And for us.

In collecting these stories, I feel honored by the chance to dust off some deserving old warhorses—familiar ones, such as "Alibi Ike," and the deliciously arcane, such as the account of Lizzie Arlington's first professional outing—insert them into a new lineup, and send them up for another cut. I have no doubt they'll connect—with that part inside every fan that dies a little bit each October only to be reborn again in the spring.

One final note about the presentation of the stories. Each arrives with its own introduction, in part to give the piece proper context and in part to give the writer his—or her—due. Not every writer in this book is as familiar as, say, Walt Whitman and Mark Twain, but each added a few worthwhile words and significant observations to baseball's long and continuing conversation. Who they were has earned at least a few moments of our time to consider their achievement. Who they were helps us appreciate what they wrote.

Jeff Silverman
Chadds Ford, Pennsylvania
January 2024

Who's on First?

Who's on First?

Abbott and Costello

Who's up first?

"*Who's on First?*"

Who wrote it?

"*Who's on First?*"

Yeah.

"*Who?*"

That's what I'm asking.

"*I don't know.*"

Third base . . .

Peel the comic genius from this most famous of all comedy baseball routines, and the question's not "Who's on First?" but who first pitched it. Like so much of what took root in the oral traditions of vaudeville, "Who's on First?" evolved over time. While other teams performed it, it's now impossible to hear voices other than Bud Abbott's and Lou Costello's playing pepper with its patter. For full effect, it begs to be heard—sorry, *Baseball Stories* doesn't come with a CD—but even when it enters through the eyes instead of the ears, it's amazingly funny.

Abbott and Costello regularly tinkered with the piece, particularly the opening, which they'd adjust to fit the demands of their audience. The version presented here aired in the mid-1940s on a baseball-themed episode of Abbott and Costello's radio show built around the Yankees. It begins with Lou called up to the club's roster with Bud coming along as coach to keep him in line.

ABBOTT: Well, Costello, I'm going to New York with you. The Yankees' manager, Bucky Harris, gave me a job as coach for as long as you're on the team.

COSTELLO: Look, Abbott, if you're the coach, you must know all the players.

ABBOTT: I certainly do.

COSTELLO: Well, you know I've never met the guys. So you'll have to tell me their names, and then I'll know who's playing on the team.

ABBOTT: Oh, I'll tell you their names, but, you know, it seems to me they give these ball players now-a-days very peculiar names.

COSTELLO: You mean funny names?

ABBOTT: Strange names, pet names . . . like Dizzy Dean . . .

COSTELLO: His brother Daffy . . .

ABBOTT: Daffy Dean . . .

COSTELLO: And their French cousin.

ABBOTT: French?

COSTELLO: Goofé.

ABBOTT: Goofé Dean. Well, let's see, we have on the bags, Who's on first, What's on second, I Don't Know is on third . . .

COSTELLO: That's what I want to find out.

ABBOTT: I say Who's on first, What's on second, I Don't Know's on third.

COSTELLO: Are you the manager?

ABBOTT: Yes.

COSTELLO: You gonna be the coach too?

ABBOTT: Yes.

COSTELLO: And you don't know the fellows' names.

ABBOTT: Well, I should.

COSTELLO: Well then who's on first?

ABBOTT: Yes.

COSTELLO: I mean the fellow's name.

ABBOTT: Who.

COSTELLO: The guy on first.

ABBOTT: Who.

COSTELLO: The first baseman.

ABBOTT: Who.

COSTELLO: The guy playing . . .

ABBOTT: Who is on first!

COSTELLO: I'm asking you who's on first.

ABBOTT: That's the man's name.

COSTELLO: That's who's name?

ABBOTT: Yes.

COSTELLO: Well go ahead and tell me.

ABBOTT: That's it.

COSTELLO: That's who?

ABBOTT: Yes.

PAUSE.

COSTELLO: Look, you gotta first baseman?

ABBOTT: Certainly.

COSTELLO: Who's playing first?

ABBOTT: That's right.

COSTELLO: When you pay off the first baseman every month, who gets the money?

ABBOTT: Every dollar of it.

THE BIG BOOK OF BASEBALL STORIES

COSTELLO: All I'm trying to find out is the fellow's name on first base.

ABBOTT: Who.

COSTELLO: The guy that gets . . .

ABBOTT: That's it.

COSTELLO: Who gets the money . . .

ABBOTT: He does, every dollar of it. Sometimes his wife comes down and collects it.

COSTELLO: Who's wife?

ABBOTT: Yes.

PAUSE.

ABBOTT: What's wrong with that?

COSTELLO: All I wanna know is when you sign up the first baseman, how does he sign his name?

ABBOTT: Who.

COSTELLO: The guy.

ABBOTT: Who.

COSTELLO: How does he sign . . .

ABBOTT: That's how he signs it.

COSTELLO: Who?

ABBOTT: Yes.

PAUSE.

COSTELLO: All I'm trying to find out is what's the guy's name on first base.

ABBOTT: No. What is on second base.

COSTELLO: I'm not asking you who's on second.

ABBOTT: Who's on first.

COSTELLO: One base at a time!

ABBOTT: Well, don't change the players around.

COSTELLO: I'm not changing nobody!

6

ABBOTT: Take it easy, buddy.

COSTELLO: I'm only asking you, who's the guy on first base?

ABBOTT: That's right.

COSTELLO: Okay.

ABBOTT: All right.

PAUSE.

COSTELLO: What's the guy's name on first base?

ABBOTT: No. What is on second.

COSTELLO: I'm not asking you who's on second.

ABBOTT: Who's on first.

COSTELLO: I don't know.

ABBOTT: He's on third, we're not talking about him.

COSTELLO: Now how did I get on third base?

ABBOTT: Why, you mentioned his name.

COSTELLO: If I mentioned the third baseman's name, who did I say is playing third?

ABBOTT: No. Who's playing first.

COSTELLO: What's on first base?

ABBOTT: What's on second.

COSTELLO: I don't know.

ABBOTT: He's on third.

COSTELLO: There I go, back on third again!

PAUSE.

COSTELLO: Would you just stay on third base and don't go off it.

ABBOTT: All right, what do you want to know?

COSTELLO: Now who's playing third base?

ABBOTT: Why do you insist on putting Who on third base?

COSTELLO: What am I putting on third.

ABBOTT: No. What is on second.

COSTELLO: You don't want who on second?

ABBOTT: Who is on first.

COSTELLO: I don't know.

TOGETHER: Third base!

PAUSE.

COSTELLO: Look, you gotta outfield?

ABBOTT: Sure.

COSTELLO: The left fielder's name?

ABBOTT: Why.

COSTELLO: I just thought I'd ask you.

ABBOTT: Well, I just thought I'd tell ya.

COSTELLO: Then tell me who's playing left field.

ABBOTT: Who's playing first.

COSTELLO: I'm not . . . stay out of the infield!!! I want to know what's the guy's name in left field?

ABBOTT: No, What is on second.

COSTELLO: I'm not asking you who's on second.

ABBOTT: Who's on first!

COSTELLO: I don't know.

TOGETHER: Third base!

PAUSE.

COSTELLO: The left fielder's name?

ABBOTT: Why.

COSTELLO: Because!

ABBOTT: Oh, he's center field.

PAUSE.

COSTELLO: Look, you gotta pitcher on this team?

ABBOTT: Sure.

COSTELLO: The pitcher's name?

ABBOTT: Tomorrow.

COSTELLO: You don't want to tell me today?

ABBOTT: I'm telling you now.

COSTELLO: Then go ahead.

ABBOTT: Tomorrow!

COSTELLO: What time?

ABBOTT: What time what?

COSTELLO: What time tomorrow are you gonna tell me who's pitching?

ABBOTT: Now listen. Who is not pitching.

COSTELLO: I'll break your arm if you say who's on first!!! I want to know what's the pitcher's name?

ABBOTT: What's on second.

COSTELLO: I don't know.

TOGETHER: Third base!

PAUSE.

COSTELLO: Gotta catcher?

ABBOTT: Certainly.

COSTELLO: The catcher's name?

ABBOTT: Today.

COSTELLO: Today, and tomorrow's pitching.

ABBOTT: Now you've got it.

COSTELLO: All we got is a couple of days on the team.

PAUSE.

COSTELLO: You know I'm a catcher too.

ABBOTT: So they tell me.

COSTELLO: I get behind the plate to do some fancy catching, Tomorrow's pitching on my team and a heavy hitter gets up. Now the heavy hitter bunts the ball. When he bunts the ball, me, being a good catcher, I'm gonna throw the guy out at first. So I pick up the ball and throw it to who?

ABBOTT: Now that's the first thing you've said right.

COSTELLO: I don't even know what I'm talking about!

PAUSE.

ABBOTT: That's all you have to do.

COSTELLO: Is to throw the ball to first base.

ABBOTT: Yes!

COSTELLO: Now who's got it?

ABBOTT: Naturally.

PAUSE.

COSTELLO: Look, if I throw the ball to first base, somebody's gotta get it. Now who has it?

ABBOTT: Naturally.

COSTELLO: Who?

ABBOTT: Naturally.

COSTELLO: Naturally?

ABBOTT: Naturally.

COSTELLO: So I pick up the ball and I throw it to Naturally.

ABBOTT: No you don't. You throw the ball to Who.

COSTELLO: Naturally.

ABBOTT: That's different.

COSTELLO: That's what I said.

ABBOTT: You're not saying it . . .

COSTELLO: I throw the ball to Naturally.

ABBOTT: You throw it to Who.

COSTELLO: Naturally.

ABBOTT: That's it.

COSTELLO: That's what I said!

ABBOTT: You ask me.

COSTELLO: I throw the ball to who?

ABBOTT: Naturally.

COSTELLO: Now you ask me.

ABBOTT: You throw the ball to Who?

COSTELLO: Naturally.

ABBOTT: That's it.

COSTELLO: Same as you! Same as YOU!!! I throw the ball to who. Whoever it is drops the ball and the guy runs to second. Who picks up the ball and throws it to What. What throws it to I Don't Know. I Don't Know throws it back to Tomorrow, triple play. Another guy gets up and hits a long fly ball to Because. Why? I don't know! He's on third and I don't give a darn!

ABBOTT: What?

COSTELLO: I said, "I don't give a darn!"

ABBOTT: Oh, that's our shortstop.

O, Baseball! My Baseball!

O, Baseball! My Baseball!

Walt Whitman

HOW FITTING THAT WALT WHITMAN (1819–1892), THE POETIC prophet of American promise and potential, would have embraced what he saw, even in the game's adolescence, something that would emerge into the sporting representation of the vibrant, young nation he sung of so passionately. "The game of ball is glorious," he enthused in an 1846 report for the *Brooklyn Eagle*; nine years later, he found a way to weave "a good game of base-ball" into the first edition of *Leaves of Grass*. Baseball captivated Whitman throughout his life. "I still find my interest in the game unabated," he underscored decades later. "I can't forget the games we used to go to . . . they are precious memories."

No surprise then that newspaper reports of the major league's first world tour of 1888–1889 had Whitman in their thrall. By spreading the game, the players—in his view—were also spreading the American spirit with every pitch, every hit, every catch, and every throw. "How I'd like to meet them," the old reporter in him noted to a friend, "talk with them. Maybe ask some questions." When the friend characterized baseball as "the hurrah game of the republic," Whitman welcomed the idea with glee. "That's beautiful," he howled with laughter, "the hurrah game! Well—it's our game: that's the chief fact in connection with it: America's game: has the snap, go, fling, of the American atmosphere—belongs as much to our institutions, fits into them as significantly, as our constitutions, laws: is just as important in the sum total of our historic life."

Oh my . . .

Given Whitman's grasp of the game's great hold on the American imagination as it evolved into the national pastime, it's somehow heartening that to the usual roles we ascribe to him—bard, journalist, and essayist extraordinaire—we can also attach baseball beat reporter—at least for one day. On June 18, 1858, the *Brooklyn Daily Times*—which he happened to then edit—ran this unsigned, but sung by himself, account of a matchup between the mighty Atlantics and the Putnams. Beat reporting might not have been Whitman's métier; he omitted the final score—17–13, Atlantics—though in his defense, it did appear prominently in the primitive box score accompanying his narrative. His spelling wasn't that hot either: The "Pierce" in the story actually turned out to be "Pearce"—as in Dickey Pearce, one of baseball's first big stars and first true professionals. His career in baseball lasted substantially longer than Whitman's, long enough for Pearce to play his last two seasons in the National League, which wasn't officially established until 1876. Along the way, he was credited with developing the position of shortstop as we know it and with inventing a maneuver at the plate he called the "tricky hit"; history's reconfigured that more familiarly into the bunt.

If Whitman spelled Pearce's name wrong, his brief game story recognized the shortstop's talents. It's somehow exhilarating to know that, for at least one day, their extraordinary careers intersected.

The game played yesterday afternoon between the Atlantic and Putnam Clubs, on the grounds of the latter club, was one of the finest and most exciting games we ever witnessed. The Atlantics beat their opponents by four runs, but the general opinion was that the defeat was as much the result of accident as of superior playing.

On the fourth innings the Putnams made several very loose plays and allowed their opponents to score nine runs, and those careless plays were sufficient to lose them the game. On every other innings, they played carefully and well, as the score will show. They were also particularly unfortunate in having three of their men injured in the course of the game. Mr. Masten, their catcher, being disabled from occupying his position on the fifth innings, was compelled to take the first base and his place taken by Mr. Burr, who in his turn was disabled on the seventh innings and his place supplied by Mr. McKinstry, the fielder, Mr. Burr taking the third base. Mr. Jackson was injured on the eighth innings so much as to be compelled to discontinue playing, and Mr. Ketcham was substituted in his stead, so that at one time no less than three men on the Putnam side were so seriously injured as to be unable to run their bases. Notwithstanding these accidents, however, the score is highly creditable to the Putnams (always excepting the fourth innings), and we doubt if any other club can show a better one in a contest with such opponents. The Atlantics, as usual, played splendidly and maintained their reputation as the Champion Club. Messrs. M. O'Brien, P. O'Brien, Boerum, Pierce, and Oliver of that club cannot easily be surpassed in their respective positions. Messrs. Masten, Gesner, and McKinstry, of the Putnam Club, also deserve special commendation.

From *A Connecticut Yankee in King Arthur's Court*

From *A Connecticut Yankee in King Arthur's Court*

Mark Twain

BY THE TIME SAMUEL CLEMONS, AKA MARK TWAIN (1835–1910), CAME up with his 1889 time-travel tale of a Connecticut engineer waking up to find himself in the Arthurian England of legend, he had already produced two of America's greatest novels—*The Adventures of Tom Sawyer* and *Adventures of Huckleberry Finn.* He'd also tried his hand at typesetting, steamboat piloting, newspaper reporting, and gold mining; thankfully, for the course of American literature, his most productive mining was internal—tapping into the vast reservoir of humor and irony that pooled within. When "Yankee" was published, Twain and his family had long been ensconced in a big house in Hartford (next to Harriet Beecher Stowe's), not too far from the Hartford Ball Club Grounds, where Twain escaped to watch his beloved Dark Blues of the National Association (precursor to the National League) as often as possible.

Twain was as educated a fan as he was an avid one. "Mark Twain contributes liberally to the support of the Hartford base ball club," noted the *Sporting News,* and the *St. Louis Post Dispatch* once described him "as a baseball fan of the most flagrant species." He liked scribbling detailed notes on the action—his own primeval scorecard—and even volunteered to umpire a July 4th weekend game, making rulings from the grandstand that he sent to the acting umpire on the field via a small messenger boy. At a particularly memorable 1875 encounter between his undefeated Hartford Dark Blues and the hated rival Red Stockings of Boston,

Twain, among the 10,000 faithful on hand that day, was so caught up in the action—"engaged in hurrahing," he called it—that a young boy made off with his prized umbrella. Two days later, he placed a notice in the *Hartford Courant*, offering five dollars for the return of the umbrella and a bonus for delivering the perpetrator to him. "I do not want the boy (in an active state)," he explained in his ad, "but"—Twain being Twain he just couldn't stop himself—"will pay two hundred dollars for his remains."

Twain's affection for baseball ran deep. He slid it into Tom Sawyer to mark change: "There was no joy in life for poor Tom. He put away his bat and his ball and dragged himself through each day." And when he found the opportunity to wedge a brief—if incongruously organic—encounter with the game into "Yankee's" Merry Olde kingdom as a respite from the messier combat entertainments of the day, he ran with it, or at least set the scene, for the big game sadly—given the two rosters—was never recorded. Coincidentally, just as Twain was finishing his novel, the 1888–1889 world tour of major league players—the tour Walt Whitman was so keen on—had come to an end. To honor the participating players—including John Montgomery Ward and Cap Anson—the enterprise was then celebrated with a valedictory banquet at the famed Delmonico's in New York. Twain was among the star-studded assembly, and he rose to "drink long life to the boys who plowed a new equator around the globe stealing bases on their bellies!" Waxing Whitmanesque, he memorably praised the game itself as "the very symbol, the outward and visible expression of the drive, and push, and rush and struggle of the raging, tearing, booming 19th century!" One reporter present was so impressed that he saluted Twain's command of the game "from A to Z."

At the end of the month I sent the vessel home for fresh supplies, and for news. We expected her back in three or four days. She would bring me, along with other news, the result of a certain experiment which I had been starting. It was a project of mine to replace the tournament with something which might furnish an escape for the extra steam of the chivalry, keep those bucks entertained and out of mischief, and at the same time preserve the best thing in them, which was their hardy spirit of emulation.

I had had a choice band of them in private training for some time, and the date was now arriving for their first public effort. This experiment was baseball. In order to give the thing vogue from the start, and place it out of the reach of criticism, I chose my nines by rank, not capacity. There wasn't a knight in either team who wasn't a sceptered sovereign. As for material of this sort, there was a glut of it always around Arthur. You couldn't throw a brick in any direction and not cripple a king. Of course, I couldn't get these people to leave off their armor; they wouldn't do that when they bathed. They consented to differentiate the armor so that a body could tell one team from the other, but that was the most they would do. So, one of the teams wore chain-mail ulsters, and the other wore plate-armor made of my new Bessemer steel. Their practice in the field was the most fantastic thing I ever saw. Being ball-proof, they never skipped out of the way, but stood still and took the result; when a Bessemer was at the bat and a ball hit him, it would bound a hundred and fifty yards sometimes. And when a man was running, and threw himself on his stomach to slide to his base, it was like an iron-clad coming into port. At first I appointed men of no rank to act as umpires, but I had to discontinue that. These people were no easier to please than other nines. The umpire's first decision was usually his last; they broke him in two with a bat, and his friends toted him home on a shutter. When it was noticed that no umpire ever survived a game, umpiring got to be unpopular. So I was obliged to appoint somebody whose rank and lofty position under the government would protect him.

Here are the names of the nines:

BESSEMERS	ULSTERS
KING ARTHUR	EMPEROR LUCIUS
KING LOT OF LOTHIAN	KING LOGRIS
KING OF NORTHGALIS	KING MARHALT OF IRELAND

KING MARSIL	KING MORGANORE
KING OF LITTLE BRITAIN	KING MARK OF CORNWALL
KING LABOR	KING NENTRES OF GARLOT
KING PELLAM OF LIONES	KING MELIODAS OF LISTENGESE
KING BAGDEMAGUS	KING OF THE LAKE
KING TOLLEME LA FEINTES	THE SOWDAN OF SYRIA

Umpire—CLARENCE

The first public game would certainly draw fifty thousand people; and for solid fun would be worth going around the world to see. Everything would be favorable; it was balmy and beautiful spring weather now, and Nature was all tailored out in her new clothes.

Alibi Ike

Alibi Ike

Ring Lardner

BATTING FOURTH . . .

The cleanup position. The spot reserved for the heaviest hitter.

In this lineup that goes to Ring Lardner (1885–1933) and his treasure, "Alibi Ike."

Lardner's career began in sports and spread into fiction, regularly blending the two with hilarious results. His work could be as biting as it was funny, and while he often wrote about seemingly simple characters, the work itself was beautifully crafted, flowing with a complex undertow.

While a sportswriter at the *Chicago Tribune*, Lardner began stitching together a series of stories in letter form about a hayseed rookie named Jack Keefe. When the *Tribune* deemed Lardner's slangy use of language inappropriate for its readership, Lardner sold the stories to the *Saturday Evening Post*. They were a smash from the get-go. Between their publication in the *Post* and their collection as *You Know Me, Al*, Lardner created another baseball character, one with an excuse for everything. Lardner sold him to the magazine, as well, and on July 31, 1915, the *Saturday Evening Post* introduced "Alibi Ike," Lardner's most enduring creation, without no extenuation whatsoever.

1

His right name was Frank X. Farrell, and I guess the X stood for "Excuse me." Because he never pulled a play, good or bad, on or off the field, without apologizin' for it.

"Alibi Ike" was the name Carey wished on him the first day he reported down south. O' course we all cut out the "Alibi" part of it right away for the fear he would overhear it and bust somebody. But we called him "Ike" right to his face and the rest of it was understood by everybody on the club except Ike himself.

He ast me one time, he says:

"What do you all call me Ike for? I ain't no Yid."

"Carey give you the name," I says. "It's his nickname for everybody he takes a likin' to."

"He mustn't have only a few friends then," says Ike. "I never heard him say 'Ike' to nobody else."

But I was goin' to tell you about Carey namin' him. We'd been workin' out two weeks and the pitchers was showin' somethin' when this bird joined us. His first day out he stood up there so good and took such a reef at the old pill that he had everyone lookin.' Then him and Carey was together in left field, catchin' fungoes, and it was after we was through for the day that Carey told me about him.

"What do you think of Alibi Ike?" ast Carey.

"Who's that?" I says.

"This here Farrell in the outfield," says Carey.

"He looks like he could hit," I says.

"Yes," says Carey, "but he can't hit near as good as he can apologize." Then Carey went on to tell me what Ike had been pullin' out there.

He'd dropped the first fly ball that was hit to him and told Carey his glove wasn't broke in good yet, and Carey says the glove could easy of been Kid Gleason's gran'father. He made a whale of a catch out o' the next one and Carey says "Nice work!" or somethin' like that, but Ike says he could of caught the ball with his back turned only he slipped when he started after it and, besides that, the air currents fooled him.

"I thought you done well to get to the ball," says Carey.

"I ought to been settin' under it," says Ike.

"What did you hit last year?" Carey ast him.

"I had malaria most o' the season," says Ike. "I wound up with .356."

"Where would I have to go to get malaria?" says Carey, but Ike didn't wise up.

I and Carey and him set at the same table together for supper. It took him half an hour longer'n us to eat because he had to excuse himself every time he lifted his fork.

"Doctor told me I needed starch," he'd say, and then toss a shovelful o' potatoes into him. Or, "They ain't much meat on one o' these chops," he'd tell us, and grab another one. Or he'd say: "Nothin' like onions for a cold," and then he'd dip into the perfumery.

"Better try that apple sauce," says Carey. "It'll help your malaria."

"Whose malaria?" says Ike. He'd forgot already why he didn't only hit .356 last year.

I and Carey begin to lead him on.

"Whereabouts did you say your home was?" I ast him.

"I live with my folks," he says. "We live in Kansas City—not right down in the business part—outside a ways."

"How's that come?" says Carey. "I should think you'd get rooms in the post office."

But Ike was too busy curin' his cold to get that one.

"Are you married?" I ast him.

"No," he says. "I never run round much with girls, except to shows onct in a wile and parties and dances and roller skatin'."

"Never take 'em to the prize fights, eh?" says Carey.

"We don't have no real good bouts," says Ike. "Just bush stuff. And I never figured a boxin' match was a place for the ladies."

Well, after supper he pulled a cigar out and lit it. I was just goin' to ask him what he done it for, but he beat me to it.

"Kind o' rests a man to smoke after a good work-out," he says. "Kind o' settles a man's supper, too."

"Looks like a pretty good cigar," says Carey.

"Yes," says Ike. "A friend o' mine give it to me—a fella in Kansas City that runs a billiard room."

"Do you play billiards?" I ast him.

"I used to play a fair game," he says. "I'm all out o' practice now—can't hardly make a shot."

We coaxed him into a four-handed battle, him and Carey against Jack Mack and I. Say, he couldn't play billiards as good as Willie Hoppe; not quite. But to hear him tell it, he didn't make a good shot all evenin'. I'd leave him an awful-lookin' layout and he'd gather 'em up in one try and then run a couple o' hundred, and between every carom he'd say he'd put too much stuff on the ball, or the English didn't take, or the table wasn't true, or his stick was crooked, or somethin'. And all the time he had the balls actin' like they was Dutch soldiers and him Kaiser William. We started out to play fifty points, but we had to make it a thousand so as I and Jack and Carey could try the table.

The four of us set round the lobby a wile after we was through playin', and when it got along toward bedtime Carey whispered to me and says:

"Ike'd like to go to bed, but he can't think up no excuse."

Carey hadn't hardly finished whisperin' when Ike got up and pulled it:

"Well, good night, boys," he says. "I ain't sleepy, but I got some gravel in my shoes and it's killin' my feet."

We knowed he hadn't never left the hotel since we'd came in from the grounds and changed our clo'es. So Carey says:

"I should think they'd take them gravel pits out o' the billiard room."

But Ike was already on his way to the elevator, limpin'.

"He's got the world beat," says Carey to Jack and I. "I've knew lots o' guys that had an alibi for every mistake they made; I've heard pitchers say that the ball slipped when somebody cracked one off'n 'em; I've heard infielders complain of a sore arm after heavin' one into the stand, and I've saw outfielders tooken sick with a dizzy spell when they've misjudged a fly ball. But this baby can't even go to bed without apologizin', and I bet he excuses himself to the razor when he gets ready to shave."

"And at that," says Jack, "he's goin' to make us a good man."

"Yes," says Carey, "unless rheumatism keeps his battin' average down to .400."

Well, sir, Ike kept whalin' away at the ball all through the trip till everybody knowed he'd won a job. Cap had him in there regular the last few exhibition games and told the newspaper boys a week before the season opened that he was goin' to start him in Kane's place.

"You're there, kid," says Carey to Ike, the night Cap made the 'nnouncement. "They ain't many boys that wins a big league berth their third year out."

"I'd of been up here a year ago," says Ike, "only I was bent over all season with lumbago."

2

It rained down in Cincinnati one day and somebody organized a little game o' cards. They was shy two men to make six and ast I and Carey to play.

"I'm with you if you get Ike and make it seven-handed," says Carey. So they got a hold of Ike and we went up to Smitty's room.

"I pretty near forgot how many you deal," says Ike. "It's been a long wile since I played."

I and Carey give each other the wink, and sure enough, he was just as ig'orant about poker as billiards. About the second hand, the pot was opened two or three ahead of him, and they was three in when it come his turn. It cost a buck, and he throwed in two.

"It's raised, boys," somebody says.

"Gosh, that's right, I did raise it," says Ike.

"Take out a buck if you didn't mean to tilt her," says Carey. "No," says Ike, "I'll leave it go."

Well, it was raised back at him and then he made another mistake and raised again. They was only three left in when the draw come. Smitty'd opened with a pair o' kings and he didn't help 'em. Ike stood pat. The guy that'd raised him back was flushin' and he didn't fill. So Smitty checked and Ike bet and didn't get no call. He tossed his hand away, but I grabbed it and give it a look. He had king, queen, jack and two tens. Alibi Ike he must have seen me peekin', for he leaned over and whispered to me.

"I overlooked my hand," he says. "I thought all the wile it was a straight."

"Yes," I says, "that's why you raised twice by mistake."

They was another pot that he come into with tens and fours. It was tilted a couple o' times and two o' the strong fellas drawed ahead of Ike. They each drawed one. So Ike threw away his little pair and come out with four tens. And they was four treys against him. Carey'd looked at Ike's discards and then he says:

"This lucky bum busted two pair."

"No, no, I didn't," says Ike.

"Yes, yes, you did," says Carey, and showed us the two fours.

"What do you know about that?" says Ike. "I'd of swore one was a five spot."

Well, we hadn't had no pay day yet, and after a wile everybody except Ike was goin' shy. I could see him gettin' restless and I was wonderin' how he'd make the get-away. He tried two or three times. "I got to buy some collars before supper," he says.

"No hurry," says Smitty. "The stores here keeps open all night in April."

After a minute he opened up again.

"My uncle out in Nebraska ain't expected to live," he says. "I ought to send a telegram."

"Would that save him?" says Carey.

"No, it sure wouldn't," says Ike, "but I ought to leave my old man know where I'm at."

"When did you hear about your uncle?" says Carey. "Just this mornin'," says Ike.

"Who told you?" ast Carey.

"I got a wire from my old man," says Ike.

"Well," says Carey, "your old man knows you're still here yet this afternoon if you was here this mornin'. Trains leavin' Cincinnati in the middle o' the day don't carry no ball clubs."

"Yes," says Ike, "that's true. But he don't know where I'm goin' to be next week."

"Ain't he got no schedule?" ast Carey.

"I sent him one openin' day," says Ike. "But it takes mail a long time to get to Idaho."

"I thought your old man lived in Kansas City," says Carey.

"He does when he's home," says Ike.

"But now," says Carey, "I s'pose he's went to Idaho so as he can be near your sick uncle in Nebraska."

"He's visitin' my other uncle in Idaho."

"Then how does he keep posted about your sick uncle?" ast Carey.

"He don't," says Ike. "He don't even know my other uncle's sick. That's why I ought to wire and tell him."

"Good night!" says Carey.

"What town in Idaho is your old man at?" I says. Ike thought it over.

"No town at all," he says. "But he's near a town."

"Near what town?" I says.

"Yuma," says Ike.

Well, by this time he'd lost two or three pots and he was desperate. We was playin' just as fast as we could, because we seen we couldn't hold him much longer. But he was tryin' so hard to frame an escape that he couldn't pay no attention to the cards, and it looked like we'd get his whole pile away from him if we could make him stick.

The telephone saved him. The minute it begun to ring, five of us jumped for it. But Ike was there first.

"Yes," he says, answerin' it. "This is him. I'll come right down."

And he slammed up the receiver and beat it out o' the door without even sayin' good-bye.

"Smitty'd ought to locked the door," says Carey. "What did he win?" ast Carey.

We figured it up—sixty-odd bucks.

"And the next time we ask him to play," says Carey, "his fingers will be so stiff he can't hold the cards."

Well, we set round a wile talkin' it over, and pretty soon the telephone rung again. Smitty answered it. It was a friend of his'n from Hamilton and he wanted to know why Smitty didn't hurry down. He was the one that had called before and Ike had told him he was Smitty.

"Ike'd ought to split with Smitty's friend," says Carey.

"No," I says, "he'll need all he won. It costs money to buy collars and to send telegrams from Cincinnati to your old man in Texas and keep him posted on the health o' your uncle in Cedar Rapids, D.C."

3

And you ought to heard him out there on that field! They wasn't a day when he didn't pull six or seven, and it didn't make no difference whether he was goin' good or bad. If he popped up in the pinch he should of made a base hit and the reason he didn't was so-and-so. And if he cracked one for three bases he ought to had a home run, only the ball wasn't lively, or the wind brought it back, or he tripped on a lump o' dirt, roundin' first base.

They was one afternoon in New York when he beat all records. Big Marquard was workin' against us and he was good.

In the first innin' Ike hit one clear over that right field stand, but it was a few feet foul. Then he got another foul and then the count come to two and two. Then Rube slipped one acrost on him and he was called out.

"What do you know about that!" he says afterward on the bench. "I lost count. I thought it was three and one, and I took a strike."

"You took a strike all right," says Carey. "Even the umps knowed it was a strike."

"Yes," says Ike, "but you can bet I wouldn't of took it if I'd knew it was the third one. The score board had it wrong."

"That score board ain't for you to look at," says Cap. "It's for you to hit that old pill against."

"Well," says Ike, "I could of hit that one over the score board if I'd knew it was the third."

"Was it a good ball?" I says.

"Well, no, it wasn't," says Ike. "It was inside."

"How far inside?" says Carey.

"Oh, two or three inches or half a foot," says Ike.

"I guess you wouldn't of threatened the score board with it then," says Cap.

"I'd of pulled it down the right foul line if I hadn't thought he'd call it a ball," says Ike.

Well, in New York's part o' the innin' Doyle cracked one and Ike run back a mile and a half and caught it with one hand. We was all sayin' what a whale of a play it was, but he had to apologize just the same as for gettin' struck out.

"That stand's so high," he says, "that a man don't never see a ball till it's right on top o' you."

"Didn't you see that one?" ast Cap.

"Not at first," says Ike, "not till it raised up above the roof o' the stand."

"Then why did you start back as soon as the ball was hit?" says Cap.

"I knowed by the sound that he'd got a good hold of it," says Ike.

"Yes," says Cap, "but how'd you know what direction to run in?"

"Doyle usually hits 'em that way, the way I run," says Ike.

"Why don't you play blindfolded?" says Carey.

"Might as well, with that big high stand to bother a man," says Ike. "If I could of saw the ball all the time I'd of got it in my hip pocket."

Along in the fifth we was one run to the bad and Ike got on with one out. On the first ball throwed to Smitty, Ike went down. The ball was outside and Meyers throwed Ike out by ten feet.

You could see Ike's lips movin' all the way to the bench and when he got there he had his piece learned.

"Why didn't he swing?" he says.

"Why didn't you wait for his sign?" says Cap.

"He give me his sign," says Ike.

"What is his sign with you?" says Cap.

"Pickin' up some dirt with his right hand," says Ike.

"Well, I didn't see him do it," Cap says.

"He done it all right," says Ike.

Well, Smitty went out and they wasn't no more argument till they come in for the next innin'. Then Cap opened it up.

"You fellas better get your signs straight," he says. "Do you mean me?" says Smitty.

"Yes," Cap says. "What's your sign with Ike?"

"Slidin' my left hand up to the end o' the bat and back," says Smitty.

"Do you hear that, Ike?" ast Cap.

"What of it?" says Ike.

"You says his sign was pickin' up dirt and he says it's slidin' his hand. Which is right?"

"I'm right," says Smitty. "But if you're arguin' about him goin' last innin', I didn't give him no sign."

"You pulled your cap down with your right hand, didn't you?" ast Ike.

"Well, s'pose I did," says Smitty. "That don't mean nothin'. I never told you to take that for a sign, did I?"

"I thought maybe you meant to tell me and forgot," says Ike.

They couldn't none of us answer that and they wouldn't of been no more said if Ike had of shut up. But wile we was settin' there Carey got on with two out and stole second clean.

"There!" says Ike. "That's what I was tryin' to do and I'd of got away with it if Smitty'd swang and bothered the Indian."

"Oh!" says Smitty. "You was tryin' to steal then, was you? I thought you claimed I give you the hit and run."

"I didn't claim no such a thing," says Ike. "I thought maybe you might of gave me a sign, but I was goin' anyway because I thought I had a good start."

Cap prob'ly would of hit him with a bat, only just about that time Doyle booted one on Hayes and Carey come acrost with the run that tied.

Well, we go into the ninth finally, one and one, and Marquard walks McDonald with nobody out.

"Lay it down," says Cap to Ike.

And Ike goes up there with orders to bunt and cracks the first ball into that right-field stand! It was fair this time, and we're two ahead, but I didn't think about that at the time. I was too busy watchin' Cap's face. First he turned pale and then he got red as fire and then he got blue and purple, and finally he just laid back and busted out laughin'. So we wasn't afraid to laugh ourself when we seen him doin' it, and when Ike come in everybody on the bench was in hysterics.

But instead o' takin' advantage, Ike had to try and excuse himself. His play was to shut up and he didn't know how to make it.

"Well," he says, "if I hadn't hit quite so quick at that one I bet it'd of cleared the center-field fence."

Cap stopped laughin'.

"It'll cost you plain fifty," he says.

"What for?" says Ike.

"When I say 'bunt' I mean 'bunt,'" says Cap.

"You didn't say 'bunt,'" says Ike.

"I says 'Lay it down,'" says Cap. "If that don't mean 'bunt,' what does it mean?"

"'Lay it down' means 'bunt' all right," says Ike, "but I understood you to say 'Lay on it.'"

"All right," says Cap, "and the little misunderstandin' will cost you fifty."

Ike didn't say nothin' for a few minutes. Then he had another bright idear.

"I was just kiddin' about misunderstandin' you," he says. "I knowed you wanted me to bunt."

"Well, then, why didn't you bunt?" ast Cap.

"I was goin' to on the next ball," says Ike. "But I thought if I took a good wallop I'd have 'em all fooled. So I walloped at the first one to fool 'em, and I didn't have no intention o' hittin' it."

"You tried to miss it, did you?" says Cap.

"Yes," says Ike.

"How'd you happen to hit it?" ast Cap.

"Well," Ike says, "I was lookin' for him to throw me a fast one and I was goin' to swing under it. But he come with a hook and I met it right square where I was swingin' to go under the fast one."

"Great!" says Cap. "Boys," he says, "Ike's learned how to hit Marquard's curve. Pretend a fast one's comin' and then try to miss it. It's a good thing to know and Ike'd ought to be willin' to pay for the lesson. So I'm goin' to make it a hundred instead o' fifty."

The game wound up 3 to 1. The fine didn't go, because Ike hit like a wild man all through that trip and we made pretty near a clean-up. The night we went to Philly I got him cornered in the car and I says to him:

"Forget them alibis for a wile and tell me somethin'. What'd you do that for, swing that time against Marquard when you was told to bunt?"

"I'll tell you," he says. "That ball he threwed me looked just like the one I struck out on in the first innin' and I wanted to show Cap what I could of done to that other one if I'd knew it was the third strike."

"But," I says, "the one you struck out on in the first innin' was a fast ball."

"So was the one I cracked in the ninth," says Ike.

4

You've saw Cap's wife, o' course. Well, her sister's about twict as good-lookin' as her, and that's goin' some.

Cap took his missus down to St. Louis the second trip and the other one come down from St. Joe to visit her. Her name is Dolly, and some doll is right.

Well, Cap was goin' to take the two sisters to a show and he wanted a beau for Dolly. He left it to her and she picked Ike. He'd hit three on the nose that afternoon—off'n Sallee, too.

They fell for each other that first evenin', Cap told us how it come off. She begin flatterin' Ike for the star game he'd played and o' course he begin excusin' himself for not doin' better. So she thought he was modest and it went strong with her. And she believed everything he said and that made her solid with him—that and her make-up. They was together every mornin' and evenin' for the five days we was there. In the afternoons Ike played the grandest ball you ever see, hittin' and runnin' the bases like a fool and catchin' everything that stayed in the park.

I told Cap, I says: "You'd ought to keep the doll with us and he'd make Cobb's figures look sick."

But Dolly had to go back to St. Joe and we come home for a long serious.

Well, for the next three weeks Ike had a letter to read every day and he'd set in the clubhouse readin' it till mornin' practice was half over. Cap didn't say nothin' to him, because he was goin' so good. But I and Carey wasted a lot of our time tryin' to get him to own up who the letters was from. Fine chanct!

"What are you readin'?" Carey'd say. "A bill?"

"No," Ike'd say, "not exactly a bill. It's a letter from a fella I used to go to school with."

"High school or college?" I'd ask him.

"College," he'd say.

Then he'd stall a wile and then he'd say:

"I didn't go to the college myself, but my friend went there."

"How did it happen you didn't go?" Carey'd ask him.

"Well," he'd say, "they wasn't no colleges near where I lived."

"Didn't you live in Kansas City?" I'd say to him.

One time he'd say he did and another time he didn't. One time he says he lived in Michigan.

"Where at?" says Carey. "Near Detroit," he says.

"Well," I says, "Detroit's near Ann Arbor and that's where they got the university."

"Yes," says Ike, "they got it there now, but they didn't have it there then."

"I come pretty near goin' to Syracuse," I says, "only they wasn't no railroads runnin' through there in them days."

"Where'd this friend o' yours go to college?" says Carey. "I forget now," says Ike.

"Was it Carlisle?" ast Carey.

"No," says Ike. "His folks wasn't very well off."

"That's what barred me from Smith," I says.

"I was goin' to tackle Cornell's," says Carey, "but the doctor told me I'd have hay fever if I didn't stay up North."

"Your friend writes long letters," I says.

"Yes," says Ike, "he's tellin' me about a ballplayer."

"Where does he play?" ast Carey.

"Down in the Texas League—Fort Wayne," says Ike.

"It looks like a girl's writin'," Carey says.

"A girl wrote it," says Ike. "That's my friend's sister, writin' for him."

"Didn't they teach writin' at this here college where he went?" says Carey.

"Sure," Ike says, "they taught writin', but he got his hand cut off in a railroad wreck."

"How long ago?" I says.

"Right after he got out o' college," says Ike.

"Well," I says, "I should think he'd of learned to write with his left hand by this time."

"It's his left hand that was cut off," says Ike, "and he was left-handed."

"You get a letter every day," says Carey. "They're all the same writin'. Is he tellin' you about a different ball player every time he writes?"

"No," Ike says. "It's the same ball player. He just tells me what he does every day."

"From the size o' the letters, they don't play nothin' but doubleheaders down there," says Carey.

We figured that Ike spent most of his evenin's answerin' the letters from his "friend's sister," so we kept tryin' to date him up for shows and parties to see how he'd duck out of 'em. He was bugs over spaghetti, so we told him one day that they was goin' to be a big feed of it over to Joe's that night and he was invited.

"How long'll it last?" he says.

"Well," we says, "we're goin' right over there after the game and stay till they close up."

"I can't go," he says, "unless they leave me come home at eight bells."

"Nothin' doin'," says Carey. "Joe'd get sore."

"I can't go then," says Ike.

"Why not?" I ast him.

"Well," he says, "my landlady locks up the house at eight and I left my key home."

"You can come and stay with me," says Carey.

"No," he says, "I can't sleep in a strange bed."

"How do you get along when we're on the road?" says I.

"I don't never sleep the first night anywheres," he says. "After that I'm all right."

"You'll have time to chase home and get your key right after the game," I told him.

"The key ain't home," says Ike. "I lent it to one o' the other fellas and he's went out o' town and took it with him."

"Couldn't you borry another key off'n the landlady?" Carey ast him.

"No," he says, "that's the only one they is."

Well, the day before we started East again, Ike come into the clubhouse all smiles.

"Your birthday?" I ast him.

"No," he says.

"What do you feel so good about?" I says.

"Got a letter from my old man," he says. "My uncle's goin' to get well."

"Is that the one in Nebraska?" says I.

"Not right in Nebraska," says Ike. "Near there."

But afterwards we got the right dope from Cap. Dolly'd blew in from Missouri and was goin' to make the trip with her sister.

5

Well, I want to alibi Carey and I for what come off in Boston. If we'd of had any idear what we was doin', we'd never did it. They wasn't nobody outside o' maybe Ike and the dame that felt worse over it than I and Carey.

The first two days we didn't see nothin' of Ike and her except out to the park. The rest o' the time they was sight-seein' over to Cambridge and down to Revere and out to Brook-a-line and all the other places where the rubes go.

But when we come into the beanery after the third game Cap's wife called us over.

"If you want to see somethin' pretty," she says, "look at the third finger on Sis's left hand."

Well, o' course we knowed before we looked that it wasn't goin' to be no hangnail. Nobody was su'prised when Dolly blew into the dinin' room with it—a rock that Ike'd bought off'n Diamond Joe the first trip to New York City. Only o' course it'd been set into a lady's-size ring instead o' the automobile tire he'd been wearin'.

Cap and his missus and Ike and Dolly ett supper together, only Ike didn't eat nothin', but just set there blushin' and spillin' things on the tablecloth. I heard him excusin' himself for not havin' no appetite. He says he couldn't never eat when he was clost to the ocean. He'd forgot about them sixty-five oysters he destroyed the first night o' the trip before.

He was goin' to take her to a show, so after supper he went upstairs to change his collar. She had to doll up, too, and o' course Ike was through long before her.

If you remember the hotel in Boston, they's a little parlor where the piano's at and then they's another little parlor openin' off o' that. Well, when Ike come down Smitty was playin' a few chords and I and Carey was harmonizin'. We seen Ike go up to the desk to leave his key and we called him in. He tried to duck away, but we wouldn't stand for it.

We ast him what he was all duded up for and he says he was goin' to the theayter.

"Goin' alone?" says Carey.

"No," he says, "a friend o' mine's goin' with me."

"What do you say if we go along?" says Carey.

"I ain't only got two tickets," he says.

"Well," says Carey, "we can go down there with you and buy our own seats; maybe we can all go together."

"No," says Ike. "They ain't no more seats. They're all sold out."

"We can buy some off'n the scalpers," says Carey.

"I wouldn't if I was you," says Ike. "They say the show's rotten."

"What are you goin' for, then?" I ast.

"I didn't hear about it bein' rotten till I got the tickets," he says.

"Well," I says, "if you don't want to go I'll buy the tickets from you."

"No," says Ike, "I wouldn't want to cheat you. I'm stung and I'll just have to stand for it."

"What are you goin' to do with the girl, leave her here at the hotel?"

"What girl?" says Ike.

"The girl you ett supper with," I says.

"Oh," he says, "we just happened to go into the dinin' room together, that's all. Cap wanted I should set down with 'em."

"I noticed," says Carey, "that she happened to be wearin' that rock you bought off'n Diamond Joe."

"Yes," says Ike. "I lent it to her for a wile."

"Did you lend her the new ring that goes with it?" I says.

"She had that already," says Ike. "She lost the set out of it."

"I wouldn't trust no strange girl with a rock o'mine," says Carey.

"Oh, I guess she's all right," Ike says. "Besides, I was tired o' the stone. When a girl asks you for somethin', what are you goin' to do?" He started out toward the desk, but we flagged him.

"Wait a minute!" Carey says. "I got a bet with Sam here, and it's up to you to settle it."

"Well," says Ike, "make it snappy. My friend'll be here any minute."

"I bet," says Carey, "that you and that girl was engaged to be married."

"Nothin to it," says Ike.

"Now look here," says Carey, "this is goin' to cost me real money if I lose. Cut out the alibi stuff and give it to us straight. Cap's wife just as good as told us you was roped."

Ike blushed like a kid.

"Well, boys," he says, "I may as well own up. You win, Carey."

"Yatta boy!" says Carey. "Congratulations!"

"You got a swell girl, Ike," I says.

"She's a peach," says Smitty.

"Well, I guess she's OK," says Ike. "I don't know much about girls."

"Didn't you never run round with 'em?" I says.

"Oh, yes, plenty of 'em," says Ike. "But I never seen none I'd fall for."

"That is, till you seen this one," says Carey.

"Well," says Ike, "this one's OK, but I wasn't thinkin' about gettin' married for a wile."

"Who done the askin'—her?" says Carey.

"O, no," says Ike, "but sometimes a man don't know what he's gettin' into. Take a good-lookin' girl, and a man gen'ally almost always does about what she wants him to."

"They couldn't no girl lasso me unless I wanted to be lassoed," says Smitty.

"Oh, I don't know," says Ike. "When a fella gets to feelin' sorry for one of 'em it's all off."

Well, we left him go after shakin' hands all round. But he didn't take Dolly to no show that night. Some time while we was talkin' she'd come into that other parlor and she'd stood there and heard us. I don't know how much she heard. But it was enough. Dolly and Cap's missus took the midnight train for New York. And from there Cap's wife sent her on her way back to Missouri.

She'd left the ring and a note for Ike with the clerk. But we didn't ask Ike if the note was from his friend in Fort Wayne, Texas.

6

When we'd came to Boston Ike was hittin' plain .397. When we got back home he'd fell off to pretty near nothin.' He hadn't drove one out o' the infield in any o' them other Eastern parks, and he didn't even give no excuse for it.

To show you how bad he was, he struck out three times in Brooklyn one day and never opened his trap when Cap ast him what was the matter. Before, if he'd whiffed oncet in a game he'd of wrote a book tellin' why.

Well, we dropped from first place to fifth in four weeks and we was still goin' down. I and Carey was about the only ones in the club that spoke to each other, and all as we did was remind ourself o' what a boner we'd pulled.

"It's goin' to beat us out o' the big money," says Carey.

"Yes," I says. "I don't want to knock my own ball club, but it looks like a one-man team, and when that one man's dauber's down we couldn't trim our whiskers."

"We ought to knew better," says Carey.

"Yes," I says, "but why should a man pull an alibi for bein' engaged to such a bearcat as she was?"

"He shouldn't," says Carey. "But I and you knowed he would or we'd never started talkin' to him about it. He wasn't no more ashamed o' the girl than I am of a regular base hit. But he just can't come clean on no subjec.'"

Cap had the whole story, and I and Carey was as pop'lar with him as an umpire.

"What do you want me to do, Cap?" Carey'd say to him before goin' up to hit.

"Use your own judgment," Cap'd tell him. "We want to lose another game."

But finally, one night in Pittsburgh, Cap had a letter from his missus and he come to us with it.

"You fellas," he says, "is the ones that put us on the bum, and if you're sorry I think theys a chancet for you to make good. The old lady's out to St. Joe and she's been tryin' her hardest to fix things up. She's explained that Ike don't mean nothin' with his talk; I've wrote and explained that to Dolly, too. But the old lady says that Dolly says that she can't believe it. But Dolly's still stuck on this baby, and she's pinin' away just the same as Ike. And the old lady says she thinks if you two fellas would write to the girl and explain how you was always kiddin' with Ike and leadin' him on, and how the ball club was all shot to pieces since Ike quit hittin,' and how he acted like he was goin' to kill himself, and this and that, she'd fall for it and maybe soften down. Dolly, the old lady says, would believe you before she'd believe I and the old lady, because she thinks it's her we're sorry for, and not him."

Well, I and Carey was only too glad to try and see what we could do. But it wasn't no snap. We wrote about eight letters before we got one that looked good. Then we give it to the stenographer and had it wrote out on a typewriter and both of us signed it.

It was Carey's idear that made the letter good. He stuck in somethin' about the world's serious money that our wives wasn't goin' to spend unless she took pity on a "boy who was so shy and modest that he was afraid to come right out and say that he had asked such a beautiful and handsome girl to become his bride."

That's prob'ly what got her, or maybe she couldn't of held out much longer anyway. It was four days after we sent the letter that Cap heard from his missus again. We was in Cincinnati.

"We've won," he says to us. "The old lady says that Dolly says she'll give him another chance. But the old lady says it won't do no good for Ike to write a letter. He'll have to go out there."

"Send him tonight," says Carey.

"I'll pay half his fare," I says.

"I'll pay the other half," says Carey.

"No," says Cap, "the club'll pay his expenses. I'll send him scoutin'."

"Are you goin' to send him tonight?"

"Sure," says Cap. "But I'm goin' to break the news to him right now. It's time we win a ball game."

So in the clubhouse, just before the game, Cap told him. And I certainly felt sorry for Rube Benton and Red Ames that afternoon! I and

45

Carey was standin' in front o' the hotel that night when Ike come out with his suitcase.

"Sent home?" I says to him.

"No," he says, "I'm goin' scoutin'."

"Where to?" I says. "Fort Wayne?"

"No, not exactly," he says.

"Well," says Carey, "have a good time."

"I ain't lookin' for no good time," says Ike. "I says I was goin' scoutin'."

"Well, then," says Carey, "I hope you see somebody you like."

"And you better have a drink before you go," I says.

"Well," says Ike, "they claim it helps a cold."

The Captain of the Orient Base-Ball 9

The Captain of the Orient Base-Ball 9

C. M. Sheldon

THROUGH HIS COLLEGE DAYS AT BROWN, CHARLES MONROE SHELDON (1857–1946) personally preferred a tennis racket to a baseball bat when it came to connecting with spheroids. But in those days, baseball still had a novel whiff to it, and the game itself frankly attracted him. "I have a vague remembrance," he wrote years later, "of sometimes stopping in my task and looking out the window at a baseball game—and wishing I could be there."

In his junior year, Sheldon contributed a short story to the writing group in his dorm, and before he could say Jackie Robinson, that story found its way into the October 1882 edition of *St. Nicholas Magazine*, an enormously popular periodical aimed at young readers. It was not only the first piece of baseball fiction ever to appear; it defined the model for a whole genre of juvenile fiction—think the Frank Merriwell or Chip Hilton books, for example—that would follow: sporting hero confronts some kind of moral dilemma, suffers the weight of his options, then connects with his better angels to make the right choice.

Moral dilemmas would turn into Sheldon's bread and butter: As a distinguished Congregationalist minister and flagbearer of Christian Socialism, he spread his gospel of "What would Jesus do?" a proposition he wove through a series of sermons he delivered as pastor of his church in Topeka, Kansas. That question was reborn—and spread farther—in his best-selling 1897 novel *In His Steps* and then born again in "WWJD" bracelets and tats sported by athletes a century later.

As a lifetime proponent of equal rights, Sheldon would have been proud that when Olivia Pichardo became the first woman to play in an NCAA Division I college baseball game in 2023, she wore the uniform of his alma mater.

The Orient Base-ball Nine, of Orient Academy, hereby challenges the Eagles, of Clayton Academy, to a match game of ball, time and place to be at the choice of the challenged.

RESPECTFULLY,
TOM DAVIS, SECRETARY OF ORIENT B. B. C.
TO SECRETARY OF EAGLE B. B. C., OF CLAYTON ACADEMY.

"There!" said Tom, as he wiped his pen on his coat-sleeve; "how'll that do?"

The Orient Base-ball nine was sitting in solemn council in Captain Gleason's room. The question had long been debated at the Orient School about playing a match game with the Eagles of Clayton, the rival Academy on the same line of railroad, about thirty miles from Orient. Until lately, the teachers of the Academy had withheld their permission for the necessary absence from school; but at last they had yielded to the petitions of the nine, and the Orient Club was now holding a meeting which had resulted in the above challenge.

"Very well put, Tom," answered Gleason, and then an animated conversation took place.

"We must beat those fellows, or they'll crow over us forever."

"Yes; do you remember, fellows, that Barton who was down here last fall when our nine played the town boys? They say he stole a ball out of Tom's pocket during the game. I hear he's short-stop this year." This from Johnny Rider, the Orient first-baseman.

"We don't know about that," said Gleason. "Don't be too sure."

"Well," put in Wagner, the popular catcher of the nine, "we *do* know some of them are not to be trusted, and will cheat, if they get a chance. You see if they don't."

"All the more reason why we should play fair, then," retorted Gleason. "Look here, boys, I haven't time to orate, and am not going to make a speech, but let's understand one another.

If we go to Clayton—and I think they will prefer to play on their own grounds—we are going to play a fair game. If we can't beat them without cheating, we won't beat them at all!"

"Three cheers for the captain!" shouted Tom, upsetting the ink-stand in his excitement. The cheers were given; and the pitcher, a short, thick-set fellow, with quick, black eyes, whispered to Wagner: "If there's any cheating done, it won't be done by Glea, that's sure."

"No," replied Wagner, "but they will beat us. You mark my words."

"We shall have something to say to that, I think," and the Orient pitcher shut his teeth together vigorously, as he thought of the latest curve which he had been practicing.

Gradually, after more talk on the merits of the two clubs, one after another dropped out of the captain's room, and at last he and Tom Davis were alone. Tom was sealing up the challenge.

"What do you think, Glea, of Rider's remark about Barton?" asked Tom, as he licked a stamp with great relish. Base-ball was food and drink to Tom.

"Why," replied Gleason, "I don't think Barton's any worse than the others. None of them are popular around here, but I think it's only on account of the jealousy of the two academies. Probably they have the same poor opinion of us."

"They're a good nine, anyway. You know they beat the Stars last Saturday."

"Yes," said Gleason, smiling, "and we beat the Rivals."

"Do you think they they'll cheat, or try to?" asked Tom.

"Well, no; there isn't much chance of cheating nowadays at base-ball. We may have some trouble with the umpire."

"Well, good-night, old fellow!" said Tom, as he rose. "I'll take this down to post, and then hie me to my downy couch. I suppose you are going to 'dig,' as usual."

"Yes; I have some Virgil to get out."

"I don't envy you. Good-night, my *pius Aeneas*."

"Good-night, my *fidus Achates*." And the captain was left alone.

He took down his books, but somehow he could not compose himself to study. The anticipated game with the Claytons filled his mind, and he could think of nothing else; so he shut the books, and took a turn up and down the room.

Young Gleason was a handsome, well-built fellow, with an open, sunny face, the very soul of honor, and a popular fellow with every one. He was all but worshiped by the nine, who adored him as a decided leader, a steady player, and a sure batsman, with a knack of wresting victory out of seeming defeat. His powers of endurance were the wonder and admiration of all the new boys, who were sure to hear of Gleason before they had been in the school two days.

He had whipped Eagen, the bully, in the cotton-mills across the river, for insulting some ladies; he had walked from Centerville to Orient in thirty-six minutes, the fastest time on record; he had won the silver cup at the last athletic tournament, for the finest exhibition of the Indian clubs; and, in short, he was a school hero, and not only the boys but the teachers of the Academy learned to admire and love him.

Perhaps the weakest point in his character was his thirst for popularity. He felt keenly any loss of it, and when Sanders carried off the first prize for original declamation, it was noticed that Gleason treated Sanders rather coldly for some time. But, in spite of this defect, Gleason was a splendid fellow, as everyone said, and sure to make his mark in the world along with the best.

For two days the nine waited impatiently for the answer to their challenge. The third day it came. The Claytons, with characteristic coolness, Wagner said, chose their own grounds, and a week from the date for the match.

"Shouldn't wonder at all if they tried to work in some outside fellow for pitcher. I hear their own is a little weak," said the ever-suspicious Wagner.

"I'm glad they've given us a week," said Francis, the pitcher. "I need about that time for practice on the new curve, and I think you will need about the same time to learn how to catch it. So stop your grumbling, old boy, and come out on the campus."

The week sped rapidly by, and at last the appointed day arrived—clear, cool, still; just the perfection of weather for ball.

A large delegation went down to the station to see the nine off.

"I say, Glea," shouted a schoolmate, "telegraph down the result, and we'll be here with a carriage to drag you up the hill when you come back."

"Yes," echoed another, "that is, if you beat. We can't turn out of our beds to get up a triumphal march for the vanquished."

"All right, fellows—we're going to beat them. We're *sure* to beat them—hey, Captain?" said Tom, looking up at Gleason.

"We'll do our best, boys," answered Gleason. Then, as the train moved off, he leaned far out of his window and whispered impressively: "You may be here with that carriage."

There was a cheer from the students, another from the nine standing on the platform and leaning out of the windows, and the Orients were whirled rapidly off to Clayton.

They reached their destination in little more than an hour and found almost as large a delegation as they had left at Orient. The talk and excitement here for the past week over the coming game had been as eager as at Orient. Nothing about the visitors escaped the notice of the Claytons. Their "points" were discussed as freely as if they were so many prize cattle at a county fair.

"Just look at that fellow's chest and arms!"

"He'll be a tough customer at the bat, I'm afraid."

"He's the fastest runner at Orient."

These and other whispers drew a large share of the attention to Gleason, and, as usual, admiration seemed to stimulate him to do his best. He summoned the nine together before the game was called, to give them final instructions.

"Keep cool. Play steady. Don't run any foolish risks in stealing bases; and, above all, let every man do honest work. Show these fellows that we know what the word *gentleman* means."

After some little delay necessary for selecting an umpire and arranging for choice of position, the game was finally called, the Orients coming first to the bat.

The crowd gathered to witness the game was the largest ever seen on the grounds, and almost every man was in sympathy with the home nine. So, as Gleason had said on the train, the only hope of his men for victory was to play together, and force the sympathy of some of the spectators, at least, by cool and steady work.

The captain himself was the first man at the bat. After two strikes he succeeded in getting a base hit, stole to second on a passed ball, reached third on a base hit by Wagner, and home on a sacrifice hit by Davis, scoring the first run for Orient amid considerable applause. The next two batters struck out in quick succession, leaving Wagner on second. Then the Claytons came to the bat, and after an exciting inning scored two runs, showing strength as batters and base-runners. In the third inning the Orients made another run, thus tying the score.

So the game went on until the ninth and last inning, when the score stood eight to seven in favor of the Orients.

The excitement by this time was intense. The playing all along had been brilliant and even. Both nines showed the same number of base hits and nearly the same number of errors. Francis, for the Orients, had done splendid work, but Wagner for some reason had not supported him as well as usual. And now, as the Claytons came to the bat for the closing inning, every one bent forward, and silence reigned over the field, broken only by the voice of the umpire.

Gleason had played a perfect game throughout. No one looking at him could imagine how much he had set his heart on the game. His coaching had been wise, his judgment at all times good, and he now, from his position in left field, awaited the issue of the closing inning with a cheerful assurance.

The inning opened with a sharp hit to short-stop. He made a fine stop and threw to first, but poor Johnny Rider, who had played so far without an error, muffed the ball, and the Clayton batsman took his first amid a perfect storm of cries and cheers.

The next batter, after a strike, drove the ball into right field, a good base hit, and the man on first took second. Then, as if to aggravate the Orients and complete their nervousness, Francis allowed the third batsman to take first on called balls; and so the bases were filled. A player on every base and no one out! It was enough to de-moralize the coolest players.

But Francis was one of those men who, after the first flurry of excitement, grow cooler. The next two Claytons struck out in turn.

Then Barton came to the bat, and all the Orients held their breath, and the Claytons watched their strongest batsman with hope. One good base hit would tie them with the Orients, and Barton had already made a two-bagger and a base hit during the game. The umpire's voice sounded out over the field:

"One ball. Two balls. One strike. Three balls. Four balls. Five balls. Two strikes." Francis ground his teeth, as he delivered the next ball directly over the plate. But Barton, quick as lightning, struck, and the ball went spinning out above short-stop, between second and third.

It was one of those balls most difficult to catch, nearly on a line, and not far enough up to allow much time for judgment as to its direction. Gleason was standing well out in the field, expecting a heavy drive of the ball there, where Barton had struck before. But he rushed forward, neck or nothing, in what seemed a useless attempt. With a marvel of dexterity and quickness, he stooped as he ran, and, reaching down his hand, caught the ball just as it touched the ground, by what is known in base-ball language as a "pick-up."

He felt the ball touch the ground, heard it distinctly, and knew that, where it had struck, a tuft of grass had been crushed down and driven into the earth; and he had straightened himself up to throw the ball home, when a perfect roar of applause struck his ears, and the umpire declared "out on the fly."

He was just on the point of rushing forward and telling the truth, but, as usual after a game, the crowd came down from the seats with a rush, the Orients came running up to him, declaring it the best play they ever saw; and before he knew what he was about, the nine had improvised a chair and carried him off, with cheers and shouts, to the station, for the game had been so long that they could not stay later, as they had planned.

It certainly was a great temptation. Besides, the umpire had declared it a fly. What right had he to dispute the umpire? And no one but himself knew that the ball had touched the ground. The whole action had been so quick, he had run forward so far after feeling the ball between his fingers, that not the least doubt existed in the minds of the Claytons that the catch was a fair one.

But, on the other hand, his conscience kept pricking him. He, the upright, the preacher to the rest of the nine on fair play, the one who had been such a stickler for the right, no matter what the result, he had been the only one to cheat! Yes, it was an ugly word. Cheat! But he could find no other name for it. And after all he had said!

He sat in silence during the ride home. The rest of the nine made noise enough, and as he was generally quiet, even after a victory, no one noticed his silence very much.

As the train ran into the station at Orient a great crowd was in waiting. Tom had telegraphed the news from Clayton, and all Orient was wild with joy. When Gleason appeared, he received a regular ovation, such an ovation as a school-boy alone can give or receive. They rushed him into the carriage, and before the order was given to pull up the hill to the Academy, some one cried out, "Speech, speech!"

It was the most trying moment of Gleason's life.

During the ride home he had fought a battle with himself, more fiercely contested than the closest game of ball, and he had won. He trembled as he rose, and those who stood nearest the lights about the station noticed that his face was pale. There was silence at once.

"Fellows, I have something to tell you which you don't expect to hear. We wouldn't have won the game to-day if I hadn't cheated."

"How's that?"

"Who cheated?"

"What's the matter?"

There was the greatest consternation among the Orients. When quiet had been partly restored, Gleason went on and related the whole event just as it happened. "And now," he concluded sadly, "I suppose you all despise me. But you can't think worse of me than I do myself." And he leaped out of the carriage, and, setting his face straight before him, walked away up the hill.

No one offered to stop him. Some hissed. A few laughed. The majority were puzzled.

"What did he want to tell for? No one would ever have known the difference."

But Tom Davis ran after the captain and caught him about half-way up the hill. School-boy fashion, he said never a word, but walked up the hill to the captain's room, shook hands with him at his door, and went away with something glittering in his eyes.

Next morning, Gleason's conduct was the talk and wonder of the whole school. But the captain himself showed true nobility. He begged the school and the nine to consider the game played with the Claytons as forfeited to them. And, after much talk, Gleason himself wrote, explaining the whole affair, and asking for another game on the Orient grounds.

The Claytons responded, came down, and defeated the Orients in a game even more hotly contested than the first. But Gleason took his defeat very calmly, and smilingly replied to Tom's almost tearful, "oh, why didn't we beat this time?" with "Ah, Tom, but I have a clear conscience, and that is worth more than all the ballgames in the world!"

The Model Baseball Player

The Model Baseball Player

Henry Chadwick

WHILE NO ONE WOULD EVER COMPARE THE LANGUAGE OF BRITISH-BORN Henry Chadwick (1824–1908) with Homer's, Chadwick was, in truth, baseball's founding bard, creator of the box score, inventor of the K, deviser of the rules, and crafter of a pair of statistics that have stood the test of time and sabermetrics: batting and earned run averages. He began his newspaper career on the cricket beat in the 1850s, and while writing for the *New York Times*, discovered its American improvement. He was soon covering the game full-time and editing the game's earliest annual guides before aligning with his friend Al Spalding—we'll meet him later—in overseeing Spalding's annual guides. He liked to call himself the "Father of the Game," which he wasn't, but he did father important ways that we document the game and immensely influenced the way sports became written about in America. He would describe his vision of what makes the ideal player in his 1868 book, *The Game of Baseball*. He later became one of the important early voices to argue against the fiction that Cooperstown's own Abner Doubleday invented the whole enterprise.

This is an individual not often seen on a ball ground, but he nevertheless exists, and as a description of his characteristics will prove advantageous, we give a pen photogram of him, in the hope that his example will be followed on all occasions, for if it were, an end would at once be put to many actions which now give rise to unpleasantness on our ball grounds.

His Moral Attributes

The principal rule of action of our model baseball player is to comport himself like a gentleman on all occasions, but especially on match days, and in doing so, he abstains from profanity and its twin and evil brother obscenity, leaving these vices to be alone cultivated by graduates of our penitentiaries.

He never takes an ungenerous advantage of his opponents, but acts towards them as he would wish them to act towards himself. Regarding the game as a healthful exercise, and a manly and exciting recreation, he plays it solely for the pleasure it affords him, and if victory crowns his efforts in a contest, well and good, but should defeat ensue he is equally ready to applaud the success obtained by his opponents; and by such action he robs defeat of half its sting, and greatly adds to the pleasure the game has afforded both himself and his adversaries. He never permits himself to be pecuniarily involved in a match, for knowing the injurious tendency of such a course of action to the best interests of the game, he values its welfare too much to make money an object in view in playing ball.

His Playing Qualifications

The physical qualifications of our model player are as follows:

To be able to throw a ball with accuracy of aim a dozen or a hundred yards.

To be fearless in facing and stopping a swiftly batted or thrown ball.

To be able to catch a ball either on the "fly" or bound, either within an inch or two of the ground, or eight or ten feet from it, with either the right or left hand, or both.

To be able to hit a swiftly pitched ball or a bothering slow one, with equal skill, and also to command his bat so as to hit the ball either within six inches of the ground or as high as his shoulder,

THE MODEL BASEBALL PLAYER

and either towards the right, centre or left fields, as occasion may require.

To be able to occupy any position on the field creditably, but to excel in one position only. To be familiar, practically and theoretically, with every rule of the game and "point" of play.

To conclude our description of a model baseball player, we have to say, that his conduct is as much marked by courtesy of demeanor and liberality of action as it is by excellence in a practical exemplification of the beauties of the game; and his highest aim is to characterize every contest in which he may be engaged, with conduct that will mark it as much as a trial as to which party excels in the moral attributes of the game, as it is one that decides any questions of physical superiority.

The Strange Case of Ed Delahanty

The Strange Case of Ed Delahanty

WHAT COULDN'T BIG ED DELAHANTY (1867–1903)—OLDEST AND BEST of the five Delahanty brothers to reach the majors—do with a baseball bat in his hands? In a sixteen-year career played primarily in Philadelphia, he hit over .400 three times, led both leagues in batting, smacked four homers in a game, and is one of only two players in baseball's long history to go six for six in a game *twice*. His career batting average of .346 is among the top ten of all time. But Delahanty was also plagued with demons, beset by the bottle, often in debt, chased by gamblers, and at the tipping point of a troubled marriage. He regularly threatened suicide.

Halfway through the 1903 season, his second after jumping to the Washington Senators in the upstart American League, Delahanty was unhappy, desperate to return to the more stable and established National League—and a bigger contract. He planned to abandon the Senators, plead his case for reinstatement to National League officials in New York, then sign with the Giants. So on July 2, he left his team in Detroit; set off by train to New York via Canada; and, well, was never heard from again. His mangled body was pulled from the waters beneath Niagara Falls a week later, his tie still in place but his diamond rings gone from his fingers. Interestingly, the second story below thickens the plot by introducing the body of a woman that surfaced right after Delahanty's, though the cash that she was supposedly carrying when she boarded the train never did.

Brother Frank Delahanty rushed to the scene to identify what was left of Big Ed. "I have some suspicion about how Ed went off that bridge," he told the inquiring press. "The poor fellow is dead now, and he can never tell his side of the story, but the others can tell just what they please."

And while certain facts revealed themselves in the pair of unsigned stories from the *New York Times* later in the week following his disappearance, questions still linger, and the death of Delahanty, arguably the greatest player of the nineteenth century, remains a mystery.

NO TRACE OF DELAHANTY
Missing Baseball Player Believed to Have Been Drowned at Buffalo

BUFFALO, July 8—A close watch is being kept along the river below the International Bridge for the reappearance of the body of a man, now believed to be Edward Delahanty, the famous baseball player, who fell through the open draw of the bridge last Thursday night. The then unknown man was put off a Pullman car on Train No. 6, on the Michigan Central Railroad at Bridgeburg. He started to walk across the bridge to Buffalo. Sam Kingston, the night watchman on the bridge, ordered him to return to shore. According to Kingston's story the man supposed to be Delahanty started to run toward the American end of the bridge. The draw had been opened to allow a boat to pass, he says, and the man fell into the river and was drowned. River men say the body should come to the surface today or tomorrow at the latest.

Superintendent Bennett of the Pullman Car Company said today:

"I found in the valise left by the passenger put off No. 6 a season pass to the Washington Baseball Park made out in the name of Ed. Delahanty. I found in the suitcase a suit of clothes with Delahanty's name on it, also the name of the tailor in Washington who made it. There was a pair of baseball shoes in the satchel. I wrote at once to the tailor in Washington and learned the address of Delahanty's family. I wrote Delahanty's wife in Washington on receipt of this information, telling her of the circumstances, and saying I believed her husband was drowned off the bridge on the night in question."

Baseball Player Swept over Niagara Falls—Woman's Body Also Recovered.

NIAGARA FALLS, N.Y., July 9.—The body of Edward Delahanty, the right fielder of the Washington baseball team of the American League, who fell from the International Bridge last Thursday night, was taken from the river at the lower Niagara gorge today. Relatives of Delahanty arrived here this afternoon and positively identified the body as that of the missing baseball player.

The body of a woman thirty-five years old was also recovered at Lewiston today. It has not been identified.

Delahanty's body was mangled. One leg was torn off, presumably by the propeller of the Maid of the Mist, near whose landing the body was found. The body will be shipped to Washington tonight. Delahanty's effects have been sent to his wife by the Pullman people.

Frank Delahanty of the Syracuse team and E.J. McGuire, a brother-in-law, from Cleveland, are here investigating the death of the player. They do not believe that Delahanty committed suicide or that he had been on a spree in Detroit. In the sleeper on the Michigan Central train on the way down from Detroit, Delahanty had five drinks of whiskey says Conductor Cole, and became so obstreperous that he had to put him off the train at Bridgeburg at the Canadian end of the bridge. Cole says Delahanty had an open razor and was terrifying others in the sleeper. When the train stopped at Bridgeburg Cole did not deliver Delahanty up to a constable, as the Canadian police say he should have done. He simply put him off the train.

After the train had disappeared across the bridge, Delahanty started to walk across, which is against the rules. The night watchman attempted to stop him, but Delahanty pushed the man to one side. The draw of the bridge had been opened for a boat, and the player plunged into the dark waters of the Niagara.

Delahanty's relatives hint at foul play, but there is nothing in the case, apparently, to bear out such a theory.

How I Pitched the First Curve

How I Pitched the First Curve

Candy Cummings

DID HE OR DIDN'T HE? SOME SAY IT'S SETTLED LAW; FOR OTHERS, THE jury is out. But the fact remains: William Arthur "Candy" Cummings (1848–1924) is credited with inventing the pitch that's come down to us as the curveball. His discovery came in the mid-1860s. That, as the *New Yorker*'s Roger Angell once observed, it would take another sixty years to come up with the slider is nothing short of a national disgrace.

Cummings pitched in an era when hurlers were required to throw underhanded from a pitching circle forty-five feet from home plate. Once he realized that a slight, imperceptible—if illegal—twist of the wrist at release could create added movement to his pitch and that for the rest of his life he could then pitch his claim for progenitorship, as in this piece from *Baseball Magazine* in 1908, Cummings had his golden ticket to baseball immortality. His National League record of 21–22 is deceptive; he pitched the bulk of his career before the league's founding. In his prime, Cummings and his curveball dominated. In 1872, the second season of National Association play, the 120-pound hurler went 33–20 for the New York Mutuals, recording fifty-three complete games. The following season, for Baltimore, his record was 28–14; in 1875, pitching for the Hartford Dark Blues—Mark Twain's favorite team—he went 35–12. And, before that, he'd reigned over amateur baseball for years. By the time the National League was born, Cummings's right arm was cooked—and other pitchers had begun figuring out their own versions of his magical pitch.

I have been asked how I first got the idea of making a ball curve. I will now explain. It is such a simple matter, though, that there is not much explanation.

In the summer of 1863 a number of boys and myself were amusing ourselves by throwing clam shells (the hard-shell variety) and watching them sail along through the air, turning now to the right and now to the left. We became interested in the mechanics of it and experimented for an hour or more.

All of a sudden it came to me that it would be a good joke on the boys if I could make a baseball curve the same way. We had been playing "three old cat" and town ball, and I had been doing the pitching. The joke seemed so good that I made a firm decision that I would try to play it.

I set to work on my theory and practiced every spare moment that I had out of school. I had no one to help me and had to fight it out alone. Time after time I would throw the ball, doubling up into all manner of positions, for I thought that my pose had something to do with it; and then I tried holding the ball in different shapes. Sometimes I thought I had it, and then maybe again in twenty-five tries I could not get the slightest curve. My visionary successes were just enough to tantalize me. Month after month I kept pegging away at my theory.

In 1864 I went to Fulton, New York, to a boarding school and remained there a year and a half. All that time I kept experimenting with my curve ball. My boyfriends began to laugh at me and to throw jokes at my theory of making a ball go sideways. I fear that some of them thought it was so preposterous that it was no joke and that I should be carefully watched over.

I don't know what made me stick at it. The great wonder to me now is that I did not give up in disgust, for I had not one single word of encouragement in all that time, while my attempts were a standing joke among my friends.

After graduating, I went back to my home in Brooklyn, New York, and joined the "Star Juniors," an amateur team. We were very successful. I was solicited to join as a junior member the Excelsior club, and I accepted the proposition.

In 1867 I, with the Excelsior club, went to Boston, where we played the Lowells, the Tri-Mountains, and Harvard clubs. During these games I kept trying to make the ball curve. It was during the Harvard game that I became fully convinced that I had succeeded in doing what all these years I had been striving to do. The batters were missing a lot of balls; I began to watch the flight of the ball through the air and distinctly saw it curve.

A surge of joy flooded over me that I shall never forget. I felt like shouting out that I had made a ball curve; I wanted to tell everybody; it was too good to keep to myself.

But I said not a word and saw many a batter at that game throw down his stick in disgust. Every time I was successful, I could scarcely keep from dancing from pure joy. The secret was mine.

There was trouble, though, for I could not make it curve when I wanted to. I would grasp it the same, but the ball seemed to do just as it pleased. It would curve, all right, but it was very erratic in its choice of places to do so. But still it curved!

The baseball came to have a new meaning to me; it almost seemed to have life.

It took time and hard work for me to master it, but I kept on pegging away until I had fairly good control.

In those days the pitcher's box was 6 feet by 4, and the ball could be thrown from any part of it; one foot could be at the forward edge of the box, while the other could be stretched back as far as the pitcher liked; but both feet had to be on the ground until the ball was delivered. It is surprising how much speed could be generated under those rules.

It was customary to swing the arm perpendicularly and to deliver the ball at the height of the knee. I still threw this way but brought in wrist action.

I found that the wind had a whole lot to do with the ball curving. With a wind against me I could get all kinds of a curve, but the trouble lay in the fact that the ball was apt not to break until it was past the batter. This was a sore trouble; but I learned not to try to curve a ball very much when the wind was unfavorable.

I have often been asked to give my theory of why a ball curves. Here it is: I give the ball a sharp twist with the middle finger, which causes it to revolve with a swift rotary motion. The air also, for a limited space around it begins to revolve, making a great swirl, until there is enough pressure to force the ball out of true line. When I first began practicing this new legerdemain, the pitchers were not the only ones who were fooled by the ball. The umpire also suffered. I would throw the ball straight at the batter; he would jump back, and then the umpire would call a ball. On this I lost, but when I started the spheroid toward the center of the plate, he would call it a strike. When it got to the batter, it was too far out, and the batter would not even swing. Then there would be a clash between the umpire and the batter. But my idlest dreams of what a curved ball would do as I dreamed of them that afternoon while throwing clam shells have been filled more than a hundred times. At that time I thought of it only as a good way to fool the boys, its real practical significance never entering my mind.

I get a great deal of pleasure now in my old age out of going to games and watching the curves, thinking that it was through my blind efforts that all this was made possible.

Why Base Ball Has Become
Our National Game

Why Base Ball Has Become Our National Game

Albert G. Spalding

CHANCES ARE IF YOU'VE EVER PUT ON A BASEBALL GLOVE OR BOUNCED A basketball, you're familiar with the name of Spalding. But before Albert Goodwill Spalding (1849–1915) cofounded what would become one of the preeminent purveyors of sporting goods on the planet, he was one heckuva ball player. Indeed, without the diamond skills to launch his name, all those Spalding tennis rackets and golf clubs would have never existed.

Playing professionally from 1871 to 1876, Spalding hurled his way to a 251–65 won–lost record, still the best by percentage ever recorded. He threw sixty-five complete games for Boston in 1874 and won fifty-two of them. After moving over to the Chicago White Stockings two years later, he helped craft the founding documents of the new National League, before heading to the mound to win forty-seven games that season, losing only twelve.

In Chicago, Spalding pitched, managed, won the first National League championship, then moved to the front office. In 1882, he took over the club entirely and in 1888–1889, organized the famed World Tour that so beguiled Walt Whitman and Mark Twain. By the early 1890s, his focus had switched from baseball to business—to his growing sporting goods empire and his publishing imprint, which in 1911 put out *America's National Game*, his memoir cum baseball credo. This essay batted leadoff in its table of contents. How much of this did Spalding write himself? Hard to say. He originally hired Henry Chadwick to pen what

Spalding envisioned as an origins and history of the game, but how much Chadwick had actually contributed before his death is uncertain. The book became a national bestseller, with more than ninety thousand copies sold in the first six months alone.

Have we, of America, a National Game? Is there in our country a form of athletic pastime which is distinctively American? Do our people recognize, among their diversified field sports, one standing apart from every other, outclassing all in its hold upon the interest and affection of the masses? If a negative reply may truthfully be given to all or any of these queries, then this book should never have been published—or written.

But, if we have a National Game; if we know a form of athletics which is peculiarly American, and have adopted it as our own; if it is American in its spirit, its character and its achievements; if it conforms in every way to the American temperament; if we have a field sport outranking all others in popularity, then it is indeed time that the writing, in personal reminiscence, of its story in book form should begin, "lest we forget" the salient points in the inception, evolution and development of so important a factor in the widespread entertainment of the American people and the physical upbuilding of our youth.

To enter upon a deliberate argument to prove that Base Ball is our National Game; that it has all the attributes of American origin, American character and unbounded public favor in America, seems a work of supererogation. It is to undertake the elucidation of a patent fact; the sober demonstration of an axiom; it is like a solemn declaration that two plus two equal four.

Every citizen of this country who is blessed with organs of vision knows that whenever the elements are favorable and wherever grounds are available, the great American game is in progress, whether in city, village or hamlet, east, west, north or south, and that countless thousands of interested spectators gather daily throughout the season to witness contests which are to determine the comparative excellence of competing local organizations or professional league teams.

The statement will not be successfully challenged that the American game of Base Ball attracts more numerous and larger gatherings of spectators than any other form of field sport in any land. It must also be admitted that it is the only game known for which the general public is willing day after day to pay the price of admission. In exciting political campaigns, Presidential candidates and brilliant orators will attract thousands; but let there be a charge of half a dollar imposed, and only Base Ball can stand the test.

I claim that Base Ball owes its prestige as our National Game to the fact that as no other form of sport it is the exponent of American Courage, Confidence, Combativeness; American Dash, Discipline, Determination; American Energy, Eagerness, Enthusiasm; American Pluck, Persistency, Performance; American Spirit, Sagacity, Success; American Vim, Vigor, Virility.

Base Ball is the American Game par excellence, because its playing demands Brain and Brawn, and American manhood supplies these ingredients in quantity sufficient to spread over the entire continent.

No man or boy can win distinction on the ball field who is not, as man or boy, an athlete, possessing all the qualifications which an intelligent, effective playing of the game demands. Having these, he has within him the elements of pronounced success in other walks of life. In demonstration of this broad statement of fact, one needs only to note the brilliant array of statesmen, judges, lawyers, preachers, teachers, engineers, physicians, surgeons, merchants, manufacturers, men of eminence in all the professions and in every avenue of commercial and industrial activity, who have graduated from the ball field to enter upon honorable careers as American citizens of the highest type, each with a sane mind in a sound body.

It seems impossible to write on this branch of the subject—to treat Base Ball as our National Game—without referring to Cricket, the national field sport of Great Britain and most of her colonies. Every writer on this theme does so. But, in instituting a comparison between these games of the two foremost nations of earth, I must not be misunderstood. Cricket is a splendid game, for Britons. It is a genteel game, a conventional game—and our cousins across the Atlantic are nothing if not conventional. They play Cricket because it accords with the traditions of their country so to do; because it is easy and does not overtax their energy or their thought. They play it because they like it and it is the proper thing to do. Their sires, and grandsires, and great-grandsires played Cricket—why not they? They play Cricket because it is their National Game, and every Briton is a Patriot. They play it persistently—and they play it well. I have played Cricket and like it. There are some features about that game which I admire more than I do some things about Baseball.

But Cricket would never do for Americans; it is too slow. It takes two and sometimes three days to complete a first-class Cricket match; but two hours of Base Ball is quite sufficient to exhaust both players and spectators. An Englishman is so constituted by nature that he can wait three days for the result of a Cricket match; while two hours is about as long as an American can wait for the close of a Base Ball game—or anything else, for that matter. The best Cricket team ever organized in America had its home in Philadelphia—and remained there. Cricket does not satisfy the red-hot blood of Young or Old America.

The genius of our institutions is democratic; Base ball is a democratic game. The spirit of our national life is combative; Base Ball is a combative game. We are a cosmopolitan people, knowing no arbitrary class distinctions, acknowledging none. The son of a President of the United States would as soon play ball with Patsy Flannigan as with Lawrence Lionel Livingstone, provided only that Patsy could put up the right article. Whether Patsy's dad was a banker or boiler-maker would never enter the mind of the White House lad. It would be quite enough for him to know that Patsy was up in the game.

I have declared that Cricket is a genteel game. It is. Our British Cricketer, having finished his day's labor at noon, may don his negligee shirt, his white trousers, his gorgeous hosiery and his canvas shoes, and sally forth to the field of sport, with his sweetheart on one arm and his Cricket bat under the other, knowing that he may engage in his national pastime without soiling his linen or neglecting his lady. He may play Cricket, drink afternoon tea, flirt, gossip, smoke, take a whiskey-and-soda at the customary hour, and have a jolly, conventional good time, don't you know?

Not so the American Ball Player. He may be a veritable Beau Brummel in social life. He may be the Swellest Swell of the Smart Set in Swelldom; but when he dons his Base Ball suit, he says good-bye to society, doffs his gentility, and becomes—just a Ball Player! He knows that his business now is to play ball, and that first of all he is expected to attend to business. It may happen to be his business to slide; hence, forgetting his beautiful new flannel uniform, he cares not if the mud is four inches deep at the base he intends to reach. His sweetheart may be in the grandstand—she probably is—but she is not for him while the game lasts.

Cricket is a gentle pastime. Base Ball is War! Cricket is an Athletic Sociable, played and applauded in a conventional, decorous and English manner. Base Ball is an Athletic Turmoil, played and applauded in an unconventional, enthusiastic and American manner.

The founder of our National Game became a Major General in the United States Army! The sport had its baptism when our country was in the preliminary agonies of a fratricidal conflict. Its early evolution was among the men, both North and South, who, during the war of the sixties, played the game to relieve the monotony of camp life in those years of melancholy struggle. It was the medium by which, in the days following the "late unpleasantness," a million warriors and their sons, from both belligerent sections, passed naturally, easily, gracefully, from a state of bitter battling to one of perfect peace. Base Ball, I repeat, is War! and the playing of the game is a battle in which every contestant is a commanding General, who, having a field of occupation, must defend it; who, having gained an advantage, must hold it by the employment of every faculty of his brain and body, by every resource of his mind and muscle.

But it is a bloodless battle; and when the struggle ends, the foes of the minute past are friends of the minute present, victims congratulating victors, conquerors pointing out the brilliant individual plays of the conquered. It would be as impossible for a Briton, who had not breathed the air of this free land as a naturalized American citizen; for one who had no part or heritage in the hopes and achievements of our country, to play Base Ball, as it would for an American, free from the trammels of English traditions, customs, conventionalities, to play the national game of Great Britain.

Let such an Englishman stand at the batter's slab on an American ball field, facing the son of an American President in the pitcher's box, and while he was ruminating upon the propriety of hitting, in his "best form," a ball delivered by the hands of so august a personage, the President's boy would probably shoot three hot ones over the plate, and the Umpire's "Three strikes; you're out," would arouse our British cousin to a realization that we have a game too lively for any but Americans to play.

On the other hand, if one of our cosmopolitan ball artists should visit England, and attempt a game of Cricket, whether it were Cobb, Lajoie, Wagner, or any American batsman of Scandinavian, Irish, French or German antecedents; simply because he was an American, and even though the Cricket ball were to be bowled at his feet by King George himself, he would probably hit the sphere in regular Base Ball style, and smash all conventionalities at the same time, in his eager effort to clear the bases with a three-bagger.

The game of Base Ball is American as to another peculiar feature. It is the only form of field sport known where spectators have an important part and actually participate in the game. Time was, and not long ago, when comparatively few understood the playing rules; but the day has come when nearly every man and boy in the land is versed in all the intricacies of the pastime; thousands of young women have learned it well enough to keep score, and the number of matrons who know the difference between the short-stop and the back-stop is daily increasing.

But neither our wives, our sisters, our daughters, nor our sweethearts, may play Base Ball on the field. They may play Cricket, but seldom do; they may play Lawn Tennis, and win championships; they may play Basket Ball, and achieve laurels; they may play Golf, and receive trophies; but Base Ball is too strenuous for womankind, except as she may take part in the grandstand, with applause for the brilliant play, with waving kerchief to the hero of the three-bagger, and, since she is ever a loyal partisan of the home team, with smiles of derision for the Umpire when he gives us the worst of it, and, for the same reason, with occasional perfectly decorous demonstrations when it becomes necessary to rattle the opposing pitcher.

But spectators of the sterner sex may play the game on field, in grandstand or on bleachers, and the influence they exert upon the contest is hardly less than that of the competitors themselves. In every town, village and city is the local wag. He is a Base Ball fan from infancy. He knows every player in the League by sight and by name. He is a veritable encyclopedia of information on the origin, evolution and history of the game. He can tell you when the Knicker-bockers were organized, and knows who led the batting list in every team of the National and American Leagues last year. He never misses a game. His witticisms, ever seasoned with spice, hurled at the visitors and now and then at the Umpire, are as thoroughly enjoyed by all who hear them as is any other feature of the sport. His words of encouragement to the home team, his shouts of derision to the opposing players, find sympathetic responses in the hearts of all present.

But it is neither the applause of the women nor the jokes of the wag which make for victory or defeat in comparison with the work of the "Rooter." He is ever present in large numbers. He is there to see the "boys" win. Nothing else will satisfy him. He is bound by no rules of the game, and too often, perhaps, by no laws of decorum. His sole object in life for two mortal hours is to gain victory for the home team, and that he is not overscrupulous as to the amount of racket emanating from his immediate vicinity need not be emphasized here.

And so it comes to pass that at every important game there is an exhibition in progress, in grandstand and on bleachers, that is quite as interesting in its features of excitement and entertainment as is the contest on the field of sport, and which, in its bearing upon the final result, is sometimes a factor nearly as potent as are the efforts of the contesting players. It must be admitted that as the game of Base Ball has become more generally known; that is, as patrons of the sport are coming to be more familiar with its rules and its requirements, their enjoyment has immeasurably increased; because, just in so far as those in attendance understand the features presented in every play, so far are they able to become participators in the game itself. And beyond doubt it is to this growing knowledge on the part of the general public with the pastime that its remarkable popularity is due. For, despite the old adage, familiarity does not breed contempt, but fondness, and all America has come to regard Base Ball as its very own, to be known throughout the civilized world as the great American National Game.

Finally, in one other particular Base Ball has won its right to be denominated the American National Game. Ever since its establishment in the hearts of the people as the foremost of field sports, Base Ball has "followed the flag." It followed the flag to the front in the sixties, and received then an impetus which has carried it to half a century of wondrous growth and prosperity. It has followed the flag to Alaska, where, under the midnight sun, it is played on Arctic ice. It has followed the flag to the Hawaiian Islands, and at once supplanted every other form of athletics in popularity. It has followed the flag to the Philippines, to Porto Rico and to Cuba, and wherever a ship floating the Stars and Stripes finds anchorage to-day, somewhere on nearby shore the American National Game is in progress.

Prejudice on the Diamond before the Color Line Was Drawn

Prejudice on the Diamond before the
Color Line Was Drawn

No surprise that the nation's great scarring shame would cut through its national pastime. Racism cut deep—and early—across the weave of organized ball.

What Moses "Fleetwood" Walker experienced as a semipro playing for a Cleveland sewing machine company against Louisville in August 1881, as reported below by the *Louisville Courier-Journal*, was emblematic of the abuse Black players would endure—and continue to even after Jackie Robinson became the first to cross the Major League Baseball color line in 1947, though to be technical about it, Robinson was third in line; the Oberlin-educated Walker crossed that barrier first, with the Toledo Blue Stockings of the American Association sixty-three years earlier. Walker's brother Weldy—he plays an important role in the next chapter—briefly joined him on the Blue Stockings roster that season, making him, thus, the second. Neither played another season at the major league level. Baseball's unwritten—though very de facto—rule barring Blacks was being laid down.

But we're getting ahead of ourselves.

As the story goes, in 1883, the year before Toledo was elevated to major league status, Walker joined the then minor league Blue Stockings, catching sixty of its eighty-four games en route to the Northwestern League championship. In August, the Chicago White Stockings, led by their powerful player–manager Cap Anson, arrived in Toledo for an exhibition game. Anson made it clear that his team wouldn't play if Walker was in the lineup. Originally, Walker hadn't been; he was nursing an injury. Then, Charlie Morton, Toledo's manager, called Anson on his threat, and sent Walker to the outfield. Anson went ballistic, but the White Stockings took the field rather than forfeit Chicago's share of the gate. Anson vowed never to play ball against a Black man again.

And when Anson and his National League champion White Stockings pulled into Newark four years later for an exhibition against the International League's Little Giants, he made good on his vow. The Giants had a dominating Black pitcher named George Stovey, and his catcher was, to firm the story's circle, Fleetwood Walker. Sadly, Newark's manager Charles Hackett was no Charlie Morton; he kept both Stovey and Walker out of the lineup. Newark won the game, but baseball lost the war. Anson's threat—and the gate receipts that would evaporate if the White Stockings refused to play—were just too much.

That night's edition of the *Newark Evening News* told the story on the front page under a headline that pulled no punches: "DRAWING THE COLOR LINE; Chicago Unwilling to Play with Stovey, No More Colored Players." Not only had Anson prevailed; that same afternoon the sages of the International League met in Buffalo and passed a resolution effectively barring Black players' contracts going forward, insisting "African players drove white men from the league." Stovey and Walker finished their season with Newark. So did other Black players in the league. But that was it.

Mark the date, then: July 14, 1887. The line was drawn. It would take baseball another sixty years to begin erasing its shame.

There were between 2,000 and 3,000 persons present to see the game at Eclipse Park yesterday between the ball-players of the White Sewing-machine Company of Cleveland and the home nines. What promised to be a very exciting gamed turned out to be a very ordinary one.

The Clevelands have won a fine reputation this season, and the score of six to three in favor of the Eclipse was not earned against the visitors on merit. The score might have told a very different story but for an incident which occurred during the second inning, in which a great deal of feeling was exhibited, and which caused considerable comment of an unfavorable nature upon the conduct of the Eclipse Club. The Cleveland Club brought with them as catcher for their nine a young [Black man] named Walker. The first trouble they experienced from Kentucky prejudice was at the St. Cloud Hotel yesterday morning at breakfast, when Walker was refused accommodations. When the club appeared on the field for practice before the game the managers and some of the players of the Eclipse Club objected to Walker playing on account of his color. In vain, the Clevelands protested that he was their regular catcher, and that his withdrawal would weaken the nine.

The prejudice of the Eclipse was either too strong, or they feared Walker, who has earned a reputation of being the best amateur catcher in the Union. He has played against other League clubs, without protest. The Louisville managers decided that he could not play, and the Clevelands were compelled to substitute West. During the inning West was "burned out" by the terrific pitching of Jones, and when the Eclipse went to bat in the second inning after one or two efforts, West said he could not face the balls with his hands so badly bruised, and refused to fill the position. The very large crowd of people present, who saw that the Clevelands were a strong nine laboring under disadvantage, at once set up a cry in good nature for [Walker]. Vice President Carroll of the Eclipse walked down in the field and called on Walker to come and play. He was disinclined to do so, after the general ill-treatment he had received; but as the game seemed to be in danger of coming to an end, he consented, and started to the catcher's stand. As he passed before the grandstand he was greeted with cheers, and from the crowd rose cries of "Walker, Walker!" He still hesitated but finally threw off his coat and vest and stepped out to catch a ball or two and feel the bases. He made several brilliant throws and fine catches while the game waited.

Then Johnnie Reccius and Fritz Pfeffer, of the Eclipse nine, walked off the field and went to the club house, while others objected to the playing of the [Black man]. The crowd was so pleased with his practice, however, that it cheered him again and again and insisted that he play. The objection of the Eclipse players, however, was too much and Walker was compelled to retire. When it was seen that he was not to play, the crowed heartily and very properly hissed the Eclipse club, and jeered their misplays for several innings, while the visitors, for whom White consented to catch, obviously under disadvantage, were cheered to the echo. Jones, the pitcher, was not supported adequately, and if Walker had caught it is probable the Eclipse would have been defeated.

It was a very small piece of business, particularly when Walker was brought out as a substitute for a disabled man and invited to play by the Vice President of the Eclipse, who acted very properly in the matter. The Clevelands acted foolishly in playing. They should have declined to play unless Walker was admitted and entered suit for gate money and damages. They could have made their point because it was understood that Walker was catcher, and no rules provide for the rejection of players on account of "race, color, or previous condition of servitude." The crowd was anxious to see Walker play, and there was no social question concerned. Walker shood the dust of Louisville from his feet last night and went home. The succeeding games will be totally uninteresting, since without him the Clevelands are not about to play the Eclipse a good game.

The Color Line

The Color Line

Sol White

LIKE SO MANY TITANS OF BASEBALL'S EARLY YEARS, SOL WHITE (1868–1955) was a multitalented, multifaceted visionary. On the field, as a player between 1887 and 1901, he was a hard-hitting infielder who could—and did—play any position on the diamond. In 1902, he added to his resume, cofounding the Philadelphia Giants; as owner, manager, and player, he led them to a series of championships across the rest of the decade. His 1905 club won 134 games. Ever the gentleman, he was inordinately proud of the fact that across his long baseball career, he was never once thrown out of a game.

And, as a Black man, White accomplished all of that in the shadow world beyond the embrace of organized baseball, which made it all the more remarkable, and worthy, certainly, of his enshrinement in the Hall of Fame. But there's more.

King Solomon's Giants were a juggernaut, winning 426 games in a four-year span, a record unsurpassed in all of professional baseball's annals. In 1905, they defeated white minor league opponents from five different leagues. Against rival Black teams that year, the Giants were undefeated. And still, White found time to finish a four-year college degree—and write one of the most important books in the game's essential library: *Sol White's History of Colored Baseball*.

A pamphlet, really, White's *History* was part of his *Official Baseball Guide*, published in 1907 and sold at Giants' games. The guide itself was something of a potpourri with chapters on hitting and pitching and profiles and photos of notable players. But its history portion was groundbreaking: an attempt to gather in one place the story of Black baseball, from before the organization of the first Black professional team in 1885 through the purge of Black players—and White was one of them—from organized baseball a few years later to the emergence of a more, well, colorful Black answer to an all-white game. His chapter on the establishment of the color line ends with a letter from Weldy Walker, the second African American to play in the majors; we met his brother Fleetwood, the first, in the previous story.

As for White's *History*, it would stand alone for another six decades before the next attempt at chronicling the story of Black baseball would be written. Sol White published his own; *Only the Ball Was White* bore the distinguished imprimatur of the Oxford University Press.

In no other profession has the color line been drawn more rigidly than in base ball. As far back as 1872 the first colored ball player of note playing on a white team was Bud Fowler, the celebrated promoter of colored ball clubs, and the sage of base ball. Bud played on a New Castle, Pennsylvania, team that year. Later the Walker Brothers, Fleet and Weldy, played on prominent college teams of the West. Fleet Walker has the distinction of being the only known colored player that ever played it in one of the big leagues. In 1884 Walker caught for Toledo in the old American Association. At this time the Walker brothers and Bud Fowler were the only negroes in the profession.

In 1886 Frank Grant joined Buffalo, of the International League. In 1887 no less than twenty colored ball players scattered among the different smaller leagues of the country.

With Walker, Grant, Stovey, Fowler, Higgins and Renfro in the International League, White, W. Walker, N. Higgins and R. Johnson in the Ohio League, and others in the West, made 1887 a banner year for colored talent in the white leagues. But this year marked the beginning of the elimination of colored players from white clubs. All the leagues, during the Winter of 1887 and 1888, drew the color line, or had a clause inserted in their constitutions limiting the number of colored players to be employed by each club.

This color line has been agitated by A. C. Anson, Captain of the Chicago National League team for years. As far back as 1883, Anson, with his team, landed in Toledo, O., to play an exhibition game with the American Association team. Walker, the colored catcher, was a member of the Toledos at the time. Anson at first absolutely refused to play his nine against Walker, the colored man, until he was told he could either play with Walker on this team or take his nine off the field. Anson in 1887 again refused to play the Newark Eastern League with Stovey, the colored pitcher, in the box. Were it not for this same man Anson, there would have been a colored player in the National League in 1887. John M. Ward, of the New York club, was anxious to secure Geo. Stovey and arrangements were about completed for his transfer from the Newark club, when a brawl was heard from Chicago to New York. The same Anson, with all the venom of hate which would be worthy of a Tillman or a Vardaman of the present day, made strenuous and fruitful opposition to any proposition looking to the admittance of a colored man into the National League. Just why Adrian C. Anson, manager and captain of the Chicago National League Club, was so strongly opposed to colored players on white teams cannot be explained. His repugnant feeling, shown at every opportunity, toward colored ball players, was a source of comment through every league in the country, and his opposition, with his great popularity and power in base ball circles, hastened the exclusion to the black man from the white leagues.

The colored players are not only barred from playing on white clubs, but at times games are canceled for no other reason than objections being raised by a Southern ball player, who refuses to play against a colored ball club. These men from the South who object to playing are, as a rule, fine ball players, and rather than lose their services, the managers will not book a colored team.

The colored ball player suffers great inconvenience, at times, while traveling. All hotels are generally filled from the cellar to the garret when they strike a town. It is a common occurrence for them to arrive in a city late at night and walk around for several hours before getting a place to lodge.

The situation is far different to-day in this respect than it was years ago. At one time the colored teams were accommodated in some of the best hotels in the country, as the entertainment in 1887 of the Cuban Giants at the McClure House in Wheeling, W. Va., will show.

The cause of this change is no doubt due to the condition of things from a racial standpoint. With the color question upper-most in the minds of the people at the present time, such proceedings on the part of hotel-keepers may be expected and will be difficult to remedy.

It is said on good authority that one of the leading players and a manager of the National League is advocating the entrance of colored players in the National League with a view of signing "Matthews," the colored man, late of Harvard. It is not expected that he will succeed in this advocacy of such a move, but when such actions come to notice there are grounds for hoping that some day the bar will drop and some good man will be chosen from out of the colored profession that will be a credit to all, and pave the way for others to follow.

This article would not be complete did we not mention the effort of John McGraw, manager of the New York National League, to sign a colored man for his Baltimore American League team.

While Manager McGraw was in Hot Springs, Ark., preparing to enter the season of 1901, he was attracted toward Chas. Grant, second baseman of the Columbia Giants of Chicago, who was also at Hot Springs, playing on a colored team. McGraw, whose knowledge of and capacity for base ball is surpassed by none, thought he saw in Grant a ball player and a card. With the color line so rigidly enforced in the American League, McGraw was at a loss as to how he could get Grant for his Baltimore bunch. The little Napoleon of base ball with a brain for solving intricate circumstances in base ball transactions, conceived the idea of introducing Grant in the league as an Indian. Had it not been for friends of Grant being so eager to show their esteem while the Baltimores were playing in Chicago, McGraw's little scheme would have worked nicely. As it was the bouquet tendered to Grant, which was meant as a gift for the colored man, was really his undoing. McGraw was immediately notified to release Grant at once, as colored players would not be tolerated in the league. This shows what a base ball man will do to get a winner and also shows why McGraw has been called by many, the greatest of all base ball managers.

The following open letter was sent to President McDermit, of the Tri-State (formerly Ohio) League, by Weldy Walker, a member of the Akron, O., team of 1887, which speaks for itself. The letter was dated March 5th, 1888. The law prohibiting the employment of colored players in the league was rescinded a few weeks later. Steubenville, O., March 5—Mr. McDermit, President Tri-State League—Sir:

I take the liberty of addressing you because noticing in The Sporting Life that the "law," permitting colored men to sign was repealed, etc., at the special meeting held at Columbus, February 22, of the above-named League of which you are the president. I ascertaining the reason of such an action I have grievances, it is a question with me whether individual loss subserves the public good in this case. This is the only question to be considered—both morally and financially—in this, as it is, or ought to be, in all cases that convinced beyond doubt that you all, as a body of men, have not been impartial and unprejudiced in your consideration of the great and important question—the success of the "National game."

The reason I say this is because you have shown partiality by making an exception with a member of the Zanesville Club, and from this one would infer that he is the only one of the three colored players Dick Johnson, alias Dick Neale, alias Dick Noyle, as the *Sporting Life* correspondent from Columbus has it; Sol White, of the Wheelings, whom I must compliment by saying was one, if not the surest hitter in the Ohio League last year, and your humble servant, who was unfortunate enough to join the Akron just ten days before they busted.

It is not because I was reserved and have been denied making my bread and butter with some clubs that I speak; but it is in hopes that the action taken at your last meeting will be called up for reconsideration at your next.

The law is a disgrace to the present age, and reflect very much upon the intelligence of your last meeting, and casts derision at the laws of Ohio—the voice of the people—that says all men are equal. I would suggest that your honorable body, in case that black law is not repealed, pass one making it criminal for a colored man or woman to be found in a ball ground.

There is now the same accommodation made for the colored patron of the game as the white, and the same provision and dispensation is made for the money of them both that finds its way into the coffers of the various clubs.

There should be some broader cause—such as lack of ability, behavior and intelligence—for barring a player, rather than his color. It is for these reasons and because I think ability and intelligence should be recognized first and last—at all times and by everyone—I ask the question again why was the "law permitting colored men to sign repealed, etc.?"

Yours truly,

Weldy W. Walker

Lady Baseballists

Lady Baseballists

When Lizzie Arlington (1877–1919) took the mound for the Philadelphia Reserves against Richmond on July 2, 1898—as the next day's *Philadelphia Inquirer* chronicled in detail—she was, indeed, the first woman to play professionally in a game with and against teams of professional men, but women were no strangers to diamonds and hadn't been for decades—even if diamonds weren't always their best friends. No one knows precisely when a woman first caught a ball or swung a bat or even joined her brothers or buddies on the local field—but when she did, she did so with enthusiasm; there are plenty of extant reports of women playing in America and even before that, in England. In her 1803 novel *Northanger Abbey*, Jane Austen's heroine "prefer[red] cricket, base ball, riding on horseback, and running about the country at the age of fourteen, to books." But as the game became more popular—and more organized—men, asserting dominion, manufactured all sorts of reasons to keep women off the field. What they really did was light a pilot until opportunity fanned the flame.

It ignited in Poughkeepsie, New York.

To promote good health and the idea of the well-rounded woman, a new fleet of women's schools began actively encouraging their students to participate in athletics; Vassar College—in 1866—gets credit for fielding the first two organized women's nines to play against each other. Other women's institutions—like Miss Porter's School and Smith College—followed. So did a cultural backlash. Parents deemed the exercise too strenuous, physicians argued that baseball's movements might damage the mechanics of reproduction, and some editorial wags simply claimed the idea of "lady baseballists" absurd.

The lady baseballists responded with raspberries, and the women's game gathered momentum.

Within a year, it was rolling out beyond the privileged confines of women's schools to cities and towns and open fields in all parts of the country. By 1868, a pair of teams had organized in Peterborough, New York, not far from Seneca Falls; Elizabeth Cady Stanton, one of the mothers of the women's rights movement, witnessed an early game. "We were delighted to find here a baseball club of girls," she wrote in a letter to *The Revolution*, the weekly paper she founded with Susan B. Anthony. "It is a very pretty sight to see the girls with their white dresses and blue ribbons flying, in full possession of the public square, last Saturday, while the boys were quiet spectators on the scene."

And so it went. The white dresses gave way to bloomers, and more women were drawn to the experience. More teams formed. The quality of play improved. In search of competition, women's clubs started traveling, sometimes to play exhibitions against men but more likely to take on other teams of women. Hats were passed to defray expenses. Then, in 1875, a savvy promoter from Springfield, Illinois, put together a team of blondes and a team of brunettes, sent them out to confront each other—and he paid them for their service, thus creating the first women pros. The game, by all accounts, seemed more theatrical than professional. But, hey, the public bought into it, and the idea of barnstorming blondes versus brunettes—though often denigrated in the press as "baseball burlesque"—took off. So did less coif-centric women's baseball. How seriously was the idea of women and baseball being taken? Seriously enough for women to have a ballpark of their own—not just an open field with stands—in 1879. Built in what's now midtown Manhattan, it was New York's first. The men had to wait for theirs—the Polo Grounds—for another year.

By the early 1890s, teams of young, single women, known as Bloomer Girls, from Boston, New York, Chicago, Kansas City, and beyond were earning good livings playing baseball—as Bloomer Girls would continue to do until they ran into the Depression. They toured the country by Pullman car and took on all comers. They played against local town's and women's clubs, semipros, and even minor league teams, and they won their fair share, though they rarely played each other; there was no league for them. If some perceived Bloomer baseball as a novelty, it may have been but only in the sense that their gender lured crowds out before their skills did. The truth is, though, they could really play ball. Fans loved them. The games were reported on in the local press. When the Chicago Bloomers became suddenly unavailable for a scheduled 1913 game in the nation's capital, the promoter tried to put one over on the ticket buyers; as the second story below—from the *Washington Post* on July 21, 1913— makes clear, the fans were none too happy.

Though Lizzie Arlington, regularly billed as the "champion lady baseball player of the world," was not an original Bloomer, she began touring with them in 1899. Her career as a professional in men's baseball was brief; it officially lasted just one more outing after her debut in Philadelphia when she pitched the ninth inning for the Reading Coal Heavers of the Atlantic League against Allentown. She allowed two hits and a walk—but no runs. More significantly, she had pitched in a sanctioned minor league game. As a Bloomer in 1899 and 1900, she led her team to a 268–87 record. She ended her career in 1901 after her marriage.

Interestingly, Ed Barrow, the Hall of Fame executive who helped build the Yankee dynasties of the twenties and thirties, was president of the Atlantic League when he saw Arlington pitch earlier in 1898. Ever the showman, he also realized she was the real deal—she could pitch, she could hit, and her presence would help fill seats. He bought her contract from the Reserves, signing Arlington for fifty dollars a game to pitch and play second base through the end of the 1898 season. When the Hartford manager protested, fearing his club could—horrors!—be bested by a woman, Barrow relented, and from then on, Arlington played only in exhibitions, not league contests. Still, if Barrow is guilty of exploiting the curiosity around Arlington, he wasn't about to embarrass himself—or the game. He knew talent when he saw it, and he knew how to think outside the box score. After all, he signed Honus Wagner to his first professional contract, then, as manager of the Red Sox, was responsible for turning a successful young pitcher named Babe Ruth into a power-hitting outfielder.

Almost a century would pass before another woman played in a minor league game. On May 31, 1997, Ila Borders pitched in relief for the St. Paul Saints of the independent Northern League.

LIZZIE ARLINGTON PLAYS GOOD BALL
Twirls the Ball Just Like a Real Man and Plays Second Base

Miss Lizzie Arlington made her debut as a professional base ball player under the shadow of Colonel Rogers' much lauded cantilever yesterday afternoon when she pitched for the Philadelphia Reserves against the Richmond Club. Miss Lizzie is a Mahanoy City maiden who learned to play ball up in the coal regions with her father and brothers. In her base ball costume she doesn't look over five feet in height, is stockily built, has brown eyes and hair, and lays claim to 22 summers, and the same number of winters. Miss Arlington has been on a visit to this city, and much of her spare time has been spent in Fairmount Park playing ball with the "Sparrows." Captain William J. Conner, well known in sporting and theatrical circles, heard of her, went out to see her play, and engaged her on sight at $100 per week to finish the season under his management. Captain Conner is very proud of his new star and sees millions in her, but was sorely disappointed at the size of the crowd, not over 500 being present. He will do better next week when he goes on the Atlantic League circuit. Tomorrow Miss Arlington will pitch for the New York Athletic Club at Norristown. On Tuesday she is booked at Reading to pitch against Allentown. On Thursday she will twirl against Reading at Allentown, on Friday at Hartford against Newark, and on Saturday at Richmond against Norfolk.

In the eight-innings game played yesterday Miss Arlington pitched four innings and played second base the other four. She is certainly a good player considering her sex: she can throw just like a real man, field a grounder, catch a fly, and can hit 'em as good as the best amateurs. In pitching the ball does not come over the plate with the cannon-ball velocity of Rusie, but she has a medium pace and her high ball is very peculiar and generally effective. Miss Lizzie has never suffered from "Charley Horse," or never had a lame arm, but she said, naively: "I don't know, but I may have both if I stick to base ball." She was attired in a pair of loose fitting bloomers, over which hung a skirt coming below the knees. A loose fitting blouse with the figure "A" on the left breast and cap, all in gray, a belt, black golf stockings, and regulation base ball shoes completed her costume. Two rows of black braid run around her cap and the bottom of her skirt. She wore a pitcher's toe plate on her right foot and used a regulation glove on her left hand.

Miss Arlington asks no favors. She told the Richmond boys to play hard against her as they could. They did, but they couldn't win, Miss Lizzie's side being victorious by a score of 18 to 5. In the four innings she pitched, six hits were made off her, two of them scratches. The first two balls she pitched were called balls, the next two were called strikes, and on the next one Hahugey struck out. The next two men gave easy chances for outs, but errors made them safe, and then two hits followed which gave the Richmonds three runs. Sheridan made a hit in the second, and in the fourth Richmond made three successive hits, which, with an error, gave them two more runs, all they got in the game. On second base Miss Arlington only had one chance. This occurred in the seventh inning when with two out and Mike Kilroy on first, his brother Bill hit to Pichon. The latter gathered the ball and made a quick throw to Miss Arlington, who covered the bag and forced Mike at second.

Miss Arlington was five times at bat and made two base hits, besides drawing a pass to first, and both of her hits were the real genuine article. She came to bat first in the second inning and poked one to right just out of the second baseman's reach. In the second she fouled out, in the fourth she lifted a high one which dropped safe back of second and sent in a run; in the sixth she was given a base on balls and in the seventh she flied out to second base. Many women witnessed the game and at its conclusion Miss Arlington was warmly congratulated by them in the pavilion. Miss Arlington was presented with two handsome bunches of roses and a bouquet of red, white and blue flowers, the donors being Mrs. William J. Conners, Mr. Church and the guests of the Junction Hotel.

BATTLE OVER 'GIRLS'
4,000 at Ball Park Storm "Chicago Bloomer Nine" Prove Men in Disguise

Four thousand fans who had gone to the Union League baseball Park, at Fifteenth and H streets northeast, to see a game between the "Bloomer Girls" and a team of young men from Locust Point, Md., yesterday afternoon participated in what was almost a riot, when they learned that the "girls" were men disguised in wigs and feminine attire. In the rush and fight to get at the players and to obtain a return of the gate receipts, one arrest was made, a policeman was struck by a brick, and the uniforms of two other policemen were torn off their backs.

Having drawn a huge crowd four weeks ago in the same park, the "Chicago Bloomer Girls," who have been touring the United States and Cuba, were advertised to play a "return engagement" yesterday, with the result that upwards of 4,000 persons poured into the park . . .

While the fans, who had paid 25 cents admission and 10 cents additional to sit in the grandstand, were nursing their disappointment, the "girl" who was playing center field threw the ball all the way from deep center to the home plate. That roused the fans' suspicions, which were confirmed when a bold small boy slipped up behind the muscular blonde girl who was cavorting about third base and snatched the wig from "her" head.

Then it was that Capt. Daley, of the Ninth precinct, and six of his men were swept away like chaff before the surging rush of the crowd, which made for the gate in one swiftly moving mass, with the bloomered players warned in time, dashing on ahead. The "girls" got through the gates a little ahead of the rain of pop bottles, bricks, and other handy little things which the crowd sent after them, and into the clubhouse in H street, opposite the park, where they barricaded themselves. Capt. Daley and the patrolmen took up a position in front of the little building and prevented the crowd from rushing the doors, though they could not stop the shower of bottles and bricks which fell about the building.

Then the fans thought of their ill-spent money. "We want our money back!" they shouted. With that they swarmed about the ticket boxes and all but mobbed the ticket sellers, who had to be hurried into the automobile patrol wagon and speeded to the Ninth police precinct for safety.

Capt. Daley in the meantime tried to quiet the crowd by announcing that nobody would get his money back because the manager had already gone away with the gate receipts. That was too much for the crowd, and somebody threw a brick at the police captain, who dodged so that it struck Bicycle Policeman Williams on the right leg . . . Policemen Hauschild and Benham were badly battered. Both will need new blouses.

The automobile patrol, having returned from the station house, was used to transport the "bloomer girls" to Union Station, where they boarded a train for Baltimore, whence they had come to play baseball. There was some difficulty in getting them into it safely, but all got away without injury, though the crowd tried hard enough to reach them . . .

It was reported last night in sporting circles that the manager hired the young men from Baltimore when he learned that the real bloomer girls, who were to play in that city yesterday, could not come to Washington. It was also said that he tried to get all of the nine to don wigs, but that only three would do so—the pitcher, third baseman, and center fielder.

That High Jump: A Story of the Diamond

That High Jump: A Story of the Diamond

Kate Upson Clark

CONSIDER THE DATE: 1898. CONSIDER THE STADIUM: BASEBALL. Now, consider the writer: Kate Upson Clark. A woman writing a story about baseball in 1898. A woman writing a story about baseball in 1898? If Clark's short story isn't the first piece of baseball fiction by a woman to reach print in a popular journal, it's certainly in contention for Founding Mother even if she had to take on a male persona to relate it.

Indeed, while women had been actively playing the game for some four decades, the first women to break the grass ceiling on the sports pages were viewed more as novelties than sports writers; the *St. Louis Republic* sent Lucy Stoughton, its society columnist, off on a lark to interview a few ballplayers. Under the pseudonym Serena Lamb, she came back with a series of disarmingly personal interviews, including one with John McGraw who admitted how much he hated his Muggsy nickname. Another player waxed freely about his collection of silk ties. For the sport pages, this was something new. Few followed Stoughton's lead. Women wouldn't be fully accepted in the press box for another half century.

That Clark (1851–1935) landed on baseball as the arena for "That High Jump"—it appeared in the prestigious *Independent*, a journal, founded in 1848 and devoted to politics, religion, and literature—is a mark of her versatility; as a writer, she was less a star than the gifted utility player able to fit several niches. Born in Alabama, she was sent north for her education. After graduating from Wheaton Female Seminary (now Wheaton College), she went to work for the *Springfield Republican*, where she met her husband, the managing editor. When he became an editorial writer for the *New York Evening Post* in the mid-1880s, they moved to Brooklyn, and she joined him on the editorial staff, continuing at the same time to write on a wide variety of subjects for such magazines as *The Atlantic*, *Harper's*, and *Leslie's Weekly*. An active suffragist, she lectured widely around the country on politics, literature, and popular culture; taught at Columbia; and wrote several books for children and one novel. She was so widely admired as a civic leader that she became known as "The Grand Old Lady of Brooklyn," which means she was able to witness the evolution of the local nine from the Grays to the Atlantics to the Grays again, then to the Bridegrooms to the Grooms, back to the Bridegrooms, and on to the Superbas, the Trolley Dodgers, the Dodgers, the Robins, and finally back to the Dodgers again, this time for good. In Brooklyn, between the mid-1880s and the early 1930s, you didn't need a scorecard just to identify the players; you needed one to put a name to the team on the field as well.

When I was a Senior in the Mackenzie High School we had a great baseball team there. Nearly all of the teams in the neighboring towns had tried us, and we had beaten every one, not only the High School and Academy nines, but several in which there were grown-up men, some of them almost twice as large as some of us. We felt no great dismay, therefore, when we learned by a letter from their manager that the Denio Shoe-shops Nine, a famous organization from the largest town in the vicinity, had the first of July free, and would like to play us then.

Altho we had heard, like everybody else, of the prowess of the Denios, we did not know until after we had accepted their challenge that they were what is called a "tough" team—of the kind that carry flasks in their pockets when they go out of town. When this little rumor was wafted to the ears of good Dr. Sheldon, our principal, he rather favored our canceling the engagement; but we protested so vigorously that he finally yielded. He had been a great pitcher in his day, and he was almost as proud of our good ball-playing as he was of the fact that Mackenzie fellows were never conditioned when they went to college.

So the arrangements for the game went on. The first of July fell on a Saturday. We had played only one match-game that week, and that was with a "scrub" nine from the next town, on Wednesday. We hadn't let Hinks, our best pitcher, play in that; we had kept him fresh for Saturday. We had three fair pitchers that year, but Hinks was the daisy of all. He had an in-curve and a drop that a professional might have envied, tho he wasn't so speedy then as he grew to be later.

It turned out to be a grand day, a trifle too cool at first for the lookers-on, but not cold enough to stiffen us. We were in first-rate trim, and had four good substitutes, while Anderson, our umpire, stood ready to serve us. When the Denios came, however, we found that they had brought their umpire. We had heard ugly stories of that individual; but the final arrangements had been made by word of mouth, and of course there had been a misunderstanding. Such matters, as we found out by hard experience, should be settled only in black and white.

The game was called at two. The Denios came on the one-thirty train, and were to return on the five. There were twelve of them and a crowd of "rooters," who proved to be a profane and disgusting lot; but our sheriff was on hand, and he managed to drive a little decency into them, so that they were not allowed to shock the large assembly of the best village people, who always came to see us play our "big games."

The Denios professed to be astonished that we objected in the least to their umpire, and there was some sense in their comments, tho we had a first-class umpire, who had never given offense—or serious offense, perhaps I should say—to the other side. "The home team," they said, "has all the advantage in every outside way—loads of their friends to cheer them, and their own familiar grounds to play on."

So Anderson, our man, went off to the further side of the grounds, and watched us from beneath the trees there. It was a shady place and near enough, and most of the on-lookers preferred that position.

The Denios drew first inning. We played a sharp, quick game, and our inning came in a few minutes. They had not made so much as first base.

When I stood up at bat, therefore, being first on the list, I was feeling "fine." Their pitcher, Clennan, gave me a clean, rather high ball, and I hit it a tremendous blow over toward left. I thought it was good for two bases at least; but they had a terror of a fellow out in their left field, and tho my ball seemed likely to pass a foot over his head, he ran like a fiend, jumped in the air what looked like two feet, but was probably only ten inches or so, and caught the ball.

There was a great clapping at this among their crowd, and they gave their yell for the first time. It was "Helter skelter, hobble gobble, siss, boom, ah! Denio, Denio, Rah, rah, rah!" The left fielder, whose name was Turner, grinned at me like a gargoyle. The fellow was a disreputable-looking chap, and made me feel sick. I determined that I would strike out next time before I would send a hit in his direction; but I changed my mind about this later, as you will see.

At first I had put my sweater on over my uniform, and I had my vest on under that. I had been really chilly while we had been waiting around for the game to begin, but now I was getting warmed up. When I went back to the corner where our fellows were gathered, I stripped off my sweater, and then I remembered for the first time that I had forgotten to take off my vest, which had my watch in it. It was a nice gold one, which one of my dearest aunts had given me, and I wouldn't have lost it for anything. We usually gave our valuables to Anderson to keep. He had the deepest pockets and the most of them that I ever saw in my life; but there was Anderson forty rods off under the trees among all the ladies, and I didn't want to take it clear over there. There was a safe dressing-room in the school; but it was an eighth of a mile across the green to the school building, and I was altogether too much excited to leave everything just now and go over there. Berrian, our scorer, was sitting right here, and I believed the watch would be secure enough under his care.

"I am going to leave my watch in my vest-pocket," I said to Gardner, our "second," who was "in the hole" and looking pretty anxious as the fellow after me at bat knocked a little grounder right into the short-stop's hands, thus making two out for us. "I guess it will be safe enough. I'm too hot to wear the vest, and Berrian's right here."

"All correct," said Gardner, absently, and listening while Berrian called Worthley to bat, Gardner on deck and Niles in the hole. "Still," he added, suddenly, "you'd better give it to Anderson. This is a hard set around here."

"Nonsense!" I said, impatiently. "Who could touch it while Berrian is close by so?"

Gardner didn't say anything. Worthley had made a base hit, and Gardner was called to bat.

I pinned the vest together hastily. Berrian was industriously jotting down the assists and put-outs. He vowed now in an aside to me that the umpire had just called two strikes on Gardner when there had been only one. He was getting very mad.

"Look out for my watch, Berrian," I said, confidentially. "It is under my sweater, right in my vest-pocket there."

Then I settled down to the game. Berrian was quivering with excitement. He probably knew as little of what I had been saying to him as a hen. Gardner was now on first base, Worthley was stealing third, and Niles, our "short," a hard batsman, was up. It looked as tho we might get in a run. Niles gave a glorious hit; but it veered of foul, and one of their long-legged fielders caught it, so that we were out without a run, in spite of two men on bases.

Turner was their first man at bat. He was a clean hitter; and the first I knew down came a swift ball in my direction, considerably above my head. Incited, probably, by his example, I gave a jump into the air which must have seemed as high as Turner's in the field; and I, too, caught the ball, and in my turn put him out.

Now I had a chance to grin. I knew that I hadn't received Turner's grin with much grace; but he received mine, as the umpire called "Out!" with a really vicious scowl. I didn't care, however, under the circumstances. We got three men out in short order, and the next inning opened without a run on either side.

We had advanced to the fourth inning, and the score stood three to two in our favor, when it occurred to me that I might as well look after my watch. I strolled up to Berrian, therefore, and remarked casually: "I suppose my watch is all right."

"Watch!" he said, crossly, keeping me waiting while he put down an error for Gardner. "Where in thunder is your watch, anyway? I haven't seen it."

I realized then that he had paid no attention to what I had said when I left the watch, and that he had not felt the slightest responsibility for it. I began to fumble nervously about among the clothes on the ground beside him. It had been growing warmer steadily all the afternoon, and several sweaters and jerseys had been piled on top of my things. Just as I had excavated down to it I heard my name called "in the hole"; but I took time to find out that the vest had been unpinned, and that the watch was missing. I searched wildly around among the miscellaneous heap of stuff, but in those few confused minutes I naturally discovered nothing. My heart seemed to melt in what the boys called a "dull, thickening sud," as I was summoned away to take my place at the bat, and felt that my precious watch was gone, probably for good and all. But my wrath was not bad for my playing. I determined that I would give that ball such a hit that no Denio man could reach it if he jumped to the moon. Two strikes and three balls had been called on me before I met my chance. Then I did give the ball a hard enough knock to send all the stuffing out of it; but I had steered it off again toward left field, and again Turner gave one of his mighty jumps and caught me out.

If the catch had not been accompanied again by one of those impish grins of his I think I could have stood it; but this grin was even worse than the other, and I was simply boiling with rage when I went back to the bench. I had time to investigate only a moment more, when we were called to the field. I had whispered my loss, however, to most of our fellows, and we had agreed that it was likely my watch was at this moment in the pocket of one of the Denio crowd, probably one of the players, as they had all been swarming around Berrian during our "outings."

The ninth inning found us neck and neck. Their first baseman had hurt his hand, and my friend Turner had been called in from the field to occupy first base. We were tired and hot and frightfully excited, and they "pulled" four runs from us in that inning, leaving the score seven to three in their favor, when we finally "outed" them. Could we make five runs in that last little inning? We all set our teeth, and steadied our nerves with fresh gum (much to our mothers' horror), and went to bat with blood in our eyes.

They felt sure that they "had us." That proved a good thing. Worthley happened to have his turn at bat to open. He made a magnificent hit, one of those grand liners which just escape the short and second, and scare both right field and center into running. Now they both ran, and in spite of their captain's yell of "Center! Center!" bumped together, giving each of them a black eye, the ball skated off serenely between them, and Worthley made the first home run of the afternoon.

Our next fellow, Gardner, batted a fly-off which sent him to first base. The next two got out. The next made a two-bagger, and on his hit we added one to Worthley's run. Oh, if the next fellow only wouldn't get out! Every fiber in my body was a-tingle as he made a base hit, and Wells, our two-bagger, slid home, scraping six inches of cuticle off his right arm, but counting the sacrifice nothing but fun. Three runs—one on first base, and two out. This was the situation when I came to bat; and as Turner, now on first base, gave me one of his most awful grins, I vowed to make my base if I broke both my arms to do it.

I wanted to give a grounder, but one can't always manage that. If one gets any sort of a hit off such a pitcher as Clennan one may be thankful. I never experienced such fierce joy as when I felt my bat hit the ball hard and square; but I had a revulsion when I saw that it was going straight ahead of me as I ran for my base with all my dead might. It was a high flyer; but Turner had already shown that he could jump like a very jack, and I grew faint as I thought he would probably get it. With all the speed I could muster I forged up to first base just in time to see him jump, as it seemed to my excited vision, six feet, or more nearly, half a mile, in the air; but he had missed the ball, which sailed calmly over the head of the right fielder also, and my base was safe. But what was that round glittering thing which reposed directly on top of the sand-bag which formed our base? I ducked like lightning and picked it up. It was my watch! In a twinkling it was in my pocket, and, as I dashed on to second, I saw Turner, who had been cursing and muttering at the right fielder so that he had not observed my motions in the least, put his hand up to the breast-pocket of his blouse—which hung open, having burst its button-hole—and then begin to stare wildly all over the ground.

"You can stare, old gargoyle!" I chuckled to myself, as I stopped at second (tho I might have made third if it hadn't been for the watch). "That watch is in my trousers pocket, and you will never see it again."

The fellow who came after me made a great hit, and that was our salvation. He never went further than second, but the fellow ahead of me and I got in, and the score stood eight to seven, so that the game closed there.

After the train had gone the doctor came around to congratulate us. His face was as red as anybody's, and he almost shook our hands off. "I never was so proud of you, never!" he cried. "You not only played ball, but your manners never showed to better advantage. You seemed like angels beside those rude, profane rowdies. I thought a score of times of Tennyson's

"'His strength is as the strength of ten,
Because his heart is pure.'

"You beat them fairly, magnificently; and it was a victory of good morals as well as of good tactics. But did you ever see anybody jump like that fielder of theirs who afterward played first base? I never imagined anything like it."

"It was the luckiest thing in life for me, Doctor," I said; and then amid great excitement, ending in a storm of congratulations I told them the strange story of my lost watch. Some of them thought that I ought to have had Turner arrested, and perhaps I ought. But I didn't, and I suppose he wonders to this day whatever became of that watch.

The Son of Rusie Returneth

The Son of Rusie Returneth

Charles Dryden

IN THE ANNALS OF THE NATIONAL PASTIME, THERE WAS NEVER A knight of the keyboard quite like Charles Dryden (1860–1931) and no column ever unfurled from a platen quite like his biblically acerbic commemoration of the Indiana Thunderbolt Amos Rusie's return to the mound after holding out in a yearlong vitriolic dispute with Giants' owner Andrew Freedman. There may be no piece of nineteenth-century baseball writing so famous and infamous at the same time as the one Dryden wrote for the *New York Journal* on April 28, 1897.

The fourth scribe to be inducted into the writer's wing of baseball's Hall of Fame, Dryden was widely acclaimed in his time—and for years after—as not just the best baseball writer of his era but the funniest and most influential as well. The *Saturday Evening Post* deemed him "the Mark Twain of baseball" and "the man to whom the game owes more, perhaps, than any other individual."

Not bad for a kid from Monmouth, Illinois, who began his working life in a foundry as a molder. But Dryden wanted to be a writer, and he became one. He wrote his first baseball story in Chicago in 1889—covering the first game he'd ever seen—then moved West to work for papers in Tacoma and San Francisco before William Randolph Hearst lured him to New York in 1896 to join the staff of his *New York Journal*. Dryden went on to star on sports pages in Philadelphia and Chicago before a stroke ended his career in 1921.

Though pretty much forgotten today, it's pretty much impossible to imagine the lingo of the game without the deftness of his touch. He's the writer who nicknamed White Sox owner Charles Comiskey "The Old Roman." He coined the constructions "pinch hit" and "horsehide," designated the 1906 Cubs "The Hitless Wonders," and characterized the 1904 Senators as "first in war, first in peace, and last in the American League." And it was Dryden who attached the unforgettable "Bonehead" sobriquet to Fred Merkle after his, well, boneheaded miscue on the basepaths cost the Giants the 1908 pennant.

But Dryden wasn't just clever; he brought the game to life on the page, entertaining as well as informing. His influence over the generation of writers who shaped the craft in his wake was enormous. Fred Lieb rhapsodized over the way Dryden "towered over the baseball writers of his day," and when Ring Lardner was cheered for his own wit on the sports pages, he quickly redirected the laurels: "Me, a humorist?" he suggested. "Have you guys read any of Charley Dryden's stuff lately? He makes me look like a novice." At his death, the *Sporting News* eulogized the way he "lifted baseball out of the commonplace and made it almost a religion."

Dryden was in full stride when he assayed Rusie's return to the Giants after his famed holdout. The piece was introduced by this explanatory note, penned, of course, by Dryden himself: "It was written by the man who reports sermons for the Monday paper. His effort shows traces of an early religious training, coupled with a smattering of baseball."

A bit more explanation. While Amosenius is obvious, Andenius is the Giants' owner; Harlenium is Harlem, home of the Polo Grounds, which sat in a valley of Manhattan overlooking Coogan's Bluff; and the army of Wagnerius is the Washington Senators.

Following Rusie's victorious return, he posted a 28–10 record, en route to a career mark of 246–174 and a plaque in Cooperstown. His legacy is carved into every adult diamond. Known as much for his wildness—he walked 298 hitters in 1890, a shame still unequaled in a single season—as for his velocity, the solons of baseball so feared that Rusie might kill someone that it prompted their 1893 decision to move the pitching rubber back an additional five feet from home plate to the sixty feet, six inches where it's resided ever since. That didn't slow down

Rusie. Four years later, he managed to bean Baltimore shortstop Hughie Jennings, sending the future Hall of Famer into a coma for three days.

Sadly, a combination of alcohol, arm trouble, and the aftermath of being hit in the head himself—with a line drive—prematurely finished Rusie's career in 1898. Despite not pitching for two seasons, the Cincinnati Reds traded for him in 1900. In return, they sent the Giants an untested college boy named Christy Mathewson. Rusie never won another ball game. Matty did somewhat better.

Now it came to pass that on the 22nd day of the fourth month, Amosenius, the son of Rusie, who dwelleth afar in the land of Indiana, waxed sore afraid in exile, and wisdom increased with his years. Therefore, he lifted up his tongue, saying in a loud voice:

"This day will I arise and get me hence to the planes of Harlenium, where Bildad, the Bleacherite, roareth, and Andenius, the Magnate, mourneth for the pennant because it is not.

"For if not graven on tablets in the temple of Andenius that I shall cop off four and twenty hundred scudi per? And I fain would clog my system with the doughnuts that the Giants do eat."

So saying, Amosenius, the son of Rusie, swart of face and stout of wing, did gird up his gunnysack with implements of war. He bestowed therein his sandals of kangaroo skin weighing 90 shekels of brass, a leather girt piece, two phials of previous charley horse ointment and many leaves of the tobacco plant, wrought into plugs and garnished with mosaics of tin, from the marts of Jersey City.

And again and again, nay, even thrice, did Amosenius speak unto himself saying in placid accents:

"Verily I am a chump, no, not, nit. No more will I waste my substance in riotous pinochle, and only with the high fast ball shall the fans of Harlenium behold me engrossed."

At these words Andenius waxed exceeding joyful and caused them to be scattered broadcast among the scribes and the Pharisees. And lo! The voice of the scoffer was hushed in the land.

Now, when the 27th day of the fourth month was come the multitude that assembled from the highways and byways of the city to roost on the wind-swept bastions numbered 10,000 human beings, and the Philistine who did serve as umpire.

And the maids and the wives of them that were tarried at home with the oil stoves.

And when the hour of 4 was struck the disciples of Andenius said, one to the other:

"Behold, Amosenius, the prodigal, has returned to the plain. He will make monkeys of the hosts of the scoffer of Wagnerius."

Verily, these words were the words of prophets, for though they wrought valiantly, yet were the invaders overcome by a score of 8 tallies to 3.

For it is written on the score card that the army of Wagnerius could not swat a marble mausoleum were it pitched into them.

And lo, and behold, as the tumult ceased and silence brooded over the plain of Harlenium, where did issue forth Colonol Cooganius, the Bluffite, who did observe the battle from his cave on the hillside.

And it was met that this man should smite himself on the bosom and proclaim from the ramparts so that all might hear:

"Behold in me the Mascot that has come out of the wilderness to save."

And straightaway the Bluffite did offer to the scribes some mixed pickles and besought them to smoke.

And it came to pass that in the midst of the battle the umpire did take from one Giant 10 pieces of silver and from another 20 pieces.

Whereat spake one who was not of the arena, saying:

"Whence cometh this man brewing turmoil? Let him depart to soak himself in the brook Harlenium, which is over against Astoria."

But they suffered him to remain, and he was an eyesore.

And when the end was come the multitude fell into the arena to touch the hand of their redeemer, Amosenius, and kiss the hem of his toga.

From *Pipetown Sandy*

From *Pipetown Sandy*

John Philip Sousa

Yes, *that* John Philip Sousa. America's "March King." Conductor of the U.S. Marine Corps Band. Composer of "The Stars and Stripes Forever," "The Liberty Bell" (aka the *Monty Python* theme), "Semper Fidelis," and "The Washington Post" march. Sousa (1854–1932) grew up in what was then known as the Pipetown section of Washington's Capitol Hill; he returned to it in 1905 for *Pipetown Sandy*, his semiauto-biographical young-adult novel about a fourteen-year-old who happens to captain the local baseball team. The brief excerpt that follows opens the chapter of the big game. However soaring his music and rococo his prose, the requirements of the game kept his feet on the ground.

Because, it turns out, the love that Sousa developed for baseball as a kid never deserted him. For years, the bandleader put together a team from his musicians; as they toured, they would suit up against nines from other bands, local communities, and military outposts. He regularly took the mound into his mid-forties. He finally hung up his cleats when a local paper observed, *"The only trouble was that the March King had no control over the ball when he started to wrap himself up and you could not tell whether the ball was coming out in the direction of the batsmen or the centerfielder."*

Our national game! What an enemy to nepotism, or any other "ism" that thrives on the favor of influence!

Oh, base-ball! thou art truly the embodiment of purest democracy; like love, thou dost level all ranks.

Of what avail is distinguished ancestry, pre-Adamite origin, cerulean blood or stainless escutcheon, when one is at the bat and strikes out! Intellectual superiority, physical perfection, social status, wealth or poverty count for nothing, if you fail to bring in the winning run.

Discovering Cy Young

Discovering Cy Young

Alfred H. Spink

WHEN ALFRED H. SPINK (1854–1928) LEARNED FROM HIS OLD FRIEND Henry Chadwick that no comprehensive history of baseball then existed, he did what anyone who knew Al Spink would have expected: he wrote it. And who better? He was there for so much of it. Throughout a long romance with the game centered primarily in Chicago and St. Louis, he'd been a player, a writer, the sports editor of the *St. Louis Chronicle*, and a principal organizer and director of the team that became the St. Louis Browns. Topping it all, he created—in 1886—and served as first editor and publisher of *The Sporting News*. Embraced as "The Bible of Baseball," the paper rolled off presses weekly for well over a century and was considered for much of that run the game's trusted national voice.

Shortly after his correspondence with Chadwick, Spink—perhaps in a race against Al Spalding, represented earlier in these pages—sat down, plowed through his knowledge and memory, and produced a monument to baseball and the people who populated it. He called his history simply, but authoritatively, *The National Game*. First published in 1910, then revised in 1911, it remains an enormous compendium, part chronicle, part narrative, part encyclopedia, and all held together by Spink's unhidden affection for the game and its fabulous cast of characters—the managers; the owners; the press; the umps; and, of course, the players, Cy Young among them, whose major league debut with the Cleveland Spiders of 1890 is recounted from its pages. Spoiler alert: Young won that first outing. And 510 more.

Cy Young, the veteran pitcher, began his career in Cleveland, and Stanley Robison late president of the St. Louis National League Club, was the man who discovered Young. At the time Robison was owner of the Cleveland franchise, and the Spiders, under Pat Tebeau, were large grapes in the major league vineyard. It happened that Patsy Tebeau was short on pitchers way back about 1893. In those days they did not have scouts combing the country for talent, and the "tipsters" on blooming talent were usually commercial travelers.

Robison was at the time looking over some of his railroad property at Fort Wayne, Ind., and he was lapping up a few "elixirs of mirth," when he happened to open up his vocal chords on baseball. There was a commercial traveler at the bar, who liked baseball, to say nothing of having a fondness for the "elixir" stuff.

Stanley invited him to have a jolt, and also to discuss baseball. "Rather odd," remarked Robison, "that it is so hard to get a good baseball pitcher nowadays. I'm looking for a man for my Cleveland club. I've offered enough real money to choke a manhole to get a fellow from one of the other clubs; but, say, I can't make the deal."

"Have another, and I'll give you the best little three-star special you've ever heard tell of since they named you after Matt Quay," returned the commercial traveler.

After the commercial traveler and M. Stanley had inhaled their mirth water the man of satchels and grips opened the conversation. "Say, old sport," said the commercial traveler, "you're looking for a pitcher. As I understand the vernacular, you are in quest of someone who can hurl an elusive leather-covered sphere, guaranteed to weigh in ringside at five ounces, and to be of 9-inch circumference, no more or no less, somewhere near a little disk they foolishly refer to as the home plate. Get me?

"Now, my friend, take my tip, pack your grip and go up to Canton. They've got a big kid up there that can do anything with a baseball except eat it. Say, he's got so much speed that he burns chunks of holes in the atmosphere. He's the shoot-'em-in-Pete of that reservation. Watched him streak 'em over last Sunday, and he struck out a flock of baseball players. I think he fanned a hundred or two hundred. I didn't keep count. He made them describe figure 'eights,' stand on their beams and wigwag for help. You get your grip, if you want a pitcher, streak it to Canton, and don't let anyone tout you off."

Robison did as he was bade, and when he arrived at Canton he went out to the ball yard. There was a big, lop-sided yap on the mound. He looked as though nature chiseled him out to pitch hay, instead of a poor, little inoffensive baseball, and Robison had to laugh when he beheld the world-renowned bearcat twirler that his friend had tipped him off to. The big boy in the box showed a lot of steam, and Robison's desire to laugh was turned to amazement. He'd never beheld anyone toss a ball with just such speed and precision and with so many curlicues on it. After the game Robison called the young hay miner aside and offered him a job at a figure which made the youth open his mouth.

Robison slipped him transportation to Cleveland, with instructions to find his way out to the ball yard and call on Pat Tebeau, admonishing him to be careful not to get run over by any street cars, as he (Robison) owned the lines and didn't want any damage suits. The lop-sided boy found his way to the ball yard, asked for Mr. Teabow, blushed like a June bride and told him what he came for.

Tebeau called Zimmer and a few of his old scouts about him, and they openly laughed at the unusual looking boy, who had the nerve to say that he might be a baseball pitcher fit for major league company.

Chicago was in Cleveland. Old fans will recall those dreaded White Stockings, with Anson at their head; and such stars as Ned Williamson, Tommy Burns, Fred Pfeffer, Dalrymple, Jimmy Ryan and that sort on the roster. Those old boys used to give great pitchers that earthquake feeling about the knees when they dragged up their hundred-pound batons to thump the bitumen out of anything that came near the plate.

Tebeau thought it would be a good joke to pitch the young man against these sluggers and see the effect. He told the boy he wanted him to pitch. Then they dug up a uniform that fitted the lad like a 14½ collar would incase the neck of Frank Gotch. Anson and his bunch were as fierce baseball pirates as ever scuttled a ship, but they had to laugh at the lad who was to aim the pill at them. They roared when they saw him go into the box. But something happened. The mere boy struck out Adrian C. Anson, world's wonder with the bat; then he fanned Fred Pfeffer, the prince of second sackers, and slipped three across that Williamson missed entirely.

Then those Chicago sluggers began to take notice. Pat Tebeau saw that the boy he mistook for a clown was a real jewel in the rough. The boy won that game. He made the White Stockings look like a young simian trying to shave. That night the young lad's name was on every tongue. He was Cy Young, farmer, who became a famous baseball pitcher in one day, and who has been making good ever since. Young is a farmer yet. He cultivates his broad acres in Ohio and is well off.

Varsity Frank

Varsity Frank

Burt L. Standish

THOUGH CHARLES SHELDON NEVER AGAIN MINED THE GENRE HE CREated in his story about "The Captain of the Orient Base-Ball Nine," others rushed down that shaft, none more successfully or prolifically than Burt Standish, the pen name for a Maine-born writer of dime novels and manager of a semiprofessional baseball team named William George Gilbert Patten (1866–1945). Patten dreamed up a character named Frank Merriwell, and the rest, as they say, is history. Merriwell made Patten one of the best-selling authors of all time.

The first Merriwell story appeared in the mass-market magazine *Tip-Top Weekly* on April 18, 1896, and they continued to appear weekly—at twenty thousand words per installment—for the next twenty years. American boys worshipped at his altar, buying into the Merriwell stories' thrillingly simple formula. Frank Merriwell—all-American youth, well bred, well mannered, exceedingly handsome, exceptionally brilliant, and an athlete nonpareil, first at prep school, then at Yale—faced moral dilemmas, solved mysteries, survived harrowing adventures, saved the girls, and excelled in everything he did, but never smoked, never drank, and never seemed to get hurt in the process. When he took the mound, as he did in this excerpt from the 1903 novel *Frank Merriwell at Yale*, something more than the game was usually on the line. Over time, Merriwell appeared in some three hundred dime novels—all but a handful penned by Patten—dozens of radio plays, a syndicated comic strip, a comic book, a serialized movie, and a Broadway musical that ran for one performance. It's amazing Frank got any studying done.

Patten also added to his mix stories about Frank's younger brother Dick and, later, his son, Frank Jr. Under other pseudonyms, Patten pounded out westerns, science fiction, and adventure stories, and under his own name, wrote an autobiography aptly titled *Frank Merriwell's Father*. In terms of baseball—and other sports for that matter—he was very good at depicting the action, and his hero became an American institution. For decades, it was not unusual for sportswriters to declare improbable ninth-inning homers or the intercepted pass run back for the game-winning touchdown as the gun went off as "Frank Merriwell finishes." In Patten's last Merriwell saga, published in 1941, a middle-aged Merriwell is still in form: he flogs a quartet of hoodlums with his cane.

The Merriwell paradigm ran rampantly through boy's fiction for generations, and in the baseball mad nation of the first half of the twentieth century, the name Burt Standish had plenty of good company on the bookshelves, and a few of those other names deserve a mention here. Writers like Ralph Henry Barbour, William Heyliger, Lester Chadwick, and Edward Stratemeyer (who also wrote the Rover Boys series) all raised the bar on the dime-novel, boy's-sport-fiction form they chose to work in, though none created a character as enduring as Merriwell. By the time I started reading in the late fifties, Merriwell was an archaeological relic; we had Chip Hilton, the hero of twenty-three books penned from the late forties to the mid-sixties by Clair Bee, the Hall of Fame basketball coach of Long Island University, who still holds the NCAA Division I mark for highest winning percentage as a head coach. Like Merriwell, Bee's Hilton was a multitalented sports star of exemplary character and class; in 1997, the NCAA established the Chip Hilton Player of the Year Award for the Division I basketball player who best embodies Hilton's talent, sportsmanship, integrity, and leadership.

Still, as much as I may have admired Hilton, to boys of the late nineteenth and early twentieth centuries, the connection with Merriwell ran to the core. Patten understood why. "As I came to know Frank better," he explained years after his last Merriwell story found its readers, "I grew fond of him and I confess that I followed his adventures almost as breathlessly as the army of boys who admired him." A telling admission from Frank's old man.

A day or two later came the very thing that had been anticipated and discussed, since the freshman game at Cambridge. Merriwell was selected as one of the pitchers on the Varsity nine, and the freshmen lost him from their team. Putnam came out frankly and confessed that he had feared something of the kind, all along, and Frank was in no mood to kick over his past treatment, so nothing was said on that point.

In the first game against a weaker team than Harvard, Merriwell was tried in the box and pitched a superb game, which Yale won in a walk. Big Hugh Heffiner, the regular pitcher, whose arm was in a bad way, complimented Merriwell on his work, which he said was "simply great."

Of course Frank felt well, as for him there was no sport he admired so much as baseball; but he remained the same old Merriwell, and his freshmen comrades could not see the least change in his manner.

The second game of the series with Harvard came off within a week, but Frank got cold in his arm, and he was not in the best possible condition to go into the box. This he told Pierson, and as Heffiner had almost entirely recovered, Frank was left on the bench. The Varsity team had another pitcher, who was known as Dad Hicks. He was a man about twenty-eight years old, and looked even older, hence the nickname of Dad. This man was most erratic and could not be relied upon. Sometimes he would do brilliant work, and at other times children could have batted him all over the lot. He was used only in desperate emergencies, and could not be counted on in a pinch.

During the whole of the second game with Harvard Frank sat on the bench, ready to go into the box if called on. At first it looked as if he would have to go in, for the Harvard boys fell upon Heffiner and pounded him severely for two innings. Then Hugh braced up and pitched the game through to the end in brilliant style, Yale winning by a score of ten to seven.

Heffiner, however, was forced to bathe his arm in witch hazel frequently, and as he went toward the box for the last time he said to Frank with a rueful smile: "You'll have to get into shape to pitch the last game of the series with these chaps. My arm is the same as gone now, and I'll finish it this inning. We must win this game anyway, regardless of arms, so here goes."

He could barely get the balls over the plate, but he used his head in a wonderful manner, and the slow ball proved a complete puzzle for Harvard after they had been batting speed all through the game, so they got but one safe hit off Heffiner that inning and no scores.

There was a wild jubilee at Yale that night. A bonfire was built on the campus, and the students blew horns, sang songs, cheered for "good old Yale," and had a real lively time.

One or two of the envious ones asked about Merriwell—why he was not allowed to pitch. Even Hartwick, a sophomore who had disliked Frank from the first, more than hinted that the freshman pitcher was being made sport of, and that he would not be allowed to go into the box when Yale was playing a team of any consequence. Jack Diamond overheard the remark, and he promptly offered to bet Hartwick any sum that Merriwell would pitch the next game against Harvard. Diamond was a freshman, and so he received a calling down from Hartwick, who told him he was altogether too new. But as Hartwick strolled away, Diamond quietly said:

"I may be new, sir, but I back up any talk I make. There are others who do not, sir."

Hartwick made no reply.

As the third and final game of the series was to be played on neutral ground, there had been some disagreement about the location, but Springfield had finally been decided upon, and accepted by Yale and Harvard.

Frank did his best to keep his arm in good condition for that game, something which Pierson approved. Hicks was used as much as possible in all other games, but Frank found it necessary to pull one or two off the coals for him.

Heffiner had indeed used his arm up in the grand struggle to win the second game from Harvard—the game that it was absolutely necessary for Yale to secure. He tended that arm as if it were a baby, but it had been strained severely and it came into shape very slowly. As soon as possible he tried to do a little throwing every day, but it was some time before he could get a ball more than ten or fifteen feet.

It became generally known that Merriwell would have to pitch at Springfield, beyond a doubt, and the greatest anxiety was felt at Yale. Every man had confidence in Heffiner, but it was believed by the majority that the freshman was still raw, and therefore was liable to make a wretched fizzle of it.

Heffiner did not think so. He coached Merriwell almost every day, and his confidence in Frank increased. "The boy is all right," was all he would say about it, but that did not satisfy the anxious ones. During the week before the deciding game was to come off Heffiner's arm improved more rapidly than it had at any time before, and scores of men urged Pierson to put Old Reliable, as Hugh was sometimes called, into the box.

A big crowd went up to Springfield on the day of the great game, but the "sons of Old Eli" were far from confident, although they were determined to root for their team to the last gasp. The most disquieting rumors had been afloat concerning Harvard. It was said her team was in a third better condition than at the opening of the season, when she took the first game from Yale; and it could not be claimed with honesty that the Yale team was apparently in any better shape. Although she had won the second game of the series with Harvard, her progress had not been satisfactory.

A monster crowd had gathered to witness the deciding game. Blue and crimson were the prevailing colors. On the bleachers at one side of the grandstand sat hundreds upon hundreds of Harvard men, cheering all together and being answered by the hundreds of Yale men on the other side of the grand stand. There were plenty of ladies and citizens present and the scene was inspiring. A band of music served to quicken the blood in the veins which were already throbbing.

There was short preliminary practice, and then at exactly three o'clock the umpire walked down behind the home plate and called: "Play ball!" Yale took the field, and as the boys in blue trotted out, the familiar Yale yell broke from hundreds of throats. Blue pennants were wildly fluttering, the band was playing a lively air, and for the moment it seemed as if the sympathy of the majority of the spectators was with Yale. But when

Hinkley, Harvard's great single hitter, who always headed the batting list, walked out with his pet "wagon tongue," a different sound swept over the multitude, and the air seemed filled with crimson pennants. Merriwell went into the box, and the umpire broke open a pasteboard box, brought out a ball that was wrapped in tin foil, removed the covering, and tossed the snowy sphere to the freshman pitcher Yale had so audaciously stacked up against Harvard.

Frank looked the box over, examined the rubber plate, and seemed to make himself familiar with every inch of the ground in his vicinity. Then he faced Hinkley, and a moment later delivered the first ball. Hinkley smashed it on the nose, and it was past Merriwell in a second, skipping along the ground and passing over second base just beyond the baseman's reach, although he made a good run for it.

The center fielder secured the ball and returned it to second, but Hinkley had made a safe single off the very first ball delivered. Harvard roared, while the Yale crowd was silent. A great mob of freshmen was up from New Haven to see the game and watch Merriwell's work, and some of them immediately expressed disappointment and dismay. "Here is where Merriwell meets his Waterloo," said Sport Harris. "He'll be batted out before the game is fairly begun."

That was quite enough to arouse Rattleton, who heard the remark.

"I'll bet you ten dollars he isn't batted out at all," spluttered Harry, fiercely. "Here's my money, too!" "Make it twenty-five and I will go you," drawled Harris. "All right, I'll make it twenty-five." The money was staked.

Derry, also a heavy hitter, was second on Harvard's list. Derry had a bat that was as long and as large as the regulations would permit, and as heavy as lead; yet, despite the weight of the stick, the strapping Vermonter handled it as if it were a feather. Frank sent up a coaxer, but Derry refused to be coaxed. The second ball was high, but Derry cracked it for two bags, and Hinkley got around to third. It began to seem as if Merriwell would be batted out in the first inning, and the Yale crowd looked weary and disgusted at the start. The next batter fouled out, however, and the next one sent a red-hot liner directly at Merriwell. There was no time to get out of the way, so Frank caught it, snapped the ball to third, found

Hinkley off the bag, and retired the side without a score. This termination of the first half of the inning was so swift and unexpected that it took some seconds for the spectators to realize what had happened. When they did, however, Yale was wildly cheered. "What do you think about it now, Harris?" demanded Harry, exultantly.

"I think Merriwell saved his neck by a dead lucky catch," was the answer. "If he had missed that ball he would have been removed within five minutes."

Pierson, who was sitting on the bench, was looking doubtful, and he held a consultation with Costigan, captain of the team, as soon as the latter came in from third base. Costigan asked Frank how he felt, and Merriwell replied that he had never felt better in his life, so it was decided to let him see what he could do in the box the next inning. Yedding, who was in the box for Harvard, could not have been in better condition, and the first three Yale men to face him went out in one-two-three order, making the first inning a whitewash for both sides.

As Merriwell went into the box the second time there were cries for Heffiner, who was on the bench, ready to pitch if forced to do so, for all of the fact that it might ruin his arm forever, so far as ball playing was concerned. In trying to deceive the first man up Merriwell gave him three balls in succession. Then he was forced to put them over. He knew the batter would take one or two, and so he sent two straight, swift ones directly over, and two strikes were called.

Then came the critical moment, for the next ball pitched would settle the matter. Frank sent in a rise and the batter struck at it, missed it, and was declared out, the ball having landed with a "plunk" in the hands of the catcher. The next batter got first on a single, but the third man sent an easy one to Frank, who gathered it in, threw the runner out at second, and the second baseman sent the ball to first in time to retire the side on a double play. "You are all right, Merriwell, old man," enthusiastically declared Heffiner, as Frank came in to the bench. "They haven't been able to score off you yet, and they won't be able to touch you at all after you get into gear."

Pierson was relieved, and Costigan looked well satisfied. "Now we must have some scores, boys," said the captain. But Yedding showed that he was out for blood, for he allowed but one safe hit, and again retired Yale without a score. Surely it was a hot game, and excitement was running high. Would Harvard be able to score the next time? That was the question everybody was asking.

Yedding came to the bat in this inning, and Merriwell struck him out with ease, while not another man got a safe hit, although one got first on the shortstop's error.

The Yale crowd cheered like Indians when Harvard was shut out for the third time, the freshmen seeming to yell louder than all the others. They originated a cry which was like this:

"He is doing very well. Who? Why, Merriwell!" Merriwell was the first man up, and Yedding did his best to get square by striking the freshman out. In this he was successful, much to his satisfaction.

But no man got a hit, and the third inning ended as had the others, neither side having made a run. The fourth opened in breathless suspense, but it was quickly over, neither side getting a man beyond second. It did not seem possible that this thing could continue much longer, but the fifth inning brought the same result, although Yale succeeded in getting a man to third with only one out. An attempt to sacrifice him home failed, and a double play was made, retiring the side. Harvard opened the sixth by batting a ball straight at Yale's shortstop, who played tag with it, chasing it around his feet long enough to allow the batter to reach first. It was not a hit, but an error for short.

This seemed to break the Yale team up somewhat. The runner tried for second on the first ball pitched, and Yale's catcher overthrew, although he had plenty of time to catch the man. The runner kept on to third and got it on a slide.

Now Harvard rejoiced. Although he had not obtained a hit, the man had reached third on two errors, and there was every prospect of scoring. Merriwell did not seem to lose his temper or his coolness. He took plenty of time to let everybody get quieted down, and then he quickly struck out the next man. The third man, however, managed to hit the ball fairly and knocked a fly into left field. It was gathered in easily, but the man on third held the bag till the fly was caught and made a desperate dash for home. The left fielder threw well, and the ball struck in the catcher's mitt. It did not stick, however, and the catcher lost the only opportunity to stop the score.

Harvard had scored at last! The Harvard cheer rent the air, and crimson fluttered on all sides.

Frank struck out the next man, and then Yale came to bat, resolved to do or die. But they did not do much. Yedding was as good as ever, and the fielders gathered in anything that came their way.

At the end of the eighth inning the score remained one to nothing in Harvard's favor. It looked as if Yale would receive a shut out, and that was something awful to contemplate. The "sons of Old Eli" were ready to do anything to win a score or two.

In the first half of the ninth Harvard went at it to make some more runs. One man got a hit, stole second, and went to third on an error that allowed the batter to reach first.

Sport Harris had been disappointed when Merriwell continued to remain in the box, but now he said: "He's rattled. Here's where they kill him."

But Frank proved that he was not rattled. He tricked the man on third into getting off the bag and then threw him out in a way that brought a yell of delight from Yale men. That fixed it so the next batter could not sacrifice with the object of letting the man on third home. Then he got down to business, and Harvard was whitewashed for the last time. "Oh, if Yale can score now!" muttered hundreds. The first man up flied out to center, and the next man was thrown out at first. That seemed to settle it. The spectators were making preparations to leave. The Yale bat-tender, with his face long and doleful, was gathering up the sticks. What's that? The next man got a safe hit, a single that placed him on first. Then Frank Merriwell was seen carefully selecting a bat. "Oh, if he were a heavy hitter!" groaned many voices.

Yedding was confident—much too confident. He laughed in Frank's face. He did not think it necessary to watch the man on first closely, and so that man found an opportunity to steal second. Two strikes and two balls had been called. Then Yedding sent in a swift one to cut the inside corner. Merriwell swung at it. Crack! Bat and ball met fairly, and away sailed the sphere over the head of the shortstop. "Run!" That word was a roar. No need to tell Frank to run. In a moment he was scudding down to first, while the left fielder was going back for the ball which had passed beyond his reach. Frank kept on for second. There was so much noise he could not hear the coachers, but he saw the fielder had not secured the ball. He made third, and the excited coacher sent him home with a furious gesture.

Every man, woman and child was standing. It seemed as if every one was shouting and waving flags, hats, or handkerchiefs. It was a moment of such thrilling, nerve-tingling excitement as is seldom experienced. If Merriwell reached home Yale won; if he failed, the score was tied, for the man in advance had scored. The fielder had secured the ball, he drove it to the shortstop, and shortstop whirled and sent it whistling home. The catcher was ready to stop Merriwell. "Slide!" That word Frank heard above all the commotion. He did slide. Forward he scooted in a cloud of dust. The catcher got the ball and put it onto Frank an instant too late!

A sudden silence. "Safe home!" rang the voice of the umpire. Then another roar, louder, wilder, full of unbounded joy! The Yale cheer! The band drowned by all the uproar! The sight of sturdy lads in blue, delirious with delight, hugging a dust-covered youth, lifting him to their shoulders, and bearing him away in triumph. Merriwell had won his own game, and his record was made. It was a glorious finish! "Never saw anything better," declared Harry. "Frank, you are a wonder!"

"He is that!" declared several others. "Old Yale can't get along without him."

The Pitcher and the Plutocrat

The Pitcher and the Plutocrat

P. G. Wodehouse

ASSOCIATE A BALL WITH P. G. WODEHOUSE (1881–1975), AND IT WILL, without question, be dimpled; his golf stories, featuring the club's Oldest Living Member, are some of the funniest and most enduring ever teed up on a typewriter. But the English-born Wodehouse wrote so much—some ninety books, twenty film scripts, and more than thirty plays and musical comedies—that mere chance would dictate he'd at least stumble onto baseball. In "The Pitcher and the Plutocrat," written in 1910 soon after he arrived in America from Britain to live, Wodehouse doesn't stumble at all. Given the game's novelty for him, he covers the bases quite splendidly.

The main difficulty in writing a story is to convey to the reader clearly yet tersely the natures and dispositions of one's leading characters. Brevity, brevity—that is the cry. Perhaps, after all, the playbill style is the best. In this drama of love, baseball, frenzied finance, and tainted millions, then, the principals are as follows, in their order of entry:

Isabel Rackstraw (a peach)

Clarence Van Puyster (a Greek god)

Old Man Van Puyster (a proud old aristocrat)

Old Man Rackstraw (a tainted millionaire)

More about Clarence later. For the moment let him go as a Greek god. There were other sides, too, to Old Man Rackstraw's character; but for the moment let him go as a Tainted Millionaire. Not that it is satisfactory. It is too mild. He was the Tainted Millionaire. The Tainted Millions of other Tainted Millionaires were as attar of roses compared with the Tainted Millions of Tainted Millionaire Rackstraw. He preferred his millions tainted. His attitude toward an untainted million was that of the sportsman toward the sitting bird. These things are purely a matter of taste. Some people like Limburger cheese.

It was at a charity bazaar that Isabel and Clarence first met. Isabel was presiding over the Billiken, Teddy Bear, and Fancy Goods stall. There she stood, that slim, radiant girl, buncoing the Younger Set out of its father's hard-earned with a smile that alone was nearly worth the money, when she observed, approaching, the handsomest man she had ever seen. It was—this is not one of those mystery stories—it was Clarence Van Puyster. Over the heads of the bevy of gilded youths who clustered round the stall their eyes met. A thrill ran through Isabel. She dropped her eyes. The next moment Clarence had bucked center; the Younger Set had shredded away like a mist; and he was leaning toward her, opening negotiations for the purchase of a yellow Teddy Bear at sixteen times its face value.

He returned at intervals during the afternoon. Over the second Teddy Bear they became friendly; over the third, intimate. He proposed as she was wrapping up the fourth Golliwog, and she gave him her heart and the parcel simultaneously. At six o'clock, carrying four Teddy Bears, seven photograph frames, five Golliwogs, and a Billiken, Clarence went home to tell the news to his father.

Clarence, when not at college, lived with his only surviving parent in an old red-brick house at the north end of Washington Square. The original Van Puyster had come over in Governor Stuyvesant's time in one of the then fashionable ninety-four-day boats. Those were the stirring days when they were giving away chunks of Manhattan Island in exchange for trading-stamps; for the bright brain which conceived the idea that the city might possibly at some remote date extend above Liberty Street had not come into existence. The original Van Puyster had acquired a square mile or so in the heart of things for ten dollars cash and a quarter interest in a pedler's outfit. "The Columbus Echo and Vespucci Intelligencer" gave him a column and a half under the heading: "Reckless Speculator. Prominent Citizen's Gamble in Land." On the proceeds of that deal his descendants had led quiet, peaceful lives ever since. If any of them ever did a day's work, the family records are silent on the point. Blood was their long suit, not Energy. They were plain, homely folk, with a refined distaste for wealth and vulgar hustle. They lived simply, without envy of their richer fellow citizens, on their three hundred thousand dollars a year. They asked no more. It enabled them to entertain on a modest scale; the boys could go to college, the girls buy an occasional new frock. They were satisfied.

Having dressed for dinner, Clarence proceeded to the library, where he found his father slowly pacing the room. Silver-haired old Vansuyther Van Puyster seemed wrapped in thought. And this was unusual, for he was not given to thinking. To be absolutely frank, the old man had just about enough brain to make a jay-bird fly crooked, and no more.

"Ah, my boy," he said, looking up as Clarence entered. "Let us go in to dinner. I have been awaiting you for some little time now. I was about to inquire as to your whereabouts. Let us be going."

Mr. Van Puyster always spoke like that. This was due to Blood.

Until the servants had left them to their coffee and cigarettes, the conversation was desultory and commonplace. But when the door had closed, Mr. Van Puyster leaned forward.

"My boy," he said quietly, "we are ruined."

Clarence looked at him inquiringly.

"Ruined much?" he asked.

"Paupers," said his father. "I doubt if when all is over, I shall have much more than a bare fifty or sixty thousand dollars a year."

A lesser man would have betrayed agitation, but Clarence was a Van Puyster. He lit a cigarette.

"Ah," he said calmly. "How's that?"

Mr. Van Puyster toyed with his coffee-spoon.

"I was induced to speculate—rashly, I fear—on the advice of a man I chanced to meet at a public dinner, in the shares of a certain mine. I did not thoroughly understand the matter, but my acquaintance appeared to be well versed in such operations, so I allowed him to—and, well, in fact, to cut a long story short, I am ruined."

"Who was the fellow?"

"A man of the name of Rackstraw. Daniel Rackstraw."

"Daniel Rackstraw!"

Not even Clarence's training and traditions could prevent a slight start as he heard the name.

"Daniel Rackstraw," repeated his father. "A man, I fear, not entirely honest. In fact it seems that he has made a very large fortune by similar transactions. Friends of mine, acquainted with these matters, tell me his behavior toward me amounted practically to theft. However, for myself I care little. We can rough it, we of the old Van Puyster stock. If there is but fifty thousand a year left, well—I must make it serve. It is for your sake that I am troubled, my poor boy. I shall be compelled to stop your allowance. I fear you will be obliged to adopt some profession." He hesitated for a moment. "In fact, work," he added.

Clarence drew at his cigarette.

"Work?" he echoed thoughtfully. "Well, of course, mind you, fellows *do* work. I met a man at the club only yesterday who knew a fellow who had met a man whose cousin worked."

He reflected for a while.

"I shall pitch," he said suddenly.

"Pitch, my boy?"

"Sign on as a professional ballplayer."

His father's fine old eyebrows rose a little.

"But, my boy, er—the-ah—family name. Our—shall I say *noblesse oblige*? Can a Van Puyster pitch and not be defiled?"

"I shall take a new name," said Clarence. "I will call myself Brown." He lit another cigarette. "I can get signed on in a minute. McGraw will jump at me."

This was no idle boast. Clarence had had a good college education, and was now an exceedingly fine pitcher. It was a pleasing sight to see him, poised on one foot in the attitude of a Salome dancer, with one eye on the batter, the other gazing coldly at the man who was trying to steal third, uncurl abruptly like the main spring of a watch and sneak over a swift one. Under Clarence's guidance a ball could do practically everything except talk. It could fly like a shot from a gun, hesitate, take the first turning to the left, go up two blocks, take the second to the right, bound in mid-air like a jack-rabbit, and end by dropping as the gentle dew from heaven upon the plate beneath. Briefly, there was class to Clarence. He was the goods.

Scarcely had he uttered these momentous words when the butler entered with the announcement that he was wanted by a lady at the telephone.

It was Isabel.

Isabel was disturbed.

"Oh, Clarence," she cried, "my precious angel wonder-child, I don't know how to begin."

"Begin just like that," said Clarence approvingly. "It's fine. You can't beat it."

"Clarence, a terrible thing has happened. I told papa of our engagement, and he wouldn't hear of it. He was furious. He c-called you a b-b-b

"A p-p-p-"

"That's a new one on me," said Clarence, wondering.

"A b-beggarly p-pauper. I knew you weren't well off, but I thought you had two or three millions. I told him so. But he said no, your father had lost all his money."

"It is too true, dearest," said Clarence. "I am a pauper. But I'm going to work. Something tells me I shall be rather good at work. I am going to work with all the accumulated energy of generations of ancestors who have never done a hand's turn. And some day when I—"

"Good-by," said Isabel hastily, "I hear papa coming."

The season during which Clarence Van Puyster pitched for the Giants is destined to live long in the memory of followers of baseball. Probably never in the history of the game has there been such persistent and widespread mortality among the more distant relatives of office-boys and junior clerks. Statisticians have estimated that if all the grandmothers alone who perished between the months of April and October that year could have been placed end to end they would have reached considerably further than Minneapolis. And it was Clarence who was responsible for this holocaust. Previous to the opening of the season skeptics had shaken their heads over the Giants' chances for the pennant. It had been assumed that as little new blood would be forthcoming as in other years, and that the fate of Our City would rest, as usual, on the shoulders of the white-haired veterans who were boys with Lafayette.

And then, like a mentor, Clarence Van Puyster had flashed upon the world of fans, bugs, chewing-gum, and nuts (pea and human). In the opening game he had done horrid things to nine men from Boston; and from then onward, except for an occasional check, the Giants had never looked back.

Among the spectators who thronged the bleachers to watch Clarence perform there appeared week after week a little, gray, dried-up man, insignificant except for a certain happy choice of language in moments of emotion and an enthusiasm far surpassing that of the ordinary spectator. To the trained eye there is a subtle but well-marked difference between the fan, the bug, and—the last phase—the nut of the baseball world. This man was an undoubted nut. It was writ clear across his brow.

Fate had made Daniel Rackstraw—for it was he—a tainted millionaire, but at heart he was a baseball spectator. He never missed a game. His baseball museum had but one equal, that of Mr. Jacob Dodson of Detroit. Between them the two had cornered, at enormous expense, the curio market of the game. It was Rackstraw who had secured the glove worn by Neal Ball, the Cleveland shortstop, when he made the only unassisted triple play in the history of the game; but it was Dodson who possessed the bat which Hans Wagner used as a boy. The two men were friends, as far as rival connoisseurs can be friends; and Mr. Dodson, when at leisure, would frequently pay a visit to Mr. Rackstraw's country home, where he would spend hours gazing wistfully at the Neal Ball glove buoyed up only by the thought of the Wagner bat at home.

Isabel saw little of Clarence during the summer months, except from a distance. She contented herself with clipping photographs of him from the evening papers. Each was a little more unlike him than the last, and this lent variety to the collection. Her father marked her new-born enthusiasm for the national game with approval. It had been secretly a great grief to the old buccaneer that his only child did not know the difference between a bunt and a swat, and, more, did not seem to care to know. He felt himself drawn closer to her. An understanding, as pleasant as it was new and strange, began to spring up between parent and child.

As for Clarence, how easy it would be to cut loose to practically an unlimited extent on the subject of his emotions at this time. One can figure him, after the game is over and the gay throng has dispersed, creeping moodily—but what's the use? Brevity. That is the cry. Brevity. Let us on.

The months sped by. August came and went, and September; and soon it was plain to even the casual follower of the game that, unless something untoward should happen, the Giants must secure the National League pennant. Those were delirious days for Daniel Rackstraw. Long before the beginning of October his voice had dwindled to a husky whisper. Deep lines appeared on his forehead; for it is an awful thing for a baseball nut to be compelled to root, in the very crisis of the season, purely by means of facial expression. In this time of affliction he found Isabel an ever-increasing comfort to him. Side by side they would sit at the Polo Grounds, and the old man's face would lose its drawn look, and light up, as her clear young soprano pealed out above the din, urging this player to slide for second, that to knock the stitching off the ball; or describing the umpire in no uncertain voice as a reincarnation of the late Mr. Jesse James.

Meanwhile, in the American League, Detroit had been heading the list with equal pertinacity; and in far-off Michigan Mr. Jacob Dodson's enthusiasm had been every whit as great as Mr. Rackstraw's in New York. It was universally admitted that when the championship series came to be played, there would certainly be something doing.

But, alas! How truly does Epictetus observe: "We know not what awaiteth us around the corner, and the hand that counteth its chickens ere they be hatched ofttimes graspeth but a lemon." The prophets who anticipated a struggle closer than any on record were destined to be proved false.

It was not that their judgment of form was at fault. By every law of averages the Giants and the Tigers should have been the two most evenly matched nines in the history of the game. In fielding there was nothing to choose between them. At hitting the Tigers held a slight superiority; but this was balanced by the inspired pitching of Clarence Van Puyster. Even the keenest supporters of either side were not confident. They argued at length, figuring out the odds with the aid of stubs of pencils and the backs of envelopes, but they were not confident. Out of all those frenzied millions two men alone had no doubts. Mr. Daniel Rackstraw said that he did not desire to be unfair to Detroit. He wished it to be clearly understood that in their own class the Tigers might quite possibly show to considerable advantage. In some rural league down South, for instance, he did not deny that they might sweep all before them. But when it came to competing with the Giants—Here words failed Mr. Rackstraw, and he had to rush to Wall Street and collect several tainted millions before he could recover his composure.

Mr. Jacob Dodson, interviewed by the Detroit "Weekly Rooter," stated that his decision, arrived at after a close and careful study of the work of both teams, was that the Giants had rather less chance in the forthcoming tourney than a lone gumdrop at an Eskimo tea party. It was his carefully considered opinion that in a contest with the Avenue B juniors the Giants might, with an effort, scrape home. But when it was a question of meeting a live team like Detroit—Here Mr. Dodson, shrugging his shoulders despairingly, sank back in his chair, and watchful secretaries brought him round with oxygen.

Throughout the whole country nothing but the approaching series was discussed. Wherever civilization reigned, and in Jersey City, one question alone was on every lip: Who would win? Octogenarians mumbled it. Infants lisped it. Tired business men, trampled under foot in the rush for the West Farms express, asked it of the ambulance attendants who carried them to hospital.

And then, one bright, clear morning, when all Nature seemed to smile, Clarence Van Puyster developed mumps.

New York was in a ferment. I could have wished to go into details to describe in crisp, burning sentences the panic that swept like a tornado through a million homes. A little encouragement, the slightest softening of the editorial austerity, and the thing would have been done. But no. Brevity. That was the cry. Brevity. Let us on.

The Tigers met the Giants at the Polo Grounds, and for five days the sweat of agony trickled unceasingly down the corrugated foreheads of the patriots who sat on the bleachers. The men from Detroit, freed from the fear of Clarence, smiled grim smiles and proceeded to knock holes through the fence. It was in vain that the home fielders skimmed like swallows around the diamond. They could not keep the score down. From start to finish the Giants were a beaten side.

Broadway during that black week was a desert. Gloom gripped Lobster Square. In distant Harlem red-eyed wives faced silently scowling husbands at the evening meal, and the children were sent early to bed. Newsboys called the extras in a whisper.

Few took the tragedy more nearly to heart than Daniel Rackstraw. Each afternoon found him more deeply plunged in sorrow. On the last day, leaving the ground with the air of a father mourning over some prodigal son, he encountered Mr. Jacob Dodson of Detroit.

Now, Mr. Dodson was perhaps the slightest bit shy on the finer feelings. He should have respected the grief of a fallen foe. He should have abstained from exulting. But he was in too exhilarated a condition to be magnanimous. Sighting Mr. Rackstraw, he addressed himself joyously to the task of rubbing the thing in. Mr. Rackstraw listened in silent anguish.

"If we had had Brown—" he said at length.

"That's what they all say," whooped Mr. Dodson. "Brown! Who's Brown?"

"If we had had Brown, we should have—" He paused. An idea had flashed upon his overwrought mind. "Dodson," he said, "listen here. Wait till Brown is well again, and let us play this thing off again for anything you like a side in my private park."

Mr. Dodson reflected.

"You're on," he said. "What side bet? A million? Two million? Three?"

Mr. Rackstraw shook his head scornfully.

"A million? Who wants a million? I'll put on my Neal Ball glove against your Hans Wagner bat. The best of three games. Does that go?"

"I should say it did," said Mr. Dodson joyfully. "I've been wanting that glove for years. It's like finding it in one's Christmas stocking."

"Very well," said Mr. Rackstraw. "Then let's get it fixed up."

Honestly, it is but a dog's life, that of the short-story writer. I partic-ularly wished at this point to introduce a description of Mr. Rackstraw's country home and estate, featuring the private ballpark with its fringe of noble trees. It would have served a double purpose, not only charming the lover of nature, but acting as a fine stimulus to the youth of the country, showing them the sort of home they would be able to buy some day if they worked hard and saved their money. But no. You shall have three guesses as to what was the cry. You give it up? It was "Brevity! Brevity!" Let us on.

The two teams arrived at the Rackstraw house in time for lunch. Clarence, his features once more reduced to their customary finely chis-eled proportions, alighted from the automobile with a swelling heart. He could see nothing of Isabel, but that did not disturb him. Letters had passed between the two. Clarence had warned her not to embrace him in public, as McGraw would not like it; and Isabel accordingly had arranged a tryst among the noble trees which fringed the ballpark.

I will pass lightly over the meeting of the two lovers. I will not describe the dewy softness of their eyes, the catching of their breath, their murmured endearments. I could, mind you. It is at just such descriptions that I am particularly happy. But I have grown discouraged. My spirit is broken. It is enough to say that Clarence had reached a level of emotional eloquence rarely met with among pitchers of the National League, when Isabel broke from him with a startled exclamation, and vanished behind a tree; and, looking over his shoulder, Clarence observed Mr. Daniel Rackstraw moving toward him.

It was evident from the millionaire's demeanor that he had seen nothing. The look on his face was anxious, but not wrathful. He sighted Clarence, and hurried up to him.

"Say, Brown," he said. "I've been looking for you. I want a word with you."

"A thousand, if you wish it," said Clarence courteously.

"Now, see here," said Mr. Rackstraw. "I want to explain to you just what this ball game means to me. Don't run away with the idea I've had you fellows down to play an exhibition game just to keep me merry and bright. If the Giants win today, it means that I shall be able to hold up my head again and look my fellow man in the face, instead of crawling around on my stomach and feeling like thirty cents. Do you get that?"

"I am hep," replied Clarence with simple dignity.

"And not only that," went on the millionaire. "There's more to it. I have put up my Neal Ball glove against Mr. Dodson's Wagner bat as a side bet. You understand what that means? It means that either you win or my life is soured for keeps. See?"

"I have got you," said Clarence.

"Good. Then what I wanted to say was this. Today is your day for pitching as you've never pitched before. Everything depends on whether you make good or not. With you pitching like mother used to make it, the Giants are some nine. Otherwise they are Nature's citrons. It's one thing or the other. It's all up to you. Win, and there's twenty thousand dollars waiting for you above what you share with the others."

Clarence waved his hand deprecatingly.

"Mr. Rackstraw," he said, "keep your dough. I care nothing for money."

"You don't?" cried the millionaire. "Then you ought to exhibit yourself in a dime museum."

"All I ask of you," proceeded Clarence, "is your consent to my engagement to your daughter."

Mr. Rackstraw looked sharply at him.

"Repeat that," he said. "I don't think I quite got it."

"All I ask is your consent to my engagement to your daughter."

"Young man," said Mr. Rackstraw, not without a touch of admiration, "you have gall."

"My friends have sometimes said so," said Clarence.

"And I admire gall. But there is a limit. That limit you have passed so far that you'd need to look for it with a telescope."

"You refuse your consent."

"I never said you weren't a clever guesser."

"Why?"

Mr. Rackstraw laughed. One of those nasty, sharp, metallic laughs that hit you like a bullet.

"How would you support my daughter?"

"I was thinking that you would help to some extent."

"You were, were you?"

"I was."

"Oh?"

Mr. Rackstraw emitted another of those laughs.

"Well," he said, "it's off. You can take that as coming from an authoritative source. No wedding-bells for you."

Clarence drew himself up, fire flashing from his eyes and a bitter smile curving his expressive lips.

"And no Wagner bat for you!" he cried.

Mr. Rackstraw started as if some strong hand had plunged an auger into him.

"What!" he shouted.

Clarence shrugged his superbly modeled shoulders in silence.

"Say," said Mr. Rackstraw, "you wouldn't let a little private difference like that influence you any in a really important thing like this ball game, would you?"

"I would."

"You would hold up the father of the girl you love?"

"Every time."

"Her white-haired old father?"

"The color of his hair would not affect me."

"Nothing would move you?"

"Nothing."

"Then, by George, you're just the son-in-law I want. You shall marry Isabel; and I'll take you into partnership this very day. I've been looking for a good, husky bandit like you for years. You make Dick Turpin look like a preliminary three-round bout. My boy, we'll be the greatest team, you and I, that ever hit Wall Street."

"Papa!" cried Isabel, bounding happily from behind her tree.

Mr. Rackstraw joined their hands, deeply moved, and spoke in low, vibrant tones:

"Play ball!"

Little remains to be said, but I am going to say it, if it snows. I am at my best in these tender scenes of idyllic domesticity.

Four years have passed. Once more we are in the Rackstraw home. A lady is coming down the stairs, leading by the hand her little son. It is Isabel. The years have dealt lightly with her. She is still the same stately, beautiful creature whom I would have described in detail long ago if I had been given half a chance. At the foot of the stairs the child stops and points at a small, wooden object in a glass case.

"Wah?" he said.

"That?" says Isabel. "That is the bat Mr. Wagner used to use when he was a little boy."

She looks at a door on the left of the hall, and puts a finger to her lip. "Hush!" she says. "We must be quiet. Daddy and grandpa are busy in there cornering wheat."

And softly mother and child go out into the sunlit garden.

Baseball May Some Day Avert War between America and Japan

Baseball May Some Day Avert War between America and Japan

COULD THE IDEA OF A TRULY WORLD WORLD SERIES CONTRIBUTE TO the lofty goals of peace and understanding between a pair of international powers separated by the Pacific Ocean? At least one Japanese prince believed so, and he chatted up the idea during a 1910 visit to New York with an unnamed reporter from the *New York Tribune*. Can you catch in his final quote just the slightest whiff of what would one day become the World Baseball Cup?

Baseball has served to entertain, thrill and excite hundreds of thousands, yes, millions, of the American people, but how many of even the most rabid "fans," the most ardent enthusiasts, ever thought of America's great national game as a peacemaker between two imperial nations, an agent possibly of averting a "terrible war," or at least a means of bringing into closer commercial and social relationship two world powers? Yet this is just what the game may do.

Prince Iyesato Tokugawa, last of the Shoguns and president of the Japanese House of Peers since 1893, paid New York a visit last week, and while here talked of the great American game to a Tribune reporter. The prince is something of a "fan" himself. He is a believer in baseball, enjoys seeing a good close game, with plenty of hitting, and knows alot about the pastime.

"Baseball in my country," said he, "is becoming more and more pop-ular. Americans introduced the game in Japan. At first we did not know what it was all about, but we used to go out and watch the teams from United States men-of-war play, and after a time we got so that we could understand it, and the better we understood it the more we thought of it.

"By degrees some of our people learned enough about it to think they would like to play it, and then a few in Tokyo started playing the game. The more they played the better they liked it, and more and more people became interested in it."

After a time, the prince said, some of the Japanese became pretty good at it, and then they decided it was about time to measure their skill with American teams. The result was the arranging of international matches with teams from the United States warships in Japanese ports. "Now our people have something like what you call the baseball fever," he continued. "Your University of Wisconsin has sent teams over and played with our University of Tokyo. And we have sent our teams over to your western coast and played with your universities there."

That the prince took considerable pride in the success of the Japanese ball tossers was easily apparent. He spoke of the showing of the Tokyo collegians against the University of Wisconsin team with just pride. As a matter of fact, those Wisconsin ball tossers have been about as good as some of the best American college teams, and when they first began visiting the land of the Mikado they thought they had a "snap," to put it mildly, but the Tokyo players gave them the surprise of their lives, and they now slap themselves on the back if they manage to get an even break in those sunny isles.

Prince Tokugawa said that he believed before long the national game of Japan would be baseball. He spoke warmly in favor of the game, and more especially of the idea of the United States sending ball teams over to play in Japan, and of his country returning the courtesy. If this was carried out to a wide extent, he thought it would result in the people of the two nations becoming better acquainted with each other and hence entertaining more cordial relations.

"Some day," said the prince, "you may see a Japanese team playing a championship series on your Polo Grounds right here in New York."

Jinxes and What They Mean
to a Ball-Player

Jinxes and What They Mean to a Ball-Player

Christy Mathewson

A TRUE DEITY OF EARLY TWENTIETH-CENTURY BASEBALL, CHRISTY Mathewson (1880–1925) was the physical embodiment of the fictional dime-novel paladin Frank Merriwell. As a man and as a ballplayer, Matty was almost too good to be true. So let the facts speak for themselves: over a seventeen-year career, all but one game with the New York Giants, Matty and his famed fadeaway pitch (aka the screwball) combined for 373 victories, still tied for tops in National League history; his all-time career ERA stands fifth; and his 79 shutouts, third. Along with Ty Cobb, Babe Ruth, Honus Wagner, and Walter Johnson—all appear elsewhere in these pages—Matty helped comprise the first class of Cooperstown enshrinees.

That said, because Matty was Matty—upstanding, levelheaded, and college educated—Matty was also something of a literary work-horse—or at least his byline became a brand. Most notably with the help of *New York Herald* sportswriter Frank Wheeler—previous attempts with other spooks, as they were then called, were DOA—he wrote a series of well-received columns covering the day-to-day progress of the 1912 World Series that led to the two teaming on the still-in-print memoir *Pitching in a Pinch, or Baseball From the Inside*, which included this examination of superstitions. Unfortunately for readers, Matty didn't stop there. His later series of books for boys—*First Base Faulkner, Second Base Sloan,* etc.—became exemplars of his most famous weapon on the mound: they just faded away. On the other hand, while the *New York Times* conscripted him to join its coverage of the 1919 World Series, he recognized good writing and the search for truth in the game he loved in others; he helped support Hugh Fullerton in his quest to shine a light into the betrayals of the 1919 White Sox by agreeing to circle suspicious plays for Fullerton on his scorecard.

A friend of mine, who took a different fork in the road when we left college from the one that I have followed, was walking down Broadway in New York with me one morning after I had joined the Giants, and we passed a cross-eyed man. I grabbed off my hat and spat in it. It was a new hat, too. "What's the matter with you, Matty?" he asked, surprised.

"Spit in your hat quick and kill that jinx," I answered, not thinking for the minute, and he followed my example.

I forgot to mention, when I said he took another fork in the road, that he had become a pitcher, too, but of a different kind. He had turned out to be sort of a conversational pitcher, for he was a minister, and, as luck would have it, on the morning we met that cross-eyed man he was wearing a silk hat. I was shocked, pained, and mortified when I saw what I had made him do. But he was the right sort, and wanted to go through with the thing according to the standards of the professional man with whom he happened to be at the time.

"What's the idea?" he asked as he replaced his hat. "Worst jinx in the world to see a cross-eyed man," I replied. "But I hope I didn't hurt your silk hat," I quickly apologized.

"Not at all. But how about these ball-players who masticate the weed? Do they kill jinxes, too?" he wanted to know. And I had to admit that they were the main exterminators of the jinx. "Then," he went on, "I'm glad that the percentage of wearers of cross eyes is small."

I have just looked into one of my favorite works for that word "jinx," and found it not. My search was in Webster's dictionary. But any ball-player can give a definition of it with his hands tied behind him— that is, any one except "Arlie" Latham, and, with his hands bound, he is deaf and dumb. A jinx is something which brings bad luck to a ball-player, and the members of the profession have built up a series of lucky and unlucky omens that should be catalogued. And besides the common or garden variety of jinxes, many stars have a series of private or pet and trained ones that are more malignant in their forms than those which come out in the open. A jinx is the child of superstition, and ball-players are among the most superstitious persons in the world, notwithstanding all this conversation lately about educated men breaking into the game and paying no attention whatever to the good and bad omens. College men are coming into both the leagues, more of them each year, and they are doing their share to make the game better and the class of men higher, but they fall the hardest for the jinxes. And I don't know as it is anything to be ashamed of at that.

A really true, on-the-level, honest-to-jiminy jinx can do all sorts of mean things to a professional ball-player. I have seen it make a bad pitcher out of a good one, and a blind batter out of a three-hundred hitter, and I have seen it make a ball club, composed of educated men, carry a Kansas farmer, with two or three screws rattling loose in his dome, around the circuit because he came as a prophet and said that he was accompanied by Miss Fickle Fortune. And that is almost a jinx record.

Jinx and Miss Fickle Fortune never go around together. And ball-players are always trying to kill this jinx, for, once he joins the club, all hope is gone. He dies hard, and many a good hat has been ruined in an effort to destroy him, as I have said before, because the wearer happened to be chewing tobacco when the jinx dropped around. But what's a new hat against a losing streak or a batting slump?

Luck is a combination of confidence and getting the breaks. Ball-players get no breaks without confidence in themselves, and lucky omens inspire this confidence. On the other hand, unlucky signs take it away. The lucky man is the one who hits the nail on the head and not his fingers, and the ability to swat the nail on its receptive end is a combination of self-confidence and an aptitude for hammering. Good ball-playing is the combination of self-confidence and the ability to play.

The next is "Red" Ames, although designated as "Leon" by his family when a very small boy before he began to play ball. (He is still called

"Leon" in the winter.) Ames is of Warren, Ohio, and the Giants, and he is said to hold the Marathon record for being the most unlucky pitcher that ever lived, and I agree with the sayers. For several seasons, Ames couldn't seem to win a ball game, no matter how well he pitched. In 1909, "Red" twirled a game on the opening day of the season against Brooklyn that was the work of a master. For nine innings he held his opponents hitless, only to have them win in the thirteenth. Time and again Ames has pitched brilliantly, to be finally beaten by a small score, because one of the men behind him made an error at a critical moment, or because the team could not give him any runs by which to win. No wonder the newspapers began to speak of Ames as the "hoodoo" pitcher and the man "who couldn't win."

There was a cross-eyed fellow who lived between Ames and the Polo Grounds, and "Red" used to make a detour of several blocks en route to the park to be sure to miss him in case he should be out walking. But one day in 1911, when it was his turn to pitch, he bumped into that cross-eyed man and, in spite of the fact that he did his duty by his hat and got three or four small boys to help him out, he failed to last two innings. When it came time to go West on the final trip of the 1911 season, Ames was badly discouraged.

"I don't see any use in taking me along, Mac," he said to McGraw a few days before we left. "The club can't win with me pitching if the other guys don't even get a foul."

The first stop was in Boston, and on the day we arrived it rained. In the mail that day, addressed to Leon Ames, came a necktie and a four-leaf clover from a prominent actress, wishing Ames good luck. The directions were inside the envelope. The four-leaf clover, if the charm were to work, must be worn on both the uniform and street clothes, and the necktie was to be worn with the street clothes and concealed in the uniform, if that necktie could be concealed anywhere. It would have done for a headlight and made Joseph's coat of many colors look like a mourning garment.

"Might as well wish good luck to a guy on the way to the morgue," murmured Ames as he surveyed the layout, but he manfully put on the necktie, taking his first dose of the prescription, as directed, at once, and he tucked the four-leaf clover away carefully in his wallet.

"You've got your work cut out for you, old boy," he remarked to the charm as he put it away, "but I'd wear you if you were a horseshoe." The first day that Ames pitched in Boston he won, and won in a stroll. "The necktie," he explained that night at dinner, and pointed to the three-sheet, colored-supplement affair he was wearing around his collar, "I don't change her until I lose."

And he did not lose a game on that trip. Once he almost did, when he was taken out in the sixth inning, and a batter put in for him, but the Giants finally pulled out the victory and he got the credit for it. He swept through the West unbeatable, letting down Pittsburg with two or three hits, cleaning up in St. Louis, and finally breaking our losing streak in Chicago after two games had gone against us. And all the time he wore that spectrum around his collar for a necktie. As it frayed with the wear and tear, more colors began to show, although I didn't think it possible. If he had had occasion to put on his evening clothes, I believe that tie would have gone with it.

For my part, I would almost rather have lost a game and changed the necktie, since it gave one the feeling all the time that he was carrying it around with him because he had had the wrong end of an election bet, or something of the sort. But not Ames! He was a game guy. He stuck with the necktie, and it stuck with him, and the combination kept right on winning ball games. Maybe he didn't mind it because he could not see it himself, unless he looked in a mirror, but it was rough on the rest of the team, except that we needed the games the necktie won, to take the pennant.

Columns were printed in the newspapers about that necktie, and it became the most famous scarf in the world. Ames used to sleep with it under his pillow alongside of his bank roll, and he didn't lose another game until the very end of the season, when he dropped one against Brooklyn.

"I don't hardly lay that up against the tie," he said afterwards. "You see, Mac put all those youngsters into it, and I didn't get any support." Analyzing is a distasteful pastime to me, but let's see what it was that made Ames win. Was it the necktie? Perhaps not. But some sliver of confidence, which resulted from that first game when he was dressed up in the scarf and the four-leaf clover, got stuck in his mind. And after that the rest was easy.

Frank Chance, the manager of the Cubs, has a funny superstition which is of the personal sort. Most ball-players have a natural prejudice against the number "13" in any form, but particularly when attached to a Pullman berth. But Chance always insists, whenever possible, that he have "lower 13." He says that if he can just crawl in under that number he is sure of a good night's rest, a safe journey, and a victory the next day. He has been in two or three minor railroad accidents, and he declares that all these occurred when he was sleeping on some other shelf besides "lower 13." He can usually satisfy his hobby, too, for most travellers steer clear of the berth.

McGraw believes a stateroom brings him good luck, or at least he always insists on having one when he can get it. "Chance can have lower 13," says "Mac," "but give me a stateroom for luck."

Most ball-players nowadays treat the superstitions of the game as jokes, probably because they are a little ashamed to acknowledge their weaknesses, but away down underneath they observe the proprieties of the ritual. Why, even I won't warm up with the third baseman while I am waiting for the catcher to get on his mask and the rest of his paraphernalia. Once, when I first broke in with the Giants, I warmed up with the third baseman between innings and in the next round they hit me hard and knocked me out of the box. Since then I have had an uncommon prejudice against the practice, and I hate to hear a man even mention it. Devlin knows of my weakness and never suggests it when he is playing the bag, but occasionally a new performer will drill into the box score at third base and yell: "Come on, Matty! Warm up here while you're waiting."

It gets me. I'll pitch to the first baseman or a substitute catcher to keep warm, but I would rather freeze to death than heat up with the third baseman. That is one of my pet jinxes. And speaking of Arthur Devlin, he has a few hand-raised jinxes of his own, too. For instance, he never likes to hear a player hum a tune on the bench, because he thinks it will keep him from getting a base hit. He nearly beat a youngster to death one day when he kept on humming after Devlin had told him to stop.

"Cut that out, Caruso," yelled Arthur, as the recruit started his melody. "You are killing base hits."

The busher continued with his air until Devlin tried another form of persuasion. Arthur also has a favorite seat on the bench which he believes is luckier than the rest, and he insists on sitting in just that one place.

But the worst blow Devlin ever had was when some young lady admirer of his in his palmy days, who unfortunately wore her eyes crossed, insisted on sitting behind third base for each game, so as to be near him. Arthur noticed her one day and, after that, it was all off. He hit the worst slump of his career. For a while no one could understand it, but at last he confessed to McGraw.

"Mac," he said one night in the clubhouse, "it's that jinx. Have you noticed her? She sits behind the bag every day, and she has got me going. She has sure slid the casters under me. I wish we could bar her out, or poison her, or shoot her, or chloroform her, or kill her in some nice, mild way because, if it isn't done, this League is going to lose a ball-player. How can you expect a guy to play with that overlooking him every afternoon?"

McGraw took Devlin out of the game for a time after that, and the newspapers printed several yards about the cross-eyed jinx who had ruined the Giants' third baseman.

With the infield weakened by the loss of Devlin, the club began to lose with great regularity. But one day the jinxess was missing and she never came back. She must have read in the newspapers what she was doing to Devlin, her hero, and quit the national pastime or moved to another part of the stand. With this weight off his shoulders, Arthur went back into the game and played like mad.

"If she'd stuck much longer," declared McGraw, joyous in his rejuvenated third baseman, "I would have had her eyes operated on and straightened. This club couldn't afford to keep on losing ball games because you are such a Romeo, Arthur, that even the cross-eyed ones fall for you."

Ball-players are very superstitious about the bats. Did you ever notice how the clubs are all laid out in a neat, even row before the bench and are scrupulously kept that way by the bat boy? If one of the sticks by any chance gets crossed, all the players will shout: "Uncross the bats! Uncross the bats!"

It's as bad as discovering a three-alarm fire in an excelsior factory. Don't believe it? Then listen to what happened to the Giants once because a careless bat boy neglected his duty. The team was playing in Cincinnati in the season of 1906 when one of the bats got crossed through the carelessness of the boy. What was the result? "Mike" Donlin, the star slugger of the team, slid into third base and came up with a broken ankle.

Ever since that time we have carried our own boy with us, because a club with championship aspirations cannot afford to take a chance with those foreign artists handling the bats. They are likely to throw you down at any time.

The Athletics have a funny superstition which is private or confined to their team as far as I know. When luck seems to be breaking against them in a game, they will take the bats and throw them wildly into the air and let them lie around in front of their bench, topsy-turvy. They call this changing the luck, but any other club would consider that it was the worst kind of a jinx. It is the same theory that cardplayers have about shuffling the deck vigorously to bring a different run of fortune. Then, if the luck changes, the Athletics throw the bats around some more to keep it. This act nearly cost them one of their best ball-players in the third game of the 1911 world's series.

The Philadelphia players had tossed their bats to break their run of luck, for the score was 1 to 0 against them, when Baker came up in the ninth inning. He cracked his now famous home run into the right-field bleachers, and the men on the bench hurled the bats wildly into the air. In jumping up and reaching for a bat to throw, Jack Barry, the shortstop, hit his head on the concrete roof of the structure and was stunned for a minute. He said that little black specks were floating in front of his eyes, but he gamely insisted on playing the contest out. "Connie" Mack was so worried over his condition that he sent Ira Thomas out on the field to inquire if he were all right, and this interrupted the game in the ninth inning. A lot of the spectators thought that Thomas was out there, bearing some secret message from "Connie" Mack. None knew that he was ascertaining the health of a player who had almost killed himself while killing a jinx.

The Athletics, for two seasons, have carried with them on all their trips a combination bat boy and mascot who is a hunchback, and he out jinxed our champion jinx killer, Charley Faust, in the 1911 world's series. A hunchback is regarded by ball-players as the best luck in the world. If a man can just touch that hump on the way to the plate, he is sure to get a hit, and any observant spectator will notice the Athletics' hitters rubbing the hunchback boy before leaving the bench. So attached to this boy have the players become that they voted him half a share of the prize money last year after the world's series. Lots of ball-players would tell you that he deserved it because he has won two world's pennants for them.

Another great piece of luck is for a ball-player to rub a colored kid's head. I've walked along the street with ball-players and seen them stop a young negro and take off his hat and run their hands through his kinky hair. Then I've seen the same ball-player go out and get two or three hits that afternoon and play the game of his life. Again, it is the confidence inspired, coupled with the ability.

Another old superstition among ball-players is that a load of empty barrels means base hits. If an athlete can just pass a flock of them on the way to the park, he is sure to step right along stride for stride with the three-hundred hitters that afternoon. McGraw once broke up a batting slump of the Giants with a load of empty barrels. That is why I maintain he is the greatest manager of them all. He takes advantage of the little things, even the superstitions of his men, and turns them to his account. He played this trick in one of the first years that he managed the New York club. The batting of all the players had slumped at the same time. None could hit, and the club was losing game after game as a result, because the easiest pitchers were making the best batters look foolish. One day Bowerman came into the clubhouse with a smile on his face for the first time in a week.

"Saw a big load of empty barrels this afternoon, boys," he announced, "and just watch me pickle the pill out there to-day."

Right at that point McGraw got an idea, as he frequently does. Bowerman went out that afternoon and made four hits out of a possible five. The next day three or four more of the players came into the park, carrying smiles and the announcement that fortunately they, too, had met a load of empty barrels. They, then, all went out and regained their old batting strides, and we won that afternoon for the first time in a week. More saw a load of barrels the next day and started to bat. At last all the members of the team had met the barrels, and men with averages of .119 were threatening to chisel into the three-hundred set. With remarkable regularity the players were meeting loads of empty barrels on their way to the park, and, with remarkable regularity and a great deal of expedition, the pitchers of opposing clubs were being driven to the shower bath.

"Say," asked "Billy" Gilbert, the old second baseman, of "Bill" Lauder, formerly the protector of the third corner, one day, "is one of that team of horses sorrel and the other white?" "Sure," answered "Bill." "Sure," echoed McGraw. "I hired that load of empty barrels by the week to drive around and meet you fellows on the way to the park, and you don't think I can afford to have them change horses every day, do you?"

Everybody had a good laugh and kept on swatting. McGraw asked for waivers on the load of empty barrels soon afterwards, but his scheme had stopped a batting slump and put the club's hitters on their feet again. He plays to the little personal qualities and superstitions in the men to get the most out of them. And just seeing those barrels gave them the idea that they were bound to get the base hits, and they got them. Once more, the old confidence, hitched up with ability.

What manager would have carried a Kansas farmer around the circuit with him besides McGraw? I refer to Charles Victor Faust of Marion, Kansas, the most famous jinx killer of them all. Faust first met the Giants in St. Louis on the next to the last trip the club made West in the season of 1911, when he wandered into the Planter's Hotel one day, asked for McGraw and announced that a fortune teller of Marion had informed him he would be a great pitcher and that for $5 he could have a full reading. This pitching announcement piqued Charles, and he reached down into his jeans, dug out his last five, and passed it over. The fortune teller informed Faust that all he had to do to get into the headlines of the newspapers and to be a great pitcher was to join the New York Giants.

He joined, and, after he once joined, it would have taken the McNamaras in their best form to separate him from the said Giants.

"Charley" came out to the ball park and amused himself warming up. Incidentally, the Giants did not lose a game while he was in the neighborhood. The night the club left for Chicago on that trip, he was down at the Union Station ready to go along.

"Did you get your contract and transportation?" asked McGraw, as the lanky Kansan appeared. "No," answered "Charley." "Pshaw," replied McGraw. "I left it for you with the clerk at the hotel. The train leaves in two minutes," he continued, glancing at his watch. "If you can run the way you say you can, you can make it and be back in time to catch it." It was the last we saw of "Charley" Faust for a time—galloping up the platform in his angular way with that contract and transportation in sight.

"I'm almost sorry we left him," remarked McGraw as "Charley" disappeared in the crowd. We played on around the circuit with indifferent luck and got back to New York with the pennant no more than a possibility, and rather a remote one at that. The first day we were in New York "Charley" Faust entered the clubhouse with several inches of dust and mud caked on him, for he had come all the way either by side-door special or blind baggage. "I'm here, all right," he announced quietly, and started to climb into a uniform. "I see you are," answered McGraw.

"Charley" stuck around for two or three days, and we won. Then McGraw decided he would have to be dropped and ordered the man on the door of the clubhouse to bar this Kansas kid out. Faust broke down and cried that day, and we lost. After that he became a member of the club, and we won game after game until some busy newspaper man obtained a vaudeville engagement for him at a salary of $100 a week. We lost three games the week he was absent from the grounds, and Faust saw at once he was not doing the right thing by the club, so, with a wave of his hand that would have gone with J.P. Morgan's income, he passed up some lucrative vaudeville contracts, much to the disgust of the newspaper man, who was cutting the remuneration with him, and settled down to business. The club did not lose a game after that, and it was decided to take Faust West with us on the last and famous trip in 1911. Daily he had been bothering McGraw and Mr. Brush for his contract, for he wanted to pitch. The club paid him some money from time to time to meet his personal expenses.

The Sunday night the club left for Boston, a vaudeville agent was at the Grand Central Station with a contract offering Faust $100 a week for five weeks, which "Charley" refused in order to stick with the club. It was the greatest trip away from home in the history of baseball. Starting with the pennant almost out of reach, the Giants won eighteen and lost four games. One contest that we dropped in St. Louis was when some of the newspaper correspondents on the trip kidnapped Faust and sat him on the St. Louis bench.

Another day in St. Louis the game had gone eleven innings, and the Cardinals needed one run to win. They had several incipient scores on the bases and "Rube" Marquard, in the box, was apparently going up in the air. Only one was out. Faust was warming up far in the suburbs when, under orders from McGraw, I ran out and sent him to the bench, for that was the place from which his charm seemed to be the most potent. "Charley" came loping to the bench as fast as his long legs would transport him and St. Louis didn't score and we won the game. It was as nice a piece of pinch mascoting as I ever saw. The first two games that "Charley" really lost were in Chicago. And all through the trip, he reiterated his weird prophecies that "the Giants with Manager McGraw were goin' ta win." The players believed in him, and none would have let him go if it had been necessary to support him out of their own pockets. And we did win.

"Charley," with his monologue and great good humor, kept the players in high spirits throughout the journey, and the feeling prevailed that we couldn't lose with him along. He was advertised all over the circuit, and spectators were going to the ball park to see Faust and Wagner. "Charley" admitted that he could fan out Hans because he had learned how to pitch out there in Kansas by correspondence school and had read of "Hans's" weakness in a book. His one "groove" was massages and manicures. He would go into the barber shop with any member of the team who happened to be getting shaved and take a massage and manicure for the purpose of sociability, as a man takes a drink. He easily was the record holder for the manicure Marathon, hanging up the figures of five in one day in St. Louis. He also liked pie for breakfast, dinner and supper, and a small half before retiring.

But, alas! "Charley" lost in the world's series. He couldn't make good. And a jinx killer never comes back. He is gone. And his expansive smile and bump-the-bumps slide are gone with him. That is, McGraw hopes he is gone. But he was a wonder while he had it. And he did a great deal toward giving the players confidence. With him on the bench, they thought they couldn't lose, and they couldn't. It has long been a superstition among ball-players that when a "bug" joins a club, it will win a championship, and the Giants believed it when "Charley" Faust arrived. Did "Charley" Faust win the championship for the Giants?

Another time-honored superstition among ball-players is that no one must say to a pitcher as he goes to the box for the eighth inning: "Come on, now. Only six more men." Or for the ninth: "Pitch hard, now. Only three left."

Ames says that he lost a game in St. Louis once because McGraw forgot himself and urged him to pitch hard because only three remained to be put out. Those three batters raised the mischief with Ames's prospects; he was knocked out of the box in that last inning, and we lost the game. That was before the days of the wonder necktie.

Ames won the third game played in Chicago on the last trip West. Coming into the ninth inning, he had the Cubs beaten, when McGraw began: "Come on, 'Red,' only—" "Nix, Mac," cut in Ames, "for the love of Mike, be reasonable."

And then he won the game. But the chances are that if McGraw had got that "only three more" out, he would have lost, because it would have been working on his strained nerves.

The Judgment Seat

The Judgment Seat

Juliet Wilbor Tompkins

SO WHAT MAKES A BASEBALL STORY A BASEBALL STORY, AND DOES "THE Judgment Seat," which appeared in the December 1906 issue of the *Atlantic*, qualify? You be the judge.

After graduating from Vassar in 1891, the Oakland-born Juliet Wilbor Tomkins (1871–1956) became a pioneering part of a new workforce: the professional woman. She was one of Frank Munsey's most trusted editors at his eponymous *Munsey's Magazine*, one of the most popular monthlies in the nation. When he needed a new editor for the *Puritan*, his "journal for gentlewomen," he tapped Tomkins for the job. She flourished, writing for the publication prolifically. By 1903, her byline was appearing with enough frequency in major publications for her to leave editing behind and do what she wanted: write full-time. Immensely popular as a short-story writer, she published her first novel in 1908. Another thirteen followed.

"This is good, Walter!" Mrs. Pender's little, withered, jeweled hands were lifted to his shoulders as he kissed her. "But why didn't you bring Alice?"

"Alice had rather a headache to-night: she wanted to be quiet, so I thought I'd come to you," Walter explained restlessly. "You can throw me out if you don't want me. You've done it before."

"Ah, that was when I was a spoiled old woman, and had you whenever I wished." The bright little eyes were kind and candid, quite satisfied with his explanation. Mrs. Pender knew everything about everybody, but she never seemed to be in process of finding it out. "I am glad you did not warn me, for now you will get your beloved lamb and mint sauce," she went on. "If I had expected you, I should have sent out for chickens. You don't like them so well, but in my bringing up company was company and had chickens; and I can't change my customs at seventy-nine." Walter's wandering attention came back with a start at the last words.

"Seventy-nine! My dear, you are not!"

Mrs. Pender smiled blandly. "It sounds better than sixty-nine, my dear. I put it ten years back as long as it was plausible! Now I find ten years ahead more effective."

"Do you call that living up to the best and the highest that is in you?" He seemed to be gloomily quoting. "I am glad you're a wicked old lady," he added impulsively, putting his arm over her minute shoulders as they turned to the dining-room. "That is why you're so lovable."

She patted his big hand.

"It is nice to have you," she repeated. "Cast your boys upon the waters of matrimony, and after many days they will return to you."

"But not 'buttered.'" Walter's laugh had a grim meaning of its own.

He was spasmodically gay at dinner, with lapses into periods of vagueness wherein he seemed to be carrying on some inner conversation: his lips shaped silent phrases, and once his fist came down on the table with a quick rap of decision or exasperation. He glanced up guiltily, and met Mrs. Pender's smiling, comprehending look. It seemed to impel confidences. He leaned his elbows on the table, pushing aside his coffee cup.

"My dear," he began, "did you know that I was on the whole rather a failure as a character?"

"No, I did not," she said stoutly, "and you will have hard work proving it to me."

"Well, it has been proved pretty thoroughly to me," and Walter lapsed into frowning silence.

"You were a good boy when I had you." Her tone was delicately detached and she did not look at him. "You can't have gone down hill very far in seven months."

He shook his head. "I haven't. It is just that I was down hill all the time. Only you and I didn't know it." He laughed resentfully. "We do now!"

"Well, I knew you were human, and a man," Mrs. Pender admitted. "Beyond those two fundamental defects—"

"Oh, they are nothing to my other failures! We've got the judgment seat established in our house now. We keep it in the back parlor and spend the evening gathered around it. I am even learning to use it myself—it's a contagious habit." He finished his coffee and rose. "Don't mind if I'm grumpy," he added, with an apologetic smile, and they went back to the drawing-room in intimate silence. When he had pulled her chair to the fire, he took his privileged position full length on the hearth rug, with his hands under his head.

"It's good to be here," he said. Presently he tipped his head back so that he might look into her face. "Do you know, I used to think I was a fairly good sort?" he began. "I was truthful, and decent, kind to my mother and all that, and people liked me: in fact, I thought I came rather high. Well, it's something of a shock to have it proved to me that my ideals are second-rate and my ambitions petty. It is, honest."

Mrs. Pender looked down thoughtfully into the sincere, worried eyes. "One says things, in anger—so many things!" she murmured.

"Oh, we don't quarrel," the barriers had suddenly dropped, leaving them deep in confidence. "We simply point out to each other, very affectionately and with the highest motives just where we fail. We don't have any hurt vanity or petty resentment in our house—we want to develop ourselves to the highest possible point, and only entire frankness with each other can get us there. We're always warm and kind, but we spend the day analyzing each other, then come together at night to report. And meanwhile"—he laughed ironically, then sighed. "She's right, you know, absolutely. I am not being misjudged—only found out. I can't deny anything enough to really mitigate it." He laid his hand for a moment on her little slippered foot. "Why didn't you bring me up better?" he accused her.

"Well, if I had caught you when I was Alice's age, I might have," she admitted. "But you see you didn't come under my eye until I was old—old enough to be humbly thankful that you were no worse!" Her glance seemed to turn back for a troubled moment to others who had been worse; then she returned to him with a smile. "If you love each other enough, criticism won't hurt you," she added.

"Oh, I can take a licking all right. But shouldn't there be intervals wherein one is merely loved and admired?"

"One should be loved and admired every moment of the twenty-four hours. I rather fancy one is!" she added, with a humorous lift of her eyebrows. He turned his face back to the fire.

"All roads lead to the judgment seat, in our house," he said. Then he began to talk of other things, as though rather ashamed.

When, at ten o'clock, he rose to go, he stood hesitating before her for a moment.

"I haven't meant to be—disloyal," he said. "I wouldn't have let out so to anyone else on earth. You believe that, don't you?"

She pulled him down and kissed him. "I know it. Hold on tight, dear boy, and wait—just wait!"

Alice's door was shut when he reached home, and her light out, so he went softly to his own room. It was a fragrantly sweet, well-kept little room: the purity of Alice's ideals showed in linen and silver and brass as clearly as in words and actions. His bookshelf had been filled with the same earnest fastidiousness: there were Amiel and Maeterlinck and Pater, Tolstoy and Browning, with a touch of Meredith and Mrs. Wharton for lighter moods. Walter had read such books with Alice devotedly during their brief engagement: He would have read Confucius in the original for the privilege of being beside her—happily and with no consciousness of guile; but that sort of thing could not go on indefinitely. He grew restless under Nietzsche after their marriage, fell asleep over Marius, and finally came to open rebellion after three nights of Plato.

"It's awful. I can't stand it," he protested. "Do let's have some good human reading for once in our lives. There's a ripping story in the new Munsey—lie down here and I'll read it to you."

Alice's quiet refusal and the dismayed look in her eyes made him feel as if he had been gross.

"But no one could listen indefinitely to that Plato stuff; and it is a good story," he muttered in bewildered self-justification when, a few minutes later, she rose and left the room. From that night dated the judgment seat: Alice had looked up from her dream and, for the first time, had seen him.

There was a pile of magazines now on the table by his bed, as well as twenty-six automobile circulars. Walter read for a while, paying scant attention. At last he threw down a half-finished story, rose, and softly opened his wife's door. A movement showed that she was awake.

"How is your head, Alice?" he asked, cheerfully ignoring the conversation on which they had parted.

"Better, dear, I think. I shall be all right in the morning," her voice tried in vain to hide the fact that she had been crying, and Walter felt a rush of irritation. "If I drank or stole!" flashed through his mind in angry protest.

"Well, I hope so. Good night," he said coldly, and closed the door. He lay awake a long time, half hoping that she would call him back; but there was no sound from the other room.

Some of Walter's natural cheerfulness of spirit reasserted itself during the course of the next day's work. The bewildered resentment that had been daily bringing him nearer and nearer to what he grimly called the breaking-point—he did not define it further—seemed relieved by his outburst to his old friend, and her hopeful, "Wait—just wait!" stayed by him comfortingly. After all, there was no real, tangible trouble between Alice and himself: and everyone knew that young couples had struggles their first year. A vision of her face—childishly rounded, brown-cheeked, wholesome, with wide, eager eyes always a little lifted, as if she were used to talking with tall people or to sitting at the feet of things: devout eyes that seemed to look through a faint mist when they were turned down to what Walter called the ordinary facts of life—made his heart warm. Dear, dear soul! Asking a little too much of man, perhaps, but deserving far more than she asked. Dear girl! He must not let himself forget the big whole of their marriage in the little struggles of the moment.

He left his office in time for a game of squash, followed by a shower and a rubdown. Encountering a twenty-seventh automobile circular, he read it absorbedly on the way home, and entered his house buoyant with health and cheer. Alice, who was bending over an Italian dictionary, pushed it away and went quickly to meet him. Evidently the day had had its warnings for her, too, for she clung to him with silent intensity. He sat down with her in his arms, talking great folly, "Old sweetness and light! Walter's bad girl!" being as sensible as any of it. After they had emerged into commonplace language again, he brought out the automobile circular.

"This really seems to be a little beauty," he explained, "and not so very expensive, either. Look here, it's got"—he reveled in technicalities, comparing it favorably with the favorites of the twenty-six previously examined. Her face had clouded, and she drew away from him: she had never shown any especial response to his automobile enthusiasm; but to-night the disapproval was too marked to be ignored.

"I'm not really going to get one, dear," he reassured her. "I may be extravagant in spots; but I am not quite so rash as all that. I am just amusing myself, honest." She rose, under pretext of rearranging the fire.

"It isn't that," she said, with her back to him. "I would almost rather you bought one and got it over with."

"You mean I bore you," said Walter quietly, returning the circular to his pocket.

"Oh, no, no! It is only"—she hesitated, then took it up as eagerly as she would have put her hand into the fire if she had believed that demanded of her; "it troubles me to see you spending all that enthusiasm and time on what is, after all, a—grown-up toy. I want your life to count, Walter!" She was facing him now, exalted by her own high desires. "There are so many fine, big things to care about, so much that means growth! Think what they are doing for the city and for science and for the poor and the sick—the men who count! Think what there is to read and study—dearest, dearest, there is so little time. How can you spend your leisure and enthusiasm over a toy?"

Walter had risen and stood with eyes on the ground, the brightness gone from his boyish face.

"The truth is, Alice," he said, after a pause, the words coming with a physical effort that made her sensitive hands clench, "the truth is, you have married the wrong man. I'm just a commonplace chap, like a million others. I haven't any vast ambitions, and I can't pump them up—I have tried, but I can't. My ideal has been to do well by my wife and—and children, to get on in my profession, and keep a decently clean record, and to have as much fun as I could on the side. To satisfy you I'd like to come higher, but I can't, honest. Now, what are we going to do about it?"

There was a new hardness in his voice, a hint of a growing intention, that made her press against a chair for steadiness. The mist seemed to gather between him and the wide, candid eyes that could see only high things.

"But you could be so much more, Walter," she pleaded. "You have all the weapons,—courage and brains and judgment. I don't want you to be what you are not—only to use what you have. You waste yourself, dearest,—undervalue your own bigness. And it is just because you have never been with people who cared for big things." She came close to him and took his arm between her hands. "Oh, can't you see how much more fun it is even, to count, to make your life matter in some one definite way? To belong to the world's great movement?"

He drew away from her with quiet hardness. "I am sorry, Alice, but I don't see life as a mission. I work fairly hard in my office: the rest of the time I want recreation. And we can't go on like this, you know."

"Ah, don't don't!" Her look was that of one who faces a physical blow. "I must. I can't stand this sort of thing another hour." He pulled out his watch, looked at it unseeingly and put it back. "I am going to do the only decent and dignified thing under the circumstances—which is to clear out." The mist seemed to be blinding her altogether: she put out her hand as though in the dark.

"To leave me!" The words were so faint that he could ignore them.

"I shall remove myself to Mrs. Pender's for a few weeks," he went on steadily. "She will understand without asking questions, and she won't misjudge you in any way. If you decide in that time that you want me as I am, if you will give up judging and love what you can in me, send me word. I will come back at any minute. Otherwise"—He turned abruptly to the door. "Goodby."

She shrank into a chair, looking white and stricken and crumpled. She could hear him moving about the room overhead, but she did not stir until his determined tread sounded on the stairs: then she bent forward, listening with strained intentness. She heard him put a bag down in the hall, then, after a horrible pause, his steps turned back and the door opened.

He stood over her a moment in silence.

"Alice, can't you take me just as I am?" he asked sadly. For all her terror, her eyes, lifted to him now, were as steady as his.

"It is you as you really are that I want! I can't compromise on the boy when the man is there. I want you, the big you." She caught his hand in both hers. "You can if you only will!"

He stooped and kissed her. "Goodby," he said.

The closing of the front door jarred and broke her restraint; but through all her desperate sobbing she whispered, "It's for his sake, for his sake!"

Mrs. Pender took Walter in with unquestioning sympathy, and for a few days the peace of her unexacting affection closed about him like relief: he believed that he was glad to be away from Alice. Then, creeping upon him like a sickness, his longing for her came back, stronger day by day. His face took on an old, tragic look under its boyishness, and he gave up trying to talk, sure of his friend's understanding. Sometimes it seemed to him that an impassable sea had rolled between him and Alice; and again he would wonder what the trouble was all about, and why he did not simply go home to her.

He did go to her after two weeks, without warning, almost without intention. She was sitting with her books about her, but she was not reading. Except for a deep breath at sight of him, she did not move or speak: the face lifted to him was all one poignant question.

"I will take up any pursuit you choose," he began, standing doggedly in front of her: "politics, religion, sanitation, Italian literature—anything whatever. They would all be an equal bore to me and I think it's rot; but I'm willing to meet you half way." The flush that had risen in her brown cheeks died out and he saw with deepened exasperation how thin she had grown. "Wait!" he added, as she started to speak. "That is my half: I will do it on condition that you drop all this analyzing and judgment now and forever, that you take me as I am, with as much love as possible, and with no comments."

If she had flashed into anger it might have been better for them both; but she was too eager for the great issue to care about her own wounds. She answered him with an unconscious forbearance that stung.

"What sort of a marriage would that be, Walter—without frankness and truth? I have to say what I think and feel: anything else would be unworthy of us both. My dear love, you don't know what you are asking."

"And you don't know what you are throwing away," he said shortly, and left her.

Until that hour Alice's faith had been strong: the big aspect must dominate the little aspect, in time; man, seeing the good thing, must inevitably choose it; she had waited in sorrow and desolation, but she had not once doubted the issue. With his last words and his last look, despair opened before her like a cleft in the solid earth, a cleft that widened daily as the ground crumbled under her, and the giant convictions rooted in her twenty-three years of life seemed to bend like twigs under her clutch. "And you don't know what you are throwing away:" the rough words bruised her afresh every hour. "It is right, it is for the truth," she cried over and over; but the words seemed to have lost their resonance.

She went painfully through every step of their trouble, trying to find herself arrogant, self-righteous, narrow-minded; but she was none of these things, and her clear mind would not let her deceive herself into the passionately desired, "I was wrong." No: she had cared loyally for what was best and biggest, she had been true to the creed of the world's greatest. Her reasoning was inexorable; but over and above it, night after night, sounded the old, primitive cry, "I want him! Oh, I want him!"

The days of her torment went by blindly; she scarcely knew evening from morning, held helpless in her anguish by the single straightness of her creed. She did not consciously rebel against her own decisions; she only crouched down under them and suffered. She might have died that way, like a martyr to whom the word "recant" conveys no meaning, but for a trivial announcement in a morning paper. Two clubs, the St. Swithin's and the Pilgrim, were to meet each other at baseball that afternoon, for the amusement of their friends and the benefit of a day nursery. The Pilgrim being Walter's club, she read the announcement for the momentary sense of nearness to him, even scanning the list of players for his friends. "Left field, Walter L. Richmond—"

"Oh, no, no!" she breathed, and read it over and over, trying not to believe. Their whole life together was at stake—and he could play amateur baseball while he waited. The agony, then, was all hers. She was utterly alone.

She spent the morning buttonholing a flannel sacque for a friend's child. One of the few violent acts of her life was to burn it, several weeks later, on sight. After a pretense of lunching, she dressed and went out into a glare of early spring sunshine. Wind was whirling the dust at the corners into flapping banners that closed round her chokingly. The world was as bald and empty as a white plate. Crowded cars went past, bearing advertisements of the charity baseball game: she tried to ignore them, but she had known all along that she must go to it. She had to see him.

She bought a reserved seat, but a glance at the crowd already installed there dismayed her: it was sure to hold friends and acquaintances. Even as she hesitated, she saw little Mrs. Pender, bright and elaborate, being helped devotedly to her place by several youths. She turned away to an uncovered stand opposite, where a crowd of another sort was cushioning the benches with newspapers, and dense clumps of little boys seemed to be chewing gum in unison. They obligingly made room for her, with a glance or two of curiosity, for well-dressed, tragic-looking young women, unescorted and evidently oblivious of the fact, were not a usual sight in the bleachers. Then the teams came out, with a pretense of being very seriously in earnest, and she was forgotten.

"There he is!" she said suddenly, as the Pilgrim team spread out on the field beneath.

"Ma'am?" said the youth beside her. She sent him a dim smile of apology and bent down again, her whole hungry, lonely soul in her gaze. Walter came past talking to a comrade, a little grave and thin, perhaps, but present-minded, ready for the occasion. Presently, when the game had begun, the old boyish gayety began to show in his movements: he ran valiantly to second, and joined in the universal chuckle when he was put out on third in spite of a dramatic slide. His voice came to her once or twice, spontaneous and alert. The loneliness closed on her like a shroud.

"I am only one element of his life," she thought; then realized into what stale old paths her bitter discovery had led her, and repeated, "a woman's whole existence!" with a new and crushing understanding.

She knew nothing of baseball, and followed the game only as it concerned Walter. The crowd seemed to watch him, too: he was often applauded, generally with friendly laughter. The game was nearly over when a ball, cracking soundly on the bat, went swinging high in his direction: Walter ran back, sprang wildly into the air and caught it. A single voice shot out from the grandstand, "Good old Walter!" and the cry was repeated in a roar of applause; even the bleachers took it up in joyous familiarity, "Good old Walter!" while he stood laughing, and the attendant Pilgrims ran to pound congratulations on his back. They were all with him, laughing, stamping, cheering: all the world was with him. Only his wife seemed to sit apart in her stifling shroud of loneliness.

"I really cannot stand it," she said quietly. "Ma'am?" repeated the youth beside her.

She rose, and they made a path out for her, thinking by her pallor that she was ill. One or two people were already leaving the grandstand opposite, and among them she saw Mrs. Pender. Alice followed her to her carriage.

"May I go home with you? May I talk with you?" She was as oblivious of greetings as a man with a bullet in his side might have been, and Mrs. Pender met her as simply. If, beneath her courtly surface, some lack of sympathy was concealed, it was gone by the time the silent drive was ended.

Alice followed her to the drawing room with the same stricken unconscious of externals and sat down facing her.

"I don't know what to do," she said. "I thought he would come back, that he must; but he seems to go farther and farther away. I wouldn't mind its killing me—but it is not saving him. I don't know what to do."

The expression, "saving him," brought back a touch of sharpness to the withered, alert little face.

"My dear Alice!" the protest came briskly, "if Sir Galahad and Savonarola and Ralph Waldo Emerson could have been rolled into one good-looking young man, you would have made him a perfect wife. But you have married Walter. Now it isn't a matter of saving him: the question is, are you going to save your marriage?"

"But it is just that that I have been trying and waiting and suffering to save," Alice broke in eagerly. "I want it to be a big and beautiful marriage, as it must be if we take it right, if we live up to what we know is highest!"

"As it won't be—" but Mrs. Pender's irritation was now plainly assumed, "if you keep on driving Walter crazy with judgments and ultimatums. Girls like you," she went on more gently under the frightened look that was searching hers, "expect a man to be entirely composed of heart and intellect; but there is a good big tract of plain man in Walter—or just plain boy. You have been trying to do in a few weeks something that in ten years—with infinite tact and patience—you might begin to accomplish. Or say twenty years. Things are as they are, Alice, not as they ought to be. You must take Walter as he is—or lose him."

"You mean I must compromise;" the girl's voice trembled; "keep my ideals to myself, put aside the big things to humor toys and games—deny in my life every day what I know is the truth?"

"If you had a son, dear," the old voice had grown wholly gentle,—"wouldn't you do very much that? Keep things till he could understand them, hide your criticisms of him under your love in nine cases out of ten, hold his heart close to yours, and so guide it when you could without wounding?"

"With a child, yes; but that isn't marriage."

Mrs. Pender rose and went to her, laying her little jeweled hands on the drooping shoulders. "My dear, that is all the marriage a woman like you can have with a man like Walter. Put away your ideal of marriage as something you have missed: take him as your son, love him, help him; above all, be his comrade—love the game because he loves it, as you would your son's. Perhaps, this way, in time he will grow nearer to the things you care about: perhaps he never will. But it is all you have left. Take him in your secret heart—your very secret heart—as your oldest son; and, Alice dear,"—she bent down and kissed her with a tremulous smile, "don't keep him an only child a minute longer than you can help!"

She went out of the room, and Alice sat for a long time motionless, staring ahead with wide, misty eyes; all that life meant to her pitted against the pain in her heart. Then the front door closed and a step sounded in the hall. She sprang to her feet, still irresolute, her face drawn with struggle.

"Alice!" Walter's voice was quick, warm, ready for overwhelming gladness. The shadows fled and she ran to him.

"Oh, my little boy!" she cried over and over, her arms about him. "My boy, my little boy!" He smiled, well content with her new name for him, hearing in it only her tenderness.

The Home Runs That Spawned a Nickname

The Home Runs That Spawned a Nickname

Grantland Rice

BASEBALL NICKNAMES CAN BE A DELICATE MATTER. MOST EVOLVE. Then there's Athletics' third baseman Frank Baker, mainstay of Connie Mack's famed $100,000 infield. The origins of his "Home Run" cognomen rests on two swings of the bat and a six-day rain delay. His go-ahead dinger off Giant pitcher Rube Marquard in Game 2 of the 1911 World Series and his ninth-inning game tyer off Christy Mathewson in Game 3 the next day gave the sporting press plenty of space filler while rain pummeled Philadelphia's Shibe Park before the fourth game could be played. And so Frank Baker, who never hit more than twelve home runs in a season and only ninety-six in his career, became a Giant-killing giant and a man whose name would always be associated with the crack of the bat and the image of baseballs flying in graceful arcs over outfield fences far away.

Now, let Grantland Rice (1880–1954), arguably the giant of American sportswriting, bring Game 3 to life, as he did on October 18, 1911, for the *Atlanta Journal*—and syndicated in papers from coast to coast.

In his almost half a century pounding keyboards and manning a mic, Rice cut an enormous swath. He arrived at the *New York Tribune* in 1914, and began batting out his nationally read Sportlight column, which magically morphed athletes—Jack Dempsey, Bobby Jones, and Babe Ruth, for just three—into American demigods. He was the editor of the *American Golfer* magazine—and its most recurring byline, as well. He was the voice of Paramount sports newsreels. He selected college football's annual All-American team. And he banged out under deadline some unforgettable prose, including the most famous lede in all of sportswriting: "Outlined against a blue-gray October sky the Four Horsemen rode again." A virtuoso of verse that primed the violins in the background, he polished the insight that became a life path, framed and hung in locker rooms and clubhouses from coast to coast: "For when the one great scorer comes to mark against your name,/He writes—not that you won or lost—but how you played the game." When Cooperstown opened its adjacent writers' wing, Rice was among the first invited in.

In the National League war, Mathewson and Marquard stood between the Giants and defeat. In the world's series they have stood as firmly until Frank Baker's mighty war club swept them both from the path. The score was 3 to 2 and Baker did it again.

John Franklin Baker of Trappe, Md.

That's the name and that's the honored village beneath today's white spotlight. For the first time in his career, pitching as grandly as he ever pitched, Christy Mathewson has gone down in a world's series defeat. His mates had cracked behind him—Johnny Coombe was pitching valiant ball and the hard-hitting visitors were rushing and assaulting Matty savagely.

Under this crimson fire the Giant premier had carried the battle into the ninth round with a 1 to 0 lead. He had led his team upon both attack and defense. He was the Giant machine, almost alone and unaided. He had put his great right arm between his people and defeat round after round. And then, with victory in sight, with his fifth Philadelphia triumph since 1905 dangling at his eager fingertips, and with only two men left to retire, John Franklin Baker threw his war club into the argument and, as the ball sailed gracefully und swiftly far and deep into the right-field crowd, the story ended.

In Mathewson's 12 campaigns of pitching, this was the roughest blow of his pitching life. There were two strikes called on Baker when

Matty broke one over with a curve that broke shoulder high. For a brief second, the gray ball seemed to hang in mid-air and then—BING—and then "good night."

No two ball clubs ever fought a more historic battle. In contrast to the first two conflicts, the third duel fairly reeked with whirl and climaxes and hair-raising episodes. Coombs pitched with spectacular effect. His support was true and staunch at the vital spots. He broke in but one round—the third—when Meyers singled, Mathewson hammered him to third and Devore's force-out put the Chief across. From this point out the Athletic iron man held the Giants spellbound, with an occasional flutter of wildness, until Herzog doubled in the eleventh and scored on Eddie Collins's fumble.

All this time the Athletic machine was outplaying the Giants, man for man, with the exception of Mathewson. Mack's men were stealing on Meyers and Mack's infield was outplaying the Giants, with both outfields steady, but Mathewson still stood guard before the door of Giant hope. He was pitching his fifth world series game and a run had to be earned from his wonderful pitching. With far less speed than Coombs and a curveball hardly as sharp, the Giant magician was still standing one of the hardest hitting ball clubs that ever played upon its beam ends. Try as they would, they could not break beneath his guard. His mates were confident of victory. The vast audience was preparing to leave the park and then, we repeat again, came Baker. Baker's wallop not only inspired his pals with new hope, it cracked the Giant machine into pieces.

Mathewson still pitched well, but his reeling support kicked away the final chance. Three infield misplays at the finish, coupled with a brace of hits which otherwise might have scored, gave the Philadelphians two runs and a deadly sure lead.

The Giants fought back briefly, when Herzog doubled to left and soon scored on Collins's fumble, but the rally died quick. Even with Baker's fame-making swipe, had Mathewson's support remained intact, he might have had a chance to win. But there was a tinge of bush to the Giants' play after Baker came through and upset the scenery.

This sudden turn at the close for the first time gave the Athletics the jump. The odds, for the first time, now belong their way. They have not only won two games to one, but play next at home with Bender ready for another start and Mathewson unavailable until Thursday, when even then he will hardly be fresh and at his best. He looked tired and worn as he left the box in the eleventh, crushed by the sudden turn which had driven him back just as the crest was reached.

The Athletics looked to be the better club Tuesday. Collins again fizzled a bit, but in the main their play was sure and keen. Coombs worked with flashing speed, which gave him a big edge upon a gray, dark day, where speed is always hardest to hit.

In only two rounds was Mathewson in deep trouble till the ninth. Herzog's error, a single by Davis which hit Connolly, and Barry's sacrifice in the fifth, put the Athletics in close scoring distance, with only one out. But Lapp and Coombs were handled with ease. In the eighth, Barry doubled and Lapp singled, as Fletcher erred, but again Mathewson came through by stopping Coombs and fanning Oldring.

All in all, it was probably the most exciting single game ever played—considering the amount of importance which lay upon almost every move. The great crowd was held in the grip of an excitement which extended its force into the field. There were any number of moments where a play one way or another might have turned the tide, but always under pressure there was too much stuff to be borne back.

With this game over, all eyes are now returned upon Philadelphia. By nightfall, the Mack men may either have the series practically won or may be back upon even terms again—the situation again close and critical. But the rebuttal is now up to McGraw, who has been forced upon a defensive, and whose pitching choice today will be one of the most vital moves of his managerial existence. For he must call upon someone who can stop Frank Baker, or the rest will count for less than naught.

On Young Walter Johnson and
Old Honus Wagner

On Young Walter Johnson and
Old Honus Wagner

ONE OF THE MOST SERVICEABLE FEATURES IN BOTH THE MONTHLY *Baseball Magazine* and the weekly newspaper *Sporting Life*, which preceded its competitor the *Sporting News* to the racks by five years, was the filler brief, or short piece, made up entirely of quotes from those in the game. The two chosen here speak volumes in their brevity.

When a nineteen-year-old Idaho farm boy named Walter Johnson was called up to the majors in August of 1907, the Senators were on their way to Detroit and Cleveland. Leading 2–1 in his debut against the Tigers, Johnson was pinch hit for in the eighth, and the Senators went on to lose. He collected his first win the following week, holding the pre–Indian Naps to just four hits, two in the ninth, in a 7–2 laugher. The Naps dazzling right-hander Addie Joss, in the midst of a 27–11 season, didn't pitch against Johnson, but he watched the kid closely from the dugout. Under the headline "Veteran's Tribute to a Youngster," *Sporting Life* recorded Joss's observation on the rook. It proved frighteningly clairvoyant:

> That young fellow is another Cy Young. I never saw a kid with more than he displayed. Of course, he is still green, but when he has a little experience he should be one of the greatest pitchers that ever broke into the game. He has terrific speed and a motion which does not put much strain on his arm. And this will all improve as he goes along.

Six years later, as shortstop Honus Wagner's career was winding down with the Pirates, *Baseball Magazine* asked longtime rival John McGraw, manager of the Giants, to assess the Dutchman and his place in the game. The assessment continues to ring with truth. Ask anyone from Pittsburgh:

The most wonderful ball player who ever lived.

I tell you that big Dutchman played great ball against us. Players may come and they may go, but Honus seems to go on forever, and to keep getting better.

He has class that no other player possesses. You can have your Cobbs, your Lajoies, your Bakers and all the rest of them, but I'll take Wagner for my pick of the greatest. He is not only a marvelous mechanical player, but he has the quickest baseball brain I have ever observed. I have watched him many and many a time, trying to pick out one time when he would fail to grasp a situation like a flash, and I have never been able to catch him yet. He is never asleep, and he always knows what the other fellow ought to do.

Pittsburgh ought to be proud of Hans. He is the greatest ever, and there is no mistake about that. He does everything better than the ordinary star can do any one thing.

One Down, 713 to Go

One Down, 713 to Go

Damon Runyon

EVERY ONCE IN A WHILE THE PLANETS LINE UP JUST RIGHT, THE UNI-
verse resonates, and the harmonic convergence that results echoes ever
after. On May 6, 1915, two giants of the sporting scene crossed paths;
neither, at the time, could have the slightest inkling that one would be
making history while the other was recording it.

Damon Runyon (1880–1946) went out to the Polo Grounds that
day to watch the Yankees host the Red Sox. Nothing unusual there. Years
before he would populate stories with such characters as Nathan Detroit,
Sky Masterson, Sorrowful Jones, and Baseball Hattie, Runyon was
already considered one of the most important sportswriters in the capital
city of American sports. And he had a game to cover for his employer, the
New York American, where his account would find its place in the sports
pages the next day.

It was a good game, certainly, but that's not why it's here. It's here
because in the third inning, a twenty-year-old Red Sox pitcher named
Ruth hit his first Major League home run. He'd hit 713 more before he
was through, which makes this a significant moment in baseball history,
though at the time, it was just another of the countless moments Runyon
would regularly filter through his typewriter.

Ruth, by the way, posted an 18–8 record as a starting pitcher in 1915,
his first full season in the majors. He also hit three more home runs.

There is not enough of Hughy High to make one good-sized hero for our story this morning, and so we add to him Luther Cook and thus compile a sufficient subject. Hughy and Luther, bunched together, make something to talk about. They assisted this community in taking a notable decision over the municipality of Boston, Mass., yesterday afternoon.

The shades of the thirteenth inning were falling fast up at the Polo Grounds, and the Wild Yanks and the Boston Red Sox, champs-presumptive of the Amur-r-r-ick-kin League, as Ban Johnson calls it, were clustered in a tie. The count was three all, with Will Evans, the gesticulator, eagerly scanning the horizon for evidence of nightfall, when Hughy and Luther amalgamated and broke up the pastime, the final tally being 4 to 3 in favor of the grand old Empire State.

In our own garrulous way we shall now endeavor to tell you just how it happened, omitting only such details as we deem unfit for publication.

Hughy High, small, but efficient, opened that thirteenth with a single to centre. Walter Pipp struck out, Hughy High stole second. Luther Cook singled over Heine Wagner's head, just out of Heine Wagner's reach and mid the mad mumble of the multitude. Hughy High came tumbling in across the h. p. with the winning run. How was that for High?

Having described the most important incident of the game, we now feel constrained to warn the compositors to clear away all obstructions below, and to either side, so we can run right on down this column, and over into the next, in telling about the goings-on prior to the moment mentioned, beginning with that hour in the ninth when we boys tied 'er up.

Luther Cook figured in that, too. One was out in the ninth, when George Ruth struck Luther with a pitched baseball. George pitched the baseball left-handed, and by giving it the body-follow-through, he succeeded in raising a tumor on Luther's shoulder. Cap'n Roger Peckinpaugh subsided without a struggle, while Luther tarried at first, rubbing his wounded torso, and glaring at George Ruth. That made two out, and it looked as this story would have to open with sighs, when Luther Boone—but by all means a separate paragraph for Luther.

Luther Boone doubled to right, a solid, smacking, soulful double that knocked the bleacherites back on the butt of their spines from the crouch that precedes the rush for the exits, and which scored Luther Cook with the tying tally.

A moment later Luther Boone went on to third, when George Ruth made a bad throw trying to catch him off second, but Leslie Nunamaker could not bring him in, and the game passed on into extra innings and to the big punch in the story as outlined above.

Well, it was quite a pastime. Everybody said it was a great game to win. Everybody was so delighted that they almost forgot about Dominick Mullaney, who was cast for the character of the bad guy in this tale. Not that we intend to make Dominick out, because you know the size of Dominick. The day that we blacken the character of Dominick is the day after Dominick leaves town, and gets well beyond the confines of this newspaper's circulation.

In the seventh inning, with we'uns needing a run to tie, Luther Cook singled. Peckinpaugh was duly expunged, and Boone hit the right field wall with a blow which put cook [sic] on third. The ball hopped back off the razorbacked sign in right into Hooper's hands, and Hooper threw to first, instead of second, as Boone anticipated.

Boone had taken "that old turn" after hitting first, in accordance with the advice of all the coachers, and was several feet off the bag when Hoblitzel got the ball. Dominick said he was out, and the rally bogged down right there. The crowd discussed Dominick in audible tones on account of that decision, and some thought it might be a good thing to assassinate him at once, but no action was taken on account of Dominick's size, and the presence of Ban Johnson.

We have been wondering ever since the season opened why Wild Bill Donovan has been keeping little Jack Warhop warmed up down there in right field, and the reason developed yesterday. It was for the purpose of having Jack pitch this game, and Jack pitched very well indeed while he was pitching, proving the efficacy of warming-up.

In the eighth inning, Charles Mullen batted for Jack, but nothing came of it, as Mike McNally, the Sox's new third baser, and the noisiest man in the whole world, next to Baumgartner, the Phil pitcher, made a smashing play on Charley's drive. Fritz Maisel got an infield hit that inning, stole second, moved to third on Carrigan's bad throw, and scored on Hartzell's out.

Cyrus Pieh finished the game for the Yanks, and this story would be wholly incomplete without an eulogy of Cyrus. Tall, thin and very interesting, Cyrus would have a column all to himself did space permit. He compiled a masterly finish. Pieh had the crust, as you might say, to use a slow curve on some of the sluggers of the Sox, and he made them appear *mighty* futile and inefficient.

In the eleventh he gathered up Scott's slow roller and made a two-base bad chuck to Pipp. Then he fanned McNally. Henricksen, who once broke up a world's series pastime on Chris Mathewson—long and long ago, that seems—batted for Cyrus Pieh any time he feels that way about it.

Henricksen singled and Scott took third, Henricksen moving to second on the throw in. Then Cyrus Pieh fanned Ruth and Hooper. How was that for Pieh?

Fanning this Ruth is not as easy as the name and occupation might indicate. In the third frame Ruth knocked the slant out of one of Jack Warhop's underhanded subterfuges, and put the baseball in the right field stand for a home run.

Ruth was discovered by Jack Dunn in a Baltimore school a year ago when he had not yet attained his lefthanded majority, and was adopted, and adapted, by Jack for the uses of the Orioles. He is now quite a pitcher and a demon hitter—when he connects.

In our boys' end of the eleventh, Pipp led off with a single, but Wild Bill had Cook up there trying to sacrifice, and after failing in two attempts to bunt, Cook struck out. Whereupon he flung his bat far from him and took on an expression of intense disgust. Evidently the only way Luther likes to bunt is from his shoe cleats.

It was in that inning that Luther Boone was purposely passed for the first time in his brief career. In other days pitchers would have passed the whole batting order to get at Luther, but yesterday Ruth let him go to fire at Nunamaker, and Leslie did not betray Ruth's confidence. He lifted a fly to Hooper.

The Greatest Game Ever Pitched

The Greatest Game Ever Pitched

F. C. Lane

THAT FERDINAND COLE LANE (1885–1984) WOULD FIND HIS WAY TO *Baseball Magazine* let alone edit the monthly for twenty-four of his twenty-five years there is one of those conundrums on life's path that go beyond deciphering. He was a scientist by training, a biologist, whose employ before walking through the magazine's door had him living in a log cabin in the Canadian wilderness for the Massachusetts Commission of Fish and Game. Then again, if he could find his way out of that, he could find his way anywhere.

Founded in 1908, *Baseball*—it soldiered on until the Mantle–Mays era of the 1950s—was the first regular publication with the luxury of exploring and analyzing the events and personalities of the National Pastime instead of reacting to them on a daily deadline. Lane quickly grew into his job, and from his arrival in 1912 to his departure in 1937, he left a legacy on the page as astute as it was prolific. He grew into a perceptive interviewer and a stylish writer, and nothing within the game lay beyond his grasp. Like the scientist he was, he enjoyed putting the game under a microscope and making sense of what he saw.

In the July 1917 issue, he focused his lens on what is, so far at least, a once-in-baseball-history event: two pitchers—Cincinnati's Fred Toney and the Cubs' Hippo Vaughn—locked in no-hit combat against each other for a full nine innings. The Reds won in the tenth on an unearned run driven in by—of course—Olympic legend and football immortal Jim Thorpe. It never left the infield.

While Lane gave the feat perspective and grace, baseball can count itself lucky that the irrepressible Charley Dryden—we met him earlier in his Biblical paean to Amos Rusie—was still at his typewriter and in the press box. On the payroll of the *Chicago Examiner*, his wit was as sharp as ever. Witness his lede: "Hippo Vaughn, the intelligent southpaw, was doomed from the beginning of his combat. He whiffed the first man up, a sure sign of defeat."

In his encomium to Vaughn and Toney, Lane paid appropriate tribute to the hookup none thought would ever be equaled: the perfect game that Cleveland's Addie Joss recorded at the end of the 1908 season against the White Sox's Ed Walsh, who struck out fifteen, giving up just four hits only to lose, like Vaughn did, on an unearned run. Amazingly, baseball would produce an even better pitched outing on September 9, 1965. That's when Sandy Koufax, the Dodgers' nonpareil, registered the fourth no-hitter of his career to pass Cy Young's and Bob Feller's once-thought unapproachable three (and since obliterated by Nolan Ryan's seven). Like Joss, Koufax tossed a perfecto—against another hard-luck Chicago hurler, the Cubs' Bob Hendley, who, in turn, pitched the game of his life. He gave up just a single hit. And he, too, lost 1–0, and, once again, the run was unearned. Koufax whiffed fourteen on the night, including the final sextet to face him, a feat that inspired Vin Sculley, the Homer of the broadcasting booth, to spin his own version of an oral epic, memorably winding down with this:

"And Sandy Koufax, whose name will always remind you of strike-outs, did it with a flourish. He struck out six consecutive batters. So when he wrote his name in capital letters in the record book, the 'K' will always loom larger than the 'O-U-F-A-X.'"

Lane would have likely admired that. Dryden too. Now, back to the past.

More than two thousand years ago, Solomon, who was the Connie Mack of his era, issued an important statement for the local press. Said the

Gifted Hebrew King, "There is nothing new under the sun." And that blunt assertion has gone unchallenged all the ages.

But Solomon was unfamiliar with baseball. What he said may have been true of his own time but it wouldn't hold water today. There is something new under the sun. It happened only the other afternoon. It was the strangest, the most unheard-of, the most unique occurrence that ever starred a game whose commonest feats are unusual.

"No two contests were ever exactly alike," said some wise umpire in a moment of lucidity. And that statement was doubtless fair to middlin' true. But the occurrence we speak of stands out head and shoulders above all similar events since Adam first hit the apple for a historic out at home.

Yes, kind friends, the event we speak of with this unusual preamble was the little set-to between the Cubs and the Reds on May 2nd. In strict fact, perhaps, we ought not to mention the Reds and Cubs at all. They were passive actors in the drama. What actually occurred was a meeting between two doughty champions, Jim Vaughn and Fred Toney. And that matching of strength has never been equalled and probably never will be equalled as long as the game endures.

Once in a while some able pitching gent hurls a two-hit game. The popular applause is only proper. Rarely a one hit game peers above the horizon and is greeted with wild huzzas. Very rarely, generally about once or twice a season, some blushing hero delivers a no-hit game. But where, O where, did you ever hear of two such red letter champions hooking up in a double acrobatic act of pitching perfection against each other on the self-same afternoon? It can't be done, but it has been done, and therefore we are a liar, although we wouldn't believe it unless the cold, clean print told the startling story and we had the facts verified by word of mouth from the principal actors in the event.

I have played poker occasionally (for matches, grains of corn, et cetera, particularly the latter) and never in all my life have I held a straight flush. I have met that beau ideal of the gambler in other hands. I have been unfortunate enough to buck one with three of a kind and bright visions of a fat pot. But I have never been on the right side of a straight flush. But if I ever do what chance would there be of someone holding a better straight flush against me? Would it be one chance in a million? I

doubt it. In fact, the odds would fade away in the nebulosity of sheer distance. It's as near certain as anything can be, that nobody would beat such
a hand. And yet that's a case parallel to Jim Vaughn's little experience on
May 2nd. Jim hurled nine innings, a full working game of hitless ball.
Not a Red Leg caromed the horsehide safely off Jim's twisters and bullet
hops. The feat which those masters of the mound, Grover Alexander
and Walter Johnson, have striven in vain to equal, was in Jim's hand. He
had done all that the pitcher can humanly accomplish. He had pitched
a no-hit game.

It wasn't so much that Jim lost the game. Other no-hit games have
been lost before. But the incredible feature of Jim's defeat was that he was
vanquished by absolutely better twirling than his own. Yes, kind friends,
the man who twirled a hitless game was defeated fairly in a pitching duel.
He held a straight flush and his opponent held a better hand.

Many years ago Addie Joss, one of the greatest pitchers who ever
lived, hooked up in a pitching duel with Ed Walsh, another of the
greatest pitchers who ever lived. Joss twirled a perfect game, not a man
hit safely, not a base runner reached first. Walsh fell a little short of this
phenomenal mark. Three lean singles wriggled snakily through the grass
as the spit ball caromed off the opposition bats. But the iron man of the
White Sox was at his best. All in all the game made quite a stir. It was
generally counted as the greatest sample of simon pure twirling baseball
had ever known. Joss felt proud to have defeated such pitching as that
of Walsh and the Spit Ball King bowed without hesitation before the
wizardly magic of Joss.

And yet, after all these years, that game has fairly been exceeded.
Perhaps neither Vaughn nor Toney did quite as well as Joss, who allowed
no one to get to first base. But on the other hand, Toney pitched not only
nine but ten full innings of hitless ball, while Vaughn was equally good
for the regulation nine. No game which has ever been played can equal
that showing. It is doubtful if it will ever be equalled again. Hats off to
Jim Vaughn and Fred Toney, in the most masterly pitching contest of
all time.

Why Blacks Belong in the Major Leagues

Why Blacks Belong in the Major Leagues
Howard A. Phelps

NOTHING TO SAY HERE THAT WOULDN'T SOUND TRITE OTHER THAN stating the obvious: the insistence of keeping baseball the province of white men was, at its core, a nonstarter. Sure, you could keep the majors lily white—until you couldn't anymore—but the urge to participate in the joys of the game could never be corralled. Separate? Yes. Equal?

Let Howard A. Phelps take that question in his 1919 response to a column by Hugh Fullerton—we'll meet him later in these pages—for the *Half Century Magazine*, a Chicago-based monthly aimed at an urban Black readership interested in fashion, culture, literature, and the blazing questions of equal rights. Phelps found a home at the magazine shortly after graduating from the University of Michigan in 1915, and while his name was ensconced on the masthead as circulation manager, his pen was as furious as its wielder was copious. Phelps jumped comfortably from business to Black history, to discrimination, and to freedom. And he relished writing about sports, especially baseball, weighing in often on its place in the national conversation. He forcefully advocated for the National Pastime to open its arms to all, less on moral grounds—though he found those—than his belief that the game would simply be more exciting.

In support of his argument, Phelps underlines how much his teammates on Michigan's track squad savored the idea of competing against the nation's best Black stars in hopes of bringing out their best. Phelps, a shot-putter, lettered twice at Michigan. His is the only Black face in the team pictures.

A short while ago, Mr. Dave Young, a New York fan, advanced the theory that to revive the waning interest in baseball Colored teams should be organized and pitted against white teams. In answer to this article Mr. Hugh S. Fullerton, the sporting editor of the New York Evening World and 18 other papers throughout the country, approved of Mr. Young's idea in so far as it concerns the organizing of Colored teams. He says that a league of Colored teams would create interest but that they would create riots and trouble also if pitted against white teams.

Mr. Fullerton is right in his contention that an organization of Colored teams in New York, Boston, Philadelphia, Chicago, Cincinnati and St. Louis would do a big stroke of business for the owners of the major league teams.

The players of the big league teams could be occupied then the whole season instead of only one-half of the season as they are under the present system of baseball. He is also right in that these Colored teams would furnish a lot of clean, healthy outdoor sport for the Colored people during the baseball season. He is also right in that the color line bars from the game some of the finest players that have been developed and in support of his theory he mentions the wonderful Monroe, now deceased, who for many years distinguished himself on different teams throughout the country. Mr. Fullerton mentions Buckner who "as a player and comedian has been for 20 years a great card, and at an age at which the majority of players retire to slippers and rheumatism he can still play a gallant third base." A little farther on in his article Mr. Fullerton pays tribute to the genius of "Rube" Foster, the manager of the American Giants Baseball team of Chicago. He says that Foster is "a great baseball man, a magnetic leader and a manager who under most difficult conditions, has made good everywhere. He has taken his team from coast to coast and from Canada to Mexico, and has played more towns and perhaps more games than any man living. His team has played as high as 225 games in a year in all sorts of towns and cities, has made money and never has had trouble of any serious nature. It has played against white teams in Southern cities and has been popular.

"His men play the game hard, fight all the line, but for conduct, for good nature, for sportsmanship and for clean language and clean play they are a model for any team of white men. Because of their color they must behave better, control their tempers and their language better than white teams, and they do it."

So much for that part of Mr. Fullerton's article which is right. Now for that part which is wrong. He claims that sooner or later the pitting of Colored teams against white teams would result in intensified race antagonism.

I fail to see the basis of such an argument. In the first place Mr. Fullerton refutes his own argument. In the quoted matter above he says that "Rube" Foster has travelled the U.S. with his teams from coast to coast and from Canada to Mexico and that Mr. Foster has played more teams and under more adverse conditions than any living man. Surely, then, the record of such a man and his teams would be a genuine test of the spirit that grows out of inter-racial contests. As Mr. Fullerton says himself there has never been any friction between Mr. Foster's team and teams they have played and yet Foster's opponents have been Colored and white in all parts of the country: North and South; East and West. If Mr. Foster can manage a team of Colored players by merely appealing to their sense of honor and manhood; if he can compete against white teams in the South where race misunderstanding is the most acute; if these white Southern teams are governed by no rule except by their love of the sport and of fair play; surely with the introduction of the rigid rules of organized baseball, a damper would be put on all rowdyism that would crop out under the present unorganized system.

Unorganized baseball still contains elements that are very irksome and disgusting to semi-professional ballplayers. Let these elements be eliminated by organized baseball and Colored teams will introduce a brand of baseball that equals anything now known. Rube Foster has demonstrated as Mr. Fullerton points out, that the Negro baseball teams play the game for all it is worth; that they have met white teams under the most trying conditions without any serious trouble cropping out between them; that they constitute a big drawing card.

I feel confident that if the Colored teams play under the same conditions as white league teams do, the great American pastime would feel
an impetus that has hither-to been foreign to the sport. The game would
be played harder and to greater crowds. A survey of inter-racial competition of the last 20 years will establish this beyond a doubt. In the professional world George Dixon, Sam Langford, Joe Gans, Jack Johnson,
and a whole retinue of other boxers have furnished the opposition when
the country felt its greatest thrill; when Irvin Cobb, Floyd Gibbons, Jack
London, rushed to Gold Field and Reno, Nevada and Havana, Cuba;
when they painted in the most lavish language the doings of the pugilists
who in each case were white against Colored. I have yet to read of any
big newspaper in the country sending writers of national fame to report
what happened at the Jeffries-Fitzsimmons fight, the Corbett-Nelson,
Ketchel-Thomas, Willard-Moran fights. Acknowledge it or not the idea
of white against black thrills the whole country. The country witnesses
men exerting every atom of their skill in order to attain victory and the
promoters reap gigantic profits when there are white men against Colored men.

In my school days at the University of Michigan, the pleasantest
moments of my athletic hours were those after a strenuous afternoon in
the hot sun when I reported to the rubbing table to hear Harold Haff,
Harold Smith, Chick Bond, Howard Seward, Joe Horner and others
plan how they were going to beat Howard Drew of Southern California, Granger of Dartmouth, Theodore Cable and Alexander Jackson of
Harvard, and Bowser of Syracuse. Never did I hear a bitter word uttered
against any of these distinguished Colored stars.

It was merely the burning of the spirit that "I must beat that Colored
man." The fastest heat I ever saw run was one afternoon on Ferry Field
in Ann Arbor in 1914 when Seward, Bond and Lapsley were having
a tryout for the Inter-Collegiate meet at Philadelphia. Lapsley, now
Dr. Lapsley, was Colored. All three men ran better than 10 seconds for
the 100-yard dash. The two white men were 4 yards behind at 80 yards.
They finished in the first places, however, with Lapsley a step behind
the winner. In the dressing room the white men said they would have
dropped dead had Lapsley beaten them. It is something in inter-racial

competition that lends greater interest and enchantment and swells the gate receipts when Colored men are pitted against white men.

It can be seen then that with the hold baseball already has on the public, the game would lend greater interest and greater receipts by the organization of Colored teams and then pitching them against white teams. I fail to see the claim of Mr. Fullerton that inter-racial baseball games would create riots and other trouble.

With the advance in salary that the Colored teams would be assured; with the better hotel and transportation facilities that would be opened; with the elimination of the disgraceful and repulsive form of betting that keep many of the Colored people away from the parks; with the attractiveness of better players; with the enthusiasm engendered by greater newspaper publicity; with the thought of tumbling down the averages of "Ty" Cobb and Joe Jackson; let these improvements and incentives be injected into the Colored baseball player's life and "Ty" Cobb and George Sisler and all the other stars will have to hustle more vigorously to retain their crowns.

Is Baseball Writing Overdone?

Is Baseball Writing Overdone?

Charles W. Murphy

COULD THE TIME HAVE BEEN MORE INTERESTING FOR THIS ESSAY BY this writer?

Both World War I and the influenza epidemic left serious scars on every level of baseball's 1918 season. At the top, more than 30 percent of Major League players were in uniform—as in military—during the war; others left their positions on the diamond for war-related industries. Both Christy Mathewson and Ty Cobb served overseas under Major Branch Rickey, then president of the St. Louis Cardinals, in the new Chemical Corps, Matty with tragic results. Back home, some teams played shorthanded, and the season itself ended prematurely—on Labor Day. Rumors spread that if the war continued, the 1919 campaign might be canceled completely.

The flu only exacerbated this *annus horribilis*. Woodrow Wilson failed to show up for Opening Day. Babe Ruth was sidelined with symptoms consistent with the virus. Other players and staff suffered in its grips. Fans stayed home. Revenues were down. Owners forced their players to take pay cuts. And in January 1919, Major Leaguers played an exhibition game in Pasadena—wearing cloth masks.

Still, Charles Murphy (1868–1931) looked to the coming season with hope.

Though Murphy was no longer involved in the game when *Baseball Magazine* asked him to share a few words for its March 1919 issue, he had owned and operated the only two Chicago Cubs teams—1907 and 1908—to win a World Series in the twentieth century. After selling the franchise in 1913, he moved home to Ohio and built a state-of-the-art movie theater. And while he was wrong about Johnny Evers's potential future as a baseball writer, the penultimate sentence of this piece is, in retrospect, chilling.

If the 1919 season began with expectation for Murphy, it ended elsewhere—in the treachery of a corrupt team and a World Series thrown away.

Does baseball get too much space from the press? That is a mooted question and it gives me much satisfaction to present my views on it. Several times when I was President of the Chicago National League Baseball Club I was solemnly informed that the Associated Press would not carry the box-scores the following season. Many times sporting editors have told me that they had been ordered to give less space to baseball. I always laughed at that sort of stuff. Here and there you will find a managing editor who makes a limousine appearance, but who has flivver brain, and he will order the sporting editor to publish less about baseball and more about other outdoor and indoor sports. When I was sporting editor of the *Cincinnati Enquirer* I held the view that baseball was bigger and better than all other sports combined and at times on a Sunday I would devote more than a page to baseball . . .

Why?

In the first place baseball is honest and for that reason alone it deserves recognition and encouragement. In the second place it is the national game and that means a whole lot to me. Uncle Sam would not have a national game that he could not be proud of. There is no need to apologize for baseball—the game as it is played on the field. On the other hand it is both a pleasure and an honor to boost it . . .

I appreciate the good that the Fourth Estate does for professional baseball by the widespread publicity that the game receives. I hope I thoroughly understand that, because I have been on both sides of the fence—the baseball side and the press pasture. I also think that most sporting editors love the grand old game of baseball and want to see it prosper. Only here and there do we find some fellow, who wishes to be a sensationalist and he takes a course opposite to the general run of fellows, simply to be different and to cause talk and make his column read. Even that type of fellow down in his heart likes the game and would be sorry to have its death-knell sounded.

My idea has always been that baseball needs the support of the press and the newspapers need baseball news to boost their circulations. I do not know of any clearer way to analyze the condition that this story has to do with. Some of the smartest men about baseball that I have ever talked with were writers about the game. That is why I say there should at least be one session annually between the writers and owners for an exchange of ideas that might result in beneficial legislation. A man does not have to own stock in a baseball club to note some evil of the sport and to be able to make a suggestion that might eradicate the mischief.

It would not surprise me greatly if Johnny Evers, who has done so much to introduce baseball in France, should eventually become a writer on the game, the same as Sam Crane and the late Tim Murnane, who also had been players. John can write his own stuff and he has a good style, which would make his stuff worthwhile. He also is a deep student of the game and a paper would make a ten-strike to secure him, in my judgment. The former Keystone King—a title, by the way, which I had the pleasure of creating, just as Charley Dryden gave Chance the title of Peerless Leader—has brains, too, and some day he may make a good man to be a member of the National Commission.

That will be when the governing body of professional baseball becomes representative and the players are given representation.

A million or more ideas will be sprung this winter and next spring as to how to aid baseball to get back on its feet and some good is bound to result from the exchange of views. Only ideas that are based on their practicability will be worth considering, however, and those who have the good of the national game at heart should not be too revolutionary in their demands for a reorganization. At least, that is what I think. Abuses should be eradicated one at a time. The press will stand by the game after things get normal again, because it is good business for the owners of the publication to take that attitude. The game will not be killed by invidious persons, or croakers, because it is too well rooted in the American temperament.

I look to see baseball more popular than it ever was in 1919.

Intimations of How White Sox Turn into Black Sox

Intimations of How White Sox
Turn into Black Sox

Hugh Fullerton

IN HIS TIME, HUGH FULLERTON (1873–1945) RANKED AS THE DEAN OF the nation's baseball writers. He was a founder of the Baseball Writers' Association of America and mentor to Ring Lardner, Grantland Rice, and Charles E. Van Loan. He pioneered an early version of sabermetrics and was noted for his ability for analyzing how teams matched up against each other on any given day. He's purported to be the first sportswriter to actually quote the players he was writing about. From his home at the *Chicago Herald and Examiner*, his game stories and columns were syndicated all over the country, as they would continue to be when he moved on to the *New York Evening World* in late 1919. His fiction and feature journalism were widely published in magazines such as *Liberty*, *Adventure*, *Redbook*, and *Blue Book*. He wrote a book with Johnny Evers, the Cubs great shortstop; another about the racetrack; and a series of juvenile novels—à la Frank Merriwell—featuring a college ballplayer named Jimmy Kirkland.

Yet his reputation evaporated over time. Perhaps it's because he was a Cassandra who could see an evil threatening the game he loved; he knew the fix was in, and with the great exception of his close colleague Ring Lardner, his fellow citizens of the press box kept their distance. Perhaps it was because he blew the whistle on what was plainly there in front of everyone, though no one wanted to believe: the Chicago White Sox took a dive in the 1919 World Series. Perhaps it was because he'd just had enough. His column below, published in the *Herald and Examiner* the day after Cincinnati's 10–5 victory in the finale, never mentions the idea of a World Series corrupted by high-stakes gamblers; he didn't have to. It was in the air and between the lines, and, alas, to too many of his fellow journalists, he crossed a line by exposing it. Ultimately, enough pieces of the truth came out—under Fullerton's own byline—to nudge baseball to take action, but by then, something in Fullerton had changed. When his new boss in New York asked him why he wasn't covering baseball anymore, he replied sadly, "I'm sick and tired of writing about a game that has gone crooked."

But, of course, Fullerton kept writing about it—thoughtfully, stylishly, passionately—and when baseball's Hall of Fame opened its writer's wing in the 1960s, Fullerton's was the third name asked to join the exclusive party.

Cincinnati's Reds are champions of the world. The Reds turned yesterday and gave the dope the worst upsetting it has had during all this surprising and upsetting series. They slashed away at Claude Williams' pitching and before the big crowd had settled to see the contest, it was over. The knockout punch was landed by Duncan, the kid who is the hero of the series and Williams was driven to his retreat and elected to the office of false alarm of the series.

The close of the series was discouraging. Wednesday the dopesters all agreed that the Reds were on the run. The Cincinnati fans who have been canonizing a lot of mediocre athletes turned upon them and declared that they were dogs, yellow curs and German quitters. Yesterday these same Reds swarmed upon the cocky White Sox and battered them into the most humiliating defeat of any world's series.

There will be a great deal written and talked about this world's series. There will be a lot of inside stuff that never will be printed, but the truth will remain that the team which was the hardest working, which fought hardest, and which stuck together to the end won. The team which excelled in mechanical skill, which had the ability, individually, to win, was beaten.

EVERYTHING GOES BACKWARD

They spilled the dope terribly. Almost everything went backward, so much so that an evil minded person might believe the stories that have been circulated during the series. The fact is that this series was lost in the first game, and lost through over confidence. Forget the suspicious and evil minded yarns that may be circulated. The Reds are not the better club. They are not even the best club in their own league, but they play ball together, fight together and hustle together, and remember that a flivver that keeps running beats a Roll Royce that is missing on several cylinders. The Sox were missing on several.

They played the game as a team only through one game, and part of another, and they deserved defeat. It is not up to me to decide why they did such things. That all probably will come out in the wash. They were licked and licked good and proper, deserved it, and got it.

Yesterday's game in all probability is the last that ever will be played in any world's series. If the club owners and those who have the interests of the game at heart have listened during this series they will call off the annual inter-league contests. If they value the good name of the sport they will do so beyond doubt.

Yesterday's game also means the disruption of the Chicago White Sox as a ball club. There are seven men on the team who will not be there when the gong sounds next Spring and some of them will not be in either major league.

The Seventh-Inning Stretch

The Seventh-Inning Stretch

Simeon Strunsky

SOMETIMES WE BECOME SO ACCUSTOMED TO BASEBALL'S DEEP-ROOTED and very American ceremonies that it takes someone from somewhere else to help us appreciate them. Simeon Strunsky (1879–1948) was certainly from elsewhere. Born in what's now called Belarus, he joined the long march of late nineteenth-century melting-pot immigrants who learned to embrace their new home and adopted culture. He spent the bulk of his working life in newspapers, the last quarter century as an editorial writer and "Topics" columnist for the *New York Times*, where he was given the luxury of chasing his curiosity where it led. When he died, the paper used its editorial pages to praise him "for his intellectual brilliance, his gifts as a master of the English tongue, [and] the wide range of his knowledge." He managed to employ all that in his majestic deconstruction of one of the game's essential protocols, written for *The Atlantic* in 1914.

A great many people have been searching during ever so many years for the religion of democracy. I believe I have found it. That is, not a religion, if by it you mean a system completely equipped with creed, formularies, organization, home and foreign missions, schisms, an empty-church problem, an underpaid-minister's problem, a Socialist and I.W.W. problem, and the like; although, if I had the time to pursue my researches, I might find a parallel to many of these things. What I have in mind is a great democratic rite, a ceremonial which is solemnized on six days in the week during six months in the year by large masses of men with such unfailing regularity and such unquestioning good faith that I cannot help thinking of it as essentially a religious performance.

It is a simple ceremonial, but impressive, like all manifestations of the soul of a multitude. I need only close my eyes to call up the picture vividly: It is a day of brilliant sunshine and a great crowd of men is seated in the open air, a crowd made up of all conditions, ages, races, temperaments, and states of mind. The crowd has sat there an hour or more, while the afternoon sun has slanted deeper into the west and the shadows have crept across greensward and hard-baked clay to the eastern horizon. Then, almost with a single motion,—the time may be somewhere between four-thirty and five o'clock, this multitude of divers minds and tempers rises to its feet and stands silent, while one might count twenty perhaps. Nothing is said; no high priest intones prayer for this vast congregation; nevertheless the impulse of ten thousand hearts is obviously focused into a single desire. When you have counted twenty the crowd sinks back to the benches. A half minute at most and the rite is over.

I am speaking, of course, of the second half of the seventh inning, when the home team comes to bat. The precise nature of this religious half-minute depends on the score. If the home team holds a safe lead of three or four runs; if the home pitcher continues to have everything, and the infield shows no sign of cracking, and the outfield isn't bothered by the sun, then I always imagine a fervent Te Deum arising from that inarticulate multitude, and the peace of a great contentment falling over men's spirits as they settle back in their seats. If the game is in the balance you must imagine the concentration of ten thousand wills on the spirit of the nine athletes in the field, ten thousand wills telepathically pouring their energies into the powerful arm of the man in the box, into the quick eye of the man on first base, and the sense of justice of the umpire.

But if the outlook for victory is gloomy, the rite does not end with the silent prayer I have described. As the crowd subsides to the benches there arises a chant which I presume harks back to the primitive litanies of the Congo forests. Voices intone unkind words addressed to the players on the other team. Ten thousand voices chanting in unison for victory, twenty thousand feet stamping confusion to the opposing pitcher—if this is not worship of the most fundamental sort, because of the most primitive sort, then what is religion?

Consider the mere number of participants in this national rite of the seventh inning. I have said a multitude of ten thousand. But if the day be Saturday and the place of worship one of the big cities of either of the major leagues, the crowd may easily be twice as large. And all over the country at almost the same moment, exultant or hopeful or despairing multitudes are rising to their feet. Multiply this number of worshipers by six days—or by seven days if you are west of the Alleghanies, where Sunday baseball has somehow been reconciled with a still vigorous Puritanism—and it is apparent that a continuous wave of spiritual ardor sweeps over this continent between three-thirty and six p.m. from the middle of April to the middle of October. We can only guess at the total number of worshipers. The three major leagues will account for five millions. Add the minor leagues and the state leagues and the interurban contests—and the total of seventh-inning communicants grows overwhelming. Take the twenty-five million males of voting age in this country, assume one visit per head to a baseball park in the season, and the result is dazzling.

It is easier to estimate the number of worshipers than the intensity of the mood. I have no gauge for measuring the spiritual fervor which exhales on the baseball stadiums of the country from mid-April to mid-October, growing in ardor with the procession of the months, until it attains a climax of orgiastic frenzy in the World's Series. Foreigners are in the habit of calling this an unspiritual nation. But what nation so frequently tastes—or for that matter has ever tasted—the emotional experience of the score tied in the ninth inning with the bases full? Foreigners call us an unspiritual people because they do not know the meaning of a double-header late in September—a double-header with two seventh innings.

The Rube's Honeymoon

The Rube's Honeymoon

Zane Grey

THINK ZANE GREY (1872–1939), AND YOU THINK WESTERNS. THE POP-ular penner of *Riders of the Purple Sage* pretty much perfected the genre. But before he romanced the west, baseball was busy romancing him.

He'd been a star on the sandlots of Ohio growing up, then a reliable outfielder and pitcher at the University of Pennsylvania. He played four years of minor league ball, and by accounts of the day, had a good shot at making the majors. He became a dentist instead.

In time, he would exchange his drill for the quill, interspersing his long shelf of westerns with a trio of baseball books. The best remains *The Redheaded Outfield and Other Baseball Stories*. Published in 1920, it included "The Rube's Honeymoon."

Baseball was a family affair for the Greys by the way. Zane's younger brother, Reddy, was the model for one of those redheaded outfielders. In 1903, he collected a pair of hits in his six at-bats with the Pittsburgh Pirates.

"He's got a new manager. Watch him pitch now!" That was what Nan Brown said to me about Rube Hurtle, my great pitcher, and I took it as her way of announcing her engagement.

My baseball career held some proud moments, but this one, wherein I realized the success of my matchmaking plans, was certainly the proudest one. So, entirely outside of the honest pleasure I got out of the

Rube's happiness, there was reason for me to congratulate myself. He was a transformed man, so absolutely renewed, so wild with joy, that on the strength of it, I decided the pennant for Worcester was a foregone conclusion, and, sure of the money promised me by the directors, Milly and I began to make plans for the cottage upon the hill.

The Rube insisted on pitching Monday's game against the Torontos, and although poor fielding gave them a couple of runs, they never had a chance. They could not see the ball. The Rube wrapped it around their necks and between their wrists and straight over the plate with such incredible speed that they might just as well have tried to bat rifle bullets.

That night I was happy. Spears, my veteran captain, was one huge smile; Radbourne quietly assured me that all was over now but the shouting; all the boys were happy.

And the Rube was the happiest of all. At the hotel he burst out with his exceeding good fortune. He and Nan were to be married upon the Fourth of July!

After the noisy congratulations were over and the Rube had gone, Spears looked at me and I looked at him.

"Con," said he soberly, "we just can't let him get married on the Fourth."

"Why not? Sure we can. We'll help him get married. I tell you it'll save the pennant for us. Look how he pitched today! Nan Brown is our salvation!" "See here, Con, you've got softenin' of the brain, too. Where's your baseball sense? We've got a pennant to win. By July Fourth we'll be close to the lead again, an' there's that three weeks' trip on the road, the longest an' hardest of the season. We've just got to break even on that trip. You know what that means. If the Rube marries Nan—what are we goin' to do? We can't leave him behind. If he takes Nan with us—why it'll be a honeymoon! An' half the gang is stuck on Nan Brown! An' Nan Brown would flirt in her bridal veil! Why Con, we're up against a worse proposition than ever."

"Good Heavens! Cap. You're right," I groaned. "I never thought of that. We've got to postpone the wedding. . . . How on earth can we? I've heard her tell Milly that. She'll never consent to it. Say, this'll drive me to drink."

"All I got to say is this, Con. If the Rube takes his wife on that trip it's goin' to be an all-fired hummer. Don't you forget that."

"I'm not likely to. But, Spears, the point is this will the Rube win his games?"

"Figurin' from his work today, I'd gamble he'll never lose another game. It ain't that. I'm thinkin' of what the gang will do to him an' Nan on the cars an' at the hotels. Oh! Lord, Con, it ain't possible to stand for that honeymoon trip! Just think!"

"If the worst comes to the worst, Cap, I don't care for anything but the games. If we get in the lead and stay there I'll stand for anything. . . . Couldn't the gang be coaxed or bought off to let the Rube and Nan alone?"

"Not on your life! There ain't enough love or money on earth to stop them. It'll be awful. Mind, I'm not responsible. Don't you go holdin' me responsible. In all my years of baseball I never went on a trip with a bride in the game. That's new on me, an' I never heard of it. It'd be bad enough if he wasn't a rube an' if she wasn't a crazy girl-fan an' a flirt to boot, an' with half the boys in love with her, but as it is—"

Spears gave up and, gravely shaking his head, he left me. I spent a little while in sober reflection, and finally came to the conclusion that, in my desperate ambition to win the pennant, I would have taken half a dozen rube pitchers and their baseball-made brides on the trip, if by so doing I could increase the percentage of games won. Nevertheless, I wanted to postpone the Rube's wedding if it was possible, and I went out to see Milly and asked her to help us. But for once in her life Milly turned traitor.

"Connie, you don't want to postpone it. Why, how perfectly lovely! Mrs. Stringer will go on that trip and Mrs. Bogart. . . . Connie, I'm going too!"

She actually jumped up and down in glee. That was the woman in her. It takes a wedding to get a woman. I remonstrated and pleaded and commanded, all to no purpose. Milly intended to go on that trip to see the games, and the fun, and the honeymoon.

She coaxed so hard that I yielded. Thereupon she called up Mrs. Stringer on the telephone, and of course found that young woman just as eager as she was. For my part, I threw anxiety and care to the four winds, and decided to be as happy as any of them. The pennant was mine! Something kept ringing that in my ears. With the Rube working his iron arm for the edification of his proud Nancy Brown, there was extreme likelihood of divers shutouts and humiliating defeats for some Eastern League teams.

How well I calculated became a matter of baseball history during that last week of June. We won six straight games, three of which fell to the Rube's credit. His opponents scored four runs in the three games, against the nineteen we made. Upon July 1, Radbourne beat Providence and Cairns won the second game. We now had a string of eight victories. Sunday we rested, and Monday was the Fourth, with morning and afternoon games with Buffalo.

Upon the morning of the Fourth, I looked for the Rube at the hotel, but could not find him. He did not show up at the grounds when the other boys did, and I began to worry. It was the Rube's turn to pitch and we were neck and neck with Buffalo for first place. If we won both games we would go ahead of our rivals. So I was all on edge, and kept going to the dressing room to see if the Rube had arrived. He came, finally, when all the boys were dressed, and about to go out for practice. He had on a new suit, a tailor-made suit at that, and he looked fine. There was about him a kind of strange radiance. He stated simply that he had arrived late because he had just been married. Before congratulations were out of our mouths, he turned to me.

"Con, I want to pitch both games today," he said. "What! Say, Whit, Buffalo is on the card today and we are only three points behind them. If we win both we'll be leading the league once more. I don't know about pitching you both games."

"I reckon we'll be in the lead tonight then," he replied, "for I'll win them both."

I was about to reply when Dave, the groundkeeper, called me to the door, saying there was a man to see me. I went out, and there stood Morrisey, manager of the Chicago American League team. We knew each other well and exchanged greetings.

"Con, I dropped off to see you about this new pitcher of yours, the one they call the Rube. I want to see him work. I've heard he's pretty fast. How about it?"

"Wait—till you see him pitch," I replied. I could scarcely get that much out, for Morrisey's presence meant a great deal and I did not want to betray my elation.

"Any strings on him?" queried the big league manager, sharply. "Well, Morrisey, not exactly. I can give you the first call. You'll have to bid high, though. Just wait till you see him work."

"I'm glad to hear that. My scout was over here watching him pitch and says he's a wonder."

What luck it was that Morrisey should have come upon this day! I could hardly contain myself. Almost I began to spend the money I would get for selling the Rube to the big league manager. We took seats in the grandstand, as Morrisey did not want to be seen by any players, and I stayed there with him until the gong sounded. There was a big attendance. I looked all over the stand for Nan, but she was lost in the gay crowd. But when I went down to the bench I saw her up in my private box with Milly. It took no second glance to see that Nan Brown was a bride and glorying in the fact.

Then, in the absorption of the game, I became oblivious to Milly and Nan; the noisy crowd; the giant firecrackers and the smoke; to the presence of Morrisey; to all except the Rube and my team and their opponents. Fortunately for my hopes, the game opened with characteristic Worcester dash. Little McCall doubled, Ashwell drew his base on four wide pitches, and Stringer drove the ball over the right-field fence—three runs!

Three runs were enough to win that game. Of all the exhibitions of pitching with which the Rube had favored us, this one was the finest. It was perhaps not so much his marvelous speed and unhittable curves that made the game one memorable in the annals of pitching; it was his perfect control in the placing of balls, in the cutting of corners; in his absolute implacable mastery of the situation. Buffalo was unable to find him at all. The game was swift, short, decisive, with the score 5 to 0 in our favor. But the score did not tell all of the Rube's work that morning. He shut out Buffalo without a hit, or a scratch, the first no-hit, no-run game of the year. He gave no base on balls; not a Buffalo player got to first base; only one fly went to the outfield.

For once I forgot Milly after a game, and I hurried to find Morrisey, and carried him off to have dinner with me.

"Your rube is a wonder, and that's a fact," he said to me several times. "Where on earth did you get him? Connelly, he's my meat. Do you understand? Can you let me have him right now?"

"No, Morrisey, I've got the pennant to win first. Then I'll sell him."

"How much? Do you hear? How much?" Morrisey hammered the table with his fist and his eyes gleamed.

Carried away as I was by his vehemence, I was yet able to calculate shrewdly, and I decided to name a very high price, from which I could come down and still make a splendid deal.

"How much?" demanded Morrisey.

"Five thousand dollars," I replied, and gulped when I got the words out.

Morrisey never batted an eye.

"Waiter, quick, pen and ink and paper!"

Presently my hand, none too firm, was signing my name to a contract whereby I was to sell my pitcher for five thousand dollars at the close of the current season. I never saw a man look so pleased as Morrisey when he folded that contract and put it in his pocket. He bade me goodbye and hurried off to catch a train, and he never knew the Rube had pitched the great game on his wedding day.

That afternoon before a crowd that had to be roped off the diamond, I put the Rube against the Bisons. How well he showed the baseball knowledge he had assimilated! He changed his style in that second game. He used a slow ball and wide curves and took things easy. He made Buffalo hit the ball and when runners got on bases once more let out his speed and held them down. He relied upon the players behind him and they were equal to the occasion. It was a totally different game from that of the morning, and perhaps one more suited to the pleasure of the audience. There was plenty of hard hitting, sharp fielding, and good base running, and the game was close and exciting up to the eighth, when

Mullancy's triple gave us two runs, and a lead that was not headed. To the deafening roar of the bleachers the Rube walked off the field, having pitched Worcester into first place in the pennant race. That night the boys planned their first job on the Rube. We had ordered a special Pullman for travel to Toronto, and when I got to the depot in the morning, the Pullman was a white fluttering mass of satin ribbons. Also, there was a brass band, and thousands of baseball fans, and barrels of old footgear. The Rube and Nan arrived in a cab and were immediately mobbed. The crowd roared, the band played, the engine whistled, the bell clanged; and the air was full of confetti and slippers, and showers of rice like hail pattered everywhere. A somewhat disheveled bride and groom boarded the Pullman and breathlessly hid in a stateroom. The train started, and the crowd gave one last rousing cheer. Old Spears yelled from the back platform:

"Fellers, an' fans, you needn't worry none about leavin' the Rube an' his bride to the tender mercies of the gang. A hundred years from now people will talk about this honeymoon baseball trip. Wait till we come back—an' say, jest to put you wise, no matter what else happens, we're comin' back in first place!" It was surely a merry party in that Pullman. The bridal couple emerged from their hiding place and held a sort of reception in which the Rube appeared shy and frightened, and Nan resembled a joyous, fluttering bird in gray. I did not see if she kissed every man on the team, but she kissed me as if she had been wanting to do it for ages. Milly kissed the Rube, and so did the other women, to his infinite embarrassment. Nan's effect upon that crowd was most singular. She was sweetness and caprice and joy personified.

We settled down presently to something approaching order, and I, for one, with very keen ears and alert eyes, because I did not want to miss anything.

"I see the lambs a-gambolin'," observed McCall, in a voice louder than was necessary to convey his meaning to Mullaney, his partner in the seat.

"Yes, it do seem as if there was joy a boundin' hereabouts," replied Mul with fervor.

"It's more springtime than summer," said Ashwell, "an' everything in nature is runnin' in pairs. There are the sheep an' the cattle an' the birds. I see two kingfishers fishin' over here. An' there's a couple of honeybees makin' honey. Oh, honey, an' by George, if there ain't two butterflies foldin' their wings round each other. See the dandelions kissin' in the field!"

Then the staid Captain Spears spoke up with an appearance of sincerity and a tone that was nothing short of remarkable.

"Reggie, see the sunshine asleep upon yon bank. Ain't it lovely? An' that white cloud sailin' thither amid the blue—how spontaneous! Joy is abroad o'er all this boo-tiful land today—Oh, yes! An' love's wings hover o'er the little lambs an' the bullfrogs in the pond an' the dicky birds in the trees. What sweetness to lie in the grass, the lap of bounteous earth, eatin' apples in the Garden of Eden, an' chasin' away the snakes an' dreamin' of Thee, Sweeth-e-a-r-t—"

Spears was singing when he got so far and there was no telling what he might have done if Mullaney, unable to stand the agony, had not jabbed a pin in him. But that only made way for the efforts of the other boys, each of whom tried to outdo the other in poking fun at the Rube and Nan. The big pitcher was too gloriously happy to note much of what went on around him, but when it dawned upon him he grew red and white by turns.

Nan, however, was more than equal to the occasion. Presently she smiled at Spears, such a smile! The captain looked as if he had just partaken of an intoxicating wine. With a heightened color in her cheeks and a dangerous flash in her roguish eyes, Nan favored McCall with a look, which was as much as to say that she remembered him with a dear sadness. She made eyes at every fellow in the car, and then bringing back her gaze to the Rube, as if glorying in comparison, she nestled her curly black head on his shoulder. He gently tried to move her; but it was not possible. Nan knew how to meet the ridicule of half a dozen old lovers. One by one they buried themselves in newspapers, and finally McCall, for once utterly beaten, showed a white feather, and sank back out of sight behind his seat.

The boys did not recover from that shock until late in the afternoon. As it was a physical impossibility for Nan to rest her head all day upon hcr husband's broad shoulder, the boys toward dinnertime came out of their jealous trance. I heard them plotting something. When dinner was called, about half of my party, including the bride and groom, went at once into the dining car. Time there flew by swiftly. And later, when we were once more in our Pullman, and I had gotten interested in a game of cards with Milly and Stringer and his wife, the Rube came marching up to me with a very red face.

"Con, I reckon some of the boys have stolen my—our grips," said he. "What?" I asked, blankly. He explained that during his absence in the dining car someone had entered his stateroom and stolen his grip and Nan's. I hastened at once to aid the Rube in his search. The boys swore by everything under and beyond the sun they had not seen the grips; they appeared very much grieved at the loss and pretended to help in searching the Pullman. At last, with the assistance of a porter, we discovered the missing grips in an upper berth. The Rube carried them off to his stateroom and we knew soon from his uncomplimentary remarks that the contents of the suitcases had been mixed and manhandled. But he did not hunt for the jokers.

We arrived at Toronto before daylight next morning, and remained in the Pullman until seven o'clock. When we got out, it was discovered that the Rube and Nan had stolen a march upon us. We traced them to the hotel, and found them at breakfast. After breakfast we formed a merry sightseeing party and rode all over the city.

That afternoon, when Raddy let Toronto down with three hits and the boys played a magnificent game behind him, and we won 7 to 2, I knew at last and for certain that the Worcester team had come into its own again. Then next day Cairns won a close, exciting game, and following that, on the third day, the matchless Rube toyed with the Torontos. Eleven straight games won! I was in the clouds, and never had I seen so beautiful a light as shone in Milly's eyes.

From that day The Honeymoon Trip of the Worcester Baseball Club, as the newspapers heralded it—was a triumphant march. We won two out of three games at Montreal, broke even with the hard-fighting Bisons, took three straight from Rochester, and won one and tied one out of three with Hartford. It would have been wonderful ball playing for a team to play on home grounds and we were doing the full circuit of the league.

Spears had called the turn when he said the trip would be a hummer. Nan Hurtle had brought us wonderful luck.

But the tricks they played on Whit and his girl-fan bride! Ashwell, who was a capital actor, disguised himself as a conductor and pretended to try to eject Whit and Nan from the train, urging that lovemaking was not permitted. Some of the team hired a clever young woman to hunt the Rube up at the hotel, and claim old acquaintance with him. Poor Whit almost collapsed when the young woman threw her arms about his neck just as Nan entered the parlor. Upon the instant Nan became wild as a little tigress, and it took much explanation and eloquence to reinstate Whit in her affections.

Another time Spears, the wily old fox, succeeded in detaining Nan on the way to the station, and the two missed the train. At first the Rube laughed with the others, but when Stringer remarked that he had noticed a growing attachment between Nan and Spears, my great pitcher experienced the first pangs of the green-eyed monster. We had to hold him to keep him from jumping from the train, and it took Milly and Mrs. Stringer to soothe him. I had to wire back to Rochester for a special train for Spears and Nan, and even then we had to play half a game without the services of our captain.

So far upon our trip I had been fortunate in securing comfortable rooms and the best of transportation for my party. At Hartford, however, I encountered difficulties. I could not get a special Pullman, and the sleeper we entered already had a number of occupants. After the ladies of my party had been assigned to berths, it was necessary for some of the boys to sleep double in upper berths.

It was late when we got aboard, the berths were already made up, and soon we had all retired. In the morning very early I was awakened by a disturbance. It sounded like a squeal. I heard an astonished exclamation, another squeal, the pattering of little feet, then hoarse uproar of laughter from the ball players in the upper berths. Following that came low, excited conversation between the porter and somebody, then an angry snort from the Rube and the thud of his heavy feet in the aisle. What took place after that was guesswork for me. But I gathered from the roars and bawls that the Rube was after some of the boys. I poked my head between the curtains and saw him digging into the berths.

"Where's McCall?" he yelled.

Mac was nowhere in that sleeper, judging from the vehement denials. But the Rube kept on digging and prodding in the upper berths.

"I'm a-goin' to lick you, Mac, so I reckon you'd better show up," shouted the Rube.

The big fellow was mad as a hornet. When he got to me he grasped me with his great fence-rail splitting hands and I cried out with pain. "Say! Whit, let up! Mac's not here. . . . What's wrong?"

"I'll show you when I find him." And the Rube stalked on down the aisle, a tragically comic figure in his pajamas. In his search for Mac he pried into several upper berths that contained occupants who were not ball players, and these protested in affright. Then the Rube began to investigate the lower berths. A row of heads protruded in a bobbing line from between the curtains of the upper berths.

"Here, you Indian! Don't you look in there! That's my wife's berth!" yelled Stringer.

Bogart, too, evinced great excitement.

"Hurtle, keep out of lower eight or I'll kill you," he shouted.

What the Rube might have done there was no telling, but as he grasped a curtain, he was interrupted by a shriek from some woman assuredly not of our party.

"Get out! you horrid wretch! Help! Porter! Help! Conductor!"

Instantly there was a deafening tumult in the car. When it had subsided somewhat, and I considered I would be safe, I descended from my berth and made my way to the dressing room. Sprawled over the leather seat was the Rube pommelling McCall with hearty goodwill. I would have interfered, had it not been for Mac's demeanor. He was half frightened, half angry, and utterly unable to defend himself or even resist, because he was laughing, too.

"Doggone it! Whit—I didn't—do it! I swear it was Spears! Stop thumpin' me now—or I'll get sore. . . . You hear me! It wasn't me, I tell you. Cheese it!"

For all his protesting Mac received a good thumping, and I doubted not in the least that he deserved it. The wonder of the affair, however, was the fact that no one appeared to know what had made the Rube so furious. The porter would not tell, and Mac was strangely reticent, though his smile was one to make a fellow exceedingly sure something out of the ordinary had befallen. It was not until I was having breakfast in Providence that I learned the true cause of Rube's conduct, and Milly confided it to me, insisting on strict confidence.

"I promised not to tell," she said. "Now you promise you'll never tell."

"Well, Connie," went on Milly, when I had promised, "it was the funniest thing yet, but it was horrid of McCall. You see, the Rube had upper seven and Nan had lower seven. Early this morning, about daylight, Nan awoke very thirsty and got up to get a drink. During her absence, probably, but anyway sometime last night, McCall changed the number on her curtain, and when Nan came back to number seven of course she almost got in the wrong berth."

"No wonder the Rube punched him!" I declared. "I wish we were safe home. Something'll happen yet on this trip."

I was faithful to my promise to Milly, but the secret leaked out somewhere; perhaps Mac told it, and before the game that day all the players knew it. The Rube, having recovered his good humor, minded it not in the least. He could not have felt ill will for any length of time. Everything seemed to get back into smooth running order, and the Honeymoon Trip bade fair to wind up beautifully.

But, somehow or other, and about something unknown to the rest of us, the Rube and Nan quarreled. It was their first quarrel. Milly and I tried to patch it up but failed.

We lost the first game to Providence and won the second. The next day, a Saturday, was the last game of the trip, and it was Rube's turn to pitch. Several times during the first two days the Rube and Nan about half made up their quarrel, only in the end to fall deeper into it. Then the last straw came in a foolish move on the part of wilful Nan. She happened to meet Henderson, her former admirer, and in a flash she took up her flirtation with him where she had left off.

"Don't go to the game with him, Nan," I pleaded. "It's a silly thing for you to do. Of course you don't mean anything, except to torment Whit. But cut it out. The gang will make him miserable and we'll lose the game. There's no telling what might happen."

"I'm supremely indifferent to what happens," she replied, with a rebellious toss of her black head. "I hope Whit gets beaten."

She went to the game with Henderson and sat in the grandstand, and the boys spied them out and told the Rube. He did not believe it at first, but finally saw them, looked deeply hurt and offended, and then grew angry. But the gong, sounding at that moment, drew his attention to his business of the day, to pitch.

His work that day reminded me of the first game he ever pitched for me, upon which occasion Captain Spears got the best out of him by making him angry. For several innings Providence was helpless before his delivery. Then something happened that showed me a crisis was near. A wag of a fan yelled from the bleachers.

"Honeymoon Rube!"

This cry was taken up by the delighted fans and it rolled around the field. But the Rube pitched on, harder than ever. Then the knowing bleacherite who had started the cry changed it somewhat.

"Nanny's Rube!" he yelled.

This, too, went the rounds, and still the Rube, though red in the face, preserved his temper and his pitching control. All would have been well if Bud Wiler, comedian of the Providence team, had not hit upon a way to rattle Rube.

"Nanny's Goat!" he shouted from the coaching lines. Every Providence player took it up.

The Rube was not proof against that. He yelled so fiercely at them, and glared so furiously, and towered so formidably, that they ceased for the moment. Then he let drive with his fast straight ball and hit the first Providence batter in the ribs. His comrades had to help him to the bench. The Rube hit the next batter on the leg, and judging from the crack of the ball, I fancied that player would walk lame for several days. The Rube tried to hit the next batter and sent him to first on balls. Thereafter it became a dodging contest with honors about equal between pitcher and batters. The Providence players stormed and the bleachers roared. But I would not take the Rube out and the game went on with the Rube forcing in runs.

With the score a tie, and three men on bases one of the players on the bench again yelled: "Nanny's Goat!" Straight as a string the Rube shot the ball at this fellow and bounded after it. The crowd rose in an uproar. The base runners began to score. I left my bench and ran across the space, but not in time to catch the Rube. I saw him hit two or three of the Providence men. Then the policemen got to him, and a real fight brought the big audience into the stamping melee. Before the Rube was collared I saw at least four blue-coats on the grass.

The game broke up, and the crowd spilled itself in streams over the field. Excitement ran high. I tried to force my way into the mass to get at the Rube and the officers, but this was impossible. I feared the Rube would be taken from the officers and treated with violence, so I waited with the surging crowd, endeavoring to get nearer. Soon we were in the street, and it seemed as if all the stands had emptied their yelling occupants.

A trolley car came along down the street, splitting the mass of people and driving them back. A dozen policemen summarily bundled the Rube upon the rear end of the car. Some of these officers boarded the car, and some remained in the street to beat off the vengeful fans.

I saw someone thrust forward a frantic young woman. The officers stopped her, then suddenly helped her on the car, just as I started. I recognized Nan. She gripped the Rube with both hands and turned a white, fearful face upon the angry crowd.

The Rube stood in the grasp of his wife and the policemen, and he looked like a ruffled lion. He shook his big fist and bawled in far-reaching voice:

"I can lick you all!"

To my infinite relief, the trolley gathered momentum and safely passed out of danger. The last thing I made out was Nan pressing close to the Rube's side. That moment saw their reconciliation and my joy that it was the end of the Rube's Honeymoon.

His Own Stuff

His Own Stuff

Charles E. Van Loan

LIKE SO MANY WRITERS WHO FOUND FAME IN THE FIRST QUARTER OF
the last century, Charles E. Van Loan (1876–1919) cut his teeth at a variety of newspapers, including a stint in the sports department of the *Los
Angeles Herald* before switching allegiance to the rival *Examiner*, a pair
of papers I'm particularly partial to; I was tied to a typewriter—and then
a computer—at their merged successor, the *Herald Examiner*, through
the first half of the eighties. That alone could have turned me into a Van
Loan fan, but it was his sporting fiction—he wrote with such grace and
humor about golf, boxing, the racetrack, and, of course, baseball that in
the years before his death, he was considered the most popular magazine writer in the nation. As a magazine writer, his base, from 1914 on,
was the *Saturday Evening Post*, but his work also appeared frequently in
Munsey's, *Collier's*, and *Outing* and collected along the way in ten volumes,
including *Score by Innings*, where "His Own Stuff" appeared in 1919. At
his death, Van Loan's friend and colleague Hugh Fullerton, the writer—
represented earlier in this volume—who broke the story of the Black Sox
scandal, wrote, "Van is dead and sports in America have lost their greatest
interpreter, and fighters, ballplayers, and athletes of all grades have lost
their best friend."

Talking about friends, when Van Loan left his post at the *New York
American* in 1911, he thought one of his pals from Denver might be a fit
replacement on the baseball beat. Turned out he would be—and more.
The guy's name was Damon Runyon.

It's a mighty fine thing for a man to know when he's had enough, but there's a piece of knowledge which beats it all hollow. That's for him to know when his friends have had too much. This is no temperance sermon, so you needn't quit reading. It's the story of a baseball player who thought he was funny and didn't know when to quit the rough-and-tumble comedy that some idiot has named practical joking.

Before I tell you what happened to Tom O'Connor because he didn't know when to quit being funny, I want to put myself on record. I don't believe that there is any such a thing as a practical joke. As I understand the word, a thing in order to be practical must have some sense to it and be of some use to people. To play it safe I looked up the dictionary definition of the word to see if I could stretch it far enough to cover the sort of stuff that Tom O'Connor pulled on us at the training camp last season. I couldn't make it answer. Here's what I found in the dictionary:

"PRACTICAL—pertaining to or governed by actual use or experience, as contrasted with ideals, speculations and theories."

That's what the big book says it means, and I string with the definition whether I understand all of it or not. Show me anything in there that applies to sawing out half the slats in a man's bed or mixing up all the shoes in a Pullman car at three o'clock in the morning! You can call it practical joking if you want to, but it won't go with me. I claim there's nothing practical about it, or sensible either. Practical joking is just another name for plain, ordinary foolishness with a mean streak in it. The main thing about a practical joke is that somebody always gets hurt—usually an innocent party.

I'm strong for a good clever joke. I get as much fun out of one as anybody and I can laugh when the joke is on me; but when it comes to the rough stuff I pass. Take 'em as a whole, baseball players are a jolly bunch. They've got youth and health and vitality. They call us the Old Guard, but we're really nothing but a lot of young fellows and we have the reputation of being the liveliest outfit in the league; but even so, we got sick of the sort of stunts that Tom O'Connor handed us at the training camp and in the early part of the season.

We didn't have much of a line on Tom when he joined the club. He'd been in the big league only part of the season previously, and he came to the Old Guard as the result of a winter trade. We needed a first-baseman the worst way, and Uncle Billy—he's our manager—gave up a pitcher, an infielder and an outfielder to get Tom O'Connor away from the Blues. The newspapers made an awful roar about that trade, and so did the fans. They said Uncle Billy was out of his head and was trying to wreck the team by letting three good men go. The noise they made wasn't a whisper to the howl that went up from the other manager when the time came to get some work out of those three good men.

When it comes to a swap, Uncle Billy is a tougher proposition than a Connecticut Yank, and a Connecticut Yank can take an Armenian pawn-broker's false teeth away from him and give him Brazil nuts in exchange for 'em. Uncle Billy always hands the other managers three or four men for one. He's so liberal and open-hearted that they feel sorry for him, and they keep right on feeling sorry after they see what he's slipped them in the trade.

In this case the pitcher had a strained ligament that even the bone-setter couldn't fix, the infielder's eyes were giving out on him and the outfielder had a permanent charley-horse in his left leg. As big-league ballplayers they were all through, but as benchwarmers and salary grabbers they were immense.

Even if they had been in condition I think that Tom O'Connor would have been worth the three, for he is a cracking good first-baseman, and now that he has settled down to business and quit being the team comedian he'll be even better than he was last year.

He joined us at the spring training camp in Louisiana. We've been going to the same place for years. It's a sort of health resort with rotten water to drink and baths; and the hotel is always full of broken-down old men with whiskers and fat wives to look after 'em.

O'Connor turned up in the main dining-room the first night with a big box of marshmallows in his hand. He is a tall, handsome chap with a tremendous head of hair and a smile that sort of warms you to him even after you know him. He stopped at every table and invited folks to help themselves. "These are very choice, madam; something new in confectionery. Prepared by a friend of mine. Won't you try one?"

That was his spiel, but the smile and the little twinkle of the eye that went with it was what did the business. The fat ladies didn't stop to think that it was rather unusual for a strange young man to be offering them candy. They smiled back at Tom and helped themselves to the marshmallows, and some of them insisted that their husbands should try one too. Tom was a smooth, rapid worker and he kept moving, not stopping long at a table and never looking back. Perhaps that was just as well, for the marshmallow had been dipped in powdered quinine instead of powdered sugar. Quinine ain't so bad when you expect it, but when your mouth is all fixed for marshmallow the disappointment and the quinine together make a strong combination. The fat ladies went out of the dining-room on the run, choking into their handkerchiefs, and the old men sent C. Q. D.s for the proprietor. He came in and Tom met him at the door and handed him one of the marshmallows, and then of course everybody laughed.

I admit that we might have begun discouraging his comedy right there. We would have done it if he'd been a minor-leaguer trying to break in, but he wasn't. He'd been five months with the Blues—a bad ball club, but still in the big league. That made him one of us. We knew and he knew that he was going to be our first-baseman and he settled down with as much assurance as if he had been with us ten years instead of ten hours. He saw right away that we were going to be a good audience for him. Not all of his stuff was on the rough-house order. Some of us were not long in finding that out.

A couple of nights afterward we were having a nice, quiet little game of draw poker in my room on the third floor of the hotel. Any poker game running after ten o'clock in the same hotel with Uncle Billy has got to be a quiet one—or it's a case of a fifty-dollar fine all round.

Uncle Billy is a great baseball manager but he's awfully narrow-gauge on certain subjects, and one of 'em is the American indoor national pastime of draw poker. He doesn't like the game for seven hundred different reasons, but mainly because he says it sets a bad example to the kid players, who get to gambling among themselves and lose more than they can afford. That's true of course, but if a kid is born with the gambling bug in his system you can't fine it out of him, not even at fifty a smash. One season Uncle Billy tried to shut down on poker altogether, and there was more poker played that year than ever before. Then he took off the lid, and now we're allowed to play twenty-five-cent limit until ten o'clock at night. Think of it! Why, if a man had all the luck in the world and filled everything he drew to he might win as much as four dollars!

I'm not saying that the rule isn't a good one for recruits and kids, but it comes hard on the veterans, especially at the training camp where there isn't a thing to do after dark. We used to sneak a real game once in a while with a blanket over the transom and paper stuffed in the cracks and the keyhole. We had to do that because we couldn't trust Uncle Billy. He was just underhanded enough to listen outside of the door, and to make it worse the poor old coot has insomnia and we never know when he's asleep and when he's not.

Well, this poker party in my room was the real thing: Pat Dunphy, Holliday, Satterfield, Meadows, Daly and myself—all deep-sea pirates. It was table-stakes of course, every man declaring fifty or a hundred behind his stack in case he should pick up something heavy and want action on it.

It got to be about two in the morning, and Dunphy was yawning his head off and looking at his watch every few minutes. He was two hundred ahead. The rest of us were up and down, seesawing along and waiting for a set of fours or something. The elevators had quit running long ago and there wasn't a sound in the hotel anywhere. What talking we did was in whispers because we never knew when Uncle Billy might take it into his head to go for a walk. I've known him to bust up a poker game at four in the morning.

Dunphy was just scooping in another nice pot—like a fool I played my pat straight against his one-card draw—when all of a sudden a board creaked in the hall outside, and then came a dry, raspy little cough that we knew mighty well.

"Holy Moses!" whispered Dunphy. "Uncle Billy! Don't move!" Then somebody pounded on the door. We were sure there wasn't any light showing through the cracks, so we sat quiet a few seconds trying to think what to do. The pounding began again, louder than before—bangety bang-bang!

Well, our only chance was to keep Uncle Billy out of the room, so I motioned to the boys and they picked up their money and chips and tiptoed into the alcove in the corner. I whipped off my shirt, kicked off my pants, put on a bathrobe, tousled up my hair to make it look as if I'd been asleep a week, switched out the light and opened the door a few inches. Then I stepped out into the hall. It was empty from end to end. There wasn't a soul in sight.

We had a long discussion about it. We all agreed that it was Uncle Billy's cough we heard; but why had he hammered on the door so hard and then gone away? That wasn't like him. Had he been round to the other rooms checking up on us? Was he so sure of us that he didn't need the actual evidence? Perhaps he was going to switch his system and begin fining people fifty dollars apiece on circumstantial evidence. It began to have all the earmarks of an expensive evening for the six of us.

"Did anybody else know about this party?" I asked. "O'Connor knew," Holliday spoke up. "I asked him if he didn't want to play a little poker. He said he couldn't take a chance of getting in Dutch with the boss so soon. That was his excuse, but maybe he was a little light in the vest pocket. He already knew about the ten o'clock rule and the fifty-dollar fine."

"Did he know we were going to play in this room?" "Sure, but I don't see where you figure him. He wouldn't have tipped it off to anybody. Probably Uncle Billy couldn't sleep and was prowling round. You can't get away from that cough. And he's got us dead to rights or he wouldn't have gone away. I'll bet he's had a pass-key and been in every one of our rooms. We'll hear from him in the morning."

It did look that way. We settled up and the boys slipped out one at a time, carrying their shoes in their hands. I don't know about the rest of 'em, but I didn't sleep much. The fifty-dollar fine didn't bother me, but Uncle Billy has got a way of throwing in a roast along with it.

I dreaded to go down to breakfast in the morning. Uncle Billy usually has a table with his wife and kids close to the door, so he can give us the once-over as we come in.

"'Morning, Bob!" says Uncle Billy, smiling over his hotcakes. "How do you feel this morning?"

"Finer'n split silk!" says I, and went on over to the main table with the gang. That started me to wondering, because if Uncle Billy had anything on me he wouldn't have smiled. The best I could have expected was a black look and a grunt. Uncle Billy was a poor hand at hiding his feelings. If he was peeved with you it showed in everything he did. I didn't know what to make of that smile, and that's what had me worried.

Dunphy and Holliday and the others were puzzled too, and the suspense was eating us up. We sat there, looking silly and fooling with our knives and forks, every little while stealing a peek at each other. We couldn't figure it at all. Tom O'Connor was at one end of the table eating like a longshoreman and saying nothing. Dunphy stood the strain as long as he could and then he cracked.

"Did Uncle Billy call on any of you fellows last night?" said he.

"No! Was he sleep-walking again, the old rascal?"

"Was anything doing?"

"He never came near the fourth floor. If he had he'd 'a' busted up a hot little crap game."

"What was he looking for—poker?"

None of the boys had seen him. It was plain that if Uncle Billy had been night-prowling we were the only ones that he had bothered. Peachy Parsons spoke up.

"Did you see him, Pat?" says he.

"Why, no," says Dunphy. "I—I heard him."

For a few seconds there was dead silence. Then Tom O'Connor shoved his chair back, stood up, looked all round the table with a queer grin on his face and coughed once—that same dry, raspy little cough. It sounded so much like Uncle Billy that we all jumped.

O'Connor didn't wait for the laugh. He walked out of the dining-room and left us looking at each other with our mouths open.

II

I knew a busher once who tore off a home run the first time he came to bat in the big league, and it would have been a lot better for him if he had struck out. The fans got to calling him Home-Run Slattery and he got to thinking he was all of that. He wouldn't have a base on balls as a gift and he wouldn't bunt. He wanted to knock the cover off every ball he saw. Uncle Billy shipped him back to Texas in June, and he's there yet. In a way O'Connor reminded me of that busher.

He had made a great start as a comedian. The stuff that he put over on the poker players was clever and legitimate; there was real fun in it. His reputation as a two-handed kidder was established then and there, and he might have rested on it until he thought of something else as good. He might have; but we laughed at him, and then of course he wanted to put the next one over the fence too.

I can see now looking back at it, that we were partly responsible. You know how it is with a comedian—the more you laugh at him, the worse he gets. Pretty soon he wants laughs all the time, and if they're not written into his part he tries to make 'em up as he goes along. If he hasn't got any new, clever ideas he pulls old stuff or rough stuff—in other words he gets to be a slapstick comedian. A good hiss or two or a few rotten eggs at the right time would teach him to stay with legitimate work.

It didn't take Tom long to run out of clever comedy and get down to the rough stuff. Rough stuff is the backbone of practical joking. Things began to happen round the training camp. We couldn't actually prove 'em on Tom at the time—and we haven't proved 'em on him yet—but the circumstantial evidence is all against him. He wouldn't have a chance with a jury of his peers—whatever they are.

Tom began easy and worked up his speed by degrees. His first stunts were mild ones, such as leaving a lot of bogus calls with the night clerk and getting a lot of people rung out of bed at four in the morning; but of course that wasn't funny enough to suit him.

There was a girl from Memphis stopping at the hotel, and Joe Holliday the pitcher thought pretty well of her. He borrowed an automobile one Sunday to take her for a ride. After they were about twenty miles from town the engine sneezed a few times and laid down cold.

"Don't worry," says Holliday, "I know all about automobiles. I'll have this bird flying again in a minute."

"It sounded to me as if you'd run out of gas," said the girl, who knew something about cars herself.

"Impossible!" says Holliday. "I had the tank filled this morning and you can see there's no leak."

"Well, I don't know all about automobiles," says the girl, "but you'd better take a look in that tank."

That made Holliday a little sore, because he'd bought twenty gallons of gasoline and paid for it. They stayed there all day and Holliday messed round in the bowels of the beast and got full of oil and grease and dirt. I'll bet he stored up enough profanity inside of him to last for the rest of his natural life. And all the time the girl kept fussing about the gasoline tank. Finally, after Joe had done everything else that he could think of, he unscrewed the cap and the gas tank was dry as a bone.

Somebody with a rare sense of humour had drawn off about seventeen gallons of gasoline.

"I told you so!" said the girl—which is just about what a girl would say under the circumstances.

They got back to the hotel late that night. Love's young dream had run out with the gasoline, and from what I could gather they must have quarrelled all the way home. Joe went down and got into a fight with the man at the garage and was hit over the head with a monkey-wrench. From now on you'll notice that Tom's comedy was mostly physical and people were getting hurt every time.

Joe's troubles lasted O'Connor for a couple of days and then he hired a darky boy to get him a water snake. I think he wrote it in the boy's contract that the snake had to be harmless or there was nothing doing. He put the snake, a whopping big striped one, between the sheets in Al Jorgenson's bed, which is my notion of no place in the world to put a snake. Jorgenson is our club secretary—a middle-aged fellow who never has much to say and attends strictly to business.

Al rolled on to the snake in the dark, but it seems he knew what it was right away. He wrecked half the furniture, tore the door off the hinges and came fluttering down into the lobby, yelling murder at every jump. It was just his luck that the old ladies were all present. They were pulling off a whist tournament that night, but they don't know yet who won. Al practically spoiled the whole evening for 'em.

The charitable way to look at it is that Tom didn't know that Jorgenson was hitting the booze pretty hard and kept a quart bottle in his room. If he had known that, maybe he would have wished the snake on to a teetotaler, like Uncle Billy. To make it a little more abundant Tom slipped in and copped the snake while Al was doing his shirt-tail specialty, and when we got him back to the room there wasn't any snake there. Tom circulated round among the old ladies and told 'em not to be alarmed in the least because maybe it wasn't a real snake that Jorgenson saw.

But Tom had his good points after all. The next morning Al found the snake tied to his door-knob, which relieved his mind a whole lot; but he was so mortified and ashamed that he had all his meals in his room after that and used to come and go by the kitchen entrance.

Tom's next stunt—which he didn't make any secret of—put four of the kid recruits out of business. He framed up a midnight hunt for killyloo birds. It's the old snipe trick. I didn't believe that there were four people left in the world who would fall for that stunt. It was invented by one of old man Pharaoh's boys in the days of the Nile Valley League. It is hard to find one man in the whole town who will fall for it, because it has been so well advertised, but Tom grabbed four in a bunch. It just goes to show how much solid ivory a baseball scout can dig up when his travelling expenses are paid.

The idea is very simple. First you catch a sucker and take him out in the woods at night. You give him a sack and a candle. He's to keep the candle lighted and hold the mouth of the sack open so that you can drive the killyloo birds into it. The main point is to make it perfectly clear to the sucker that a killyloo bird when waked out of a sound sleep always walks straight to the nearest light to get his feet warm. After the sucker understands that thoroughly you can leave him and go home to bed. He sits there with his candle, fighting mosquitoes and wondering what has become of you and why the killyloo birds don't show up.

Tom staged his production in fine style. He rented a livery rig and drove those poor kids eleven miles into a swamp. If you have ever seen a Louisiana swamp you can begin laughing now. He got 'em planted so far apart that they couldn't do much talking, explained all about the peculiar habits of the sleepy killyloos, saw that their candles were burning nicely and then went away to herd in the game. He was back at the hotel by eleven o'clock.

About midnight the boys held a conference and decided that maybe it was a bad time of the year for killyloo birds but that the sucker crop hadn't been cut down any. They started back for the hotel on foot and got lost in mud clear up to their necks. They stayed in the swamp all night and it's a wonder that they got out alive. And that wasn't all: Uncle Billy listened to their tales of woe and said if they didn't have any more sense than that they wouldn't make ballplayers, so he sent 'em home.

The night before we were to leave for the North there was a little informal dance at the hotel and the town folks came in to meet the ballplayers and learn the tango and the hesitation waltz.

It was a perfectly bully party and everything went along fine until the punch was brought in. We'd decided not to have any liquor in it on account of the strong prohibition sentiment in the community, so we had a kind of a fruit lemonade with grape juice in it.

Well, those fat old ladies crowded round the bowl as if they were perishing of thirst. They took one swig of the punch and went sailing for the elevators like full-rigged ships in a gale of wind.

Of course I thought I knew what was wrong. It's always considered quite a joke to slip something into the punch. I'd been dancing with a swell little girl and as we started for the punch-bowl I said:

"You won't mind if this punch has got a wee bit of a kick in it, will you?"

"Not in the least," said she. "Father always puts a little brandy in ours."

So that was all right and I ladled her out a sample. I would have got mine at the same time, but an old lady behind me started to choke and I turned round to see what was the matter. When I turned back to the girl again there were tears in her eyes and she was sputtering about rowdy ballplayers. She said that she had a brother at college who could lick all the big-leaguers in the world, and she hoped he'd begin on me. Then she went out of the room with her nose in the air.

I was terribly upset about it because I couldn't think what I had done that was wrong, and just because I had the glass in my hand I began drinking the punch. Then I went out and climbed a telegraph pole and yelled for the fire department. Talk about going crazy with the heat. It can be done, believe me! I felt like a general-alarm fire for the rest of the evening.

There was an awful fuss about that, and some of us held a council of war. We decided to put it up to O'Connor. He stood pat in a very dignified way and said that he must positively refuse to take the blame for anything unless there was proof that he did it. About that time the cook found two empty tabasco sauce bottles under the kitchen sink. That didn't prove anything. We already knew what the stuff was and that too much of it had been used. One bottle would have been a great plenty.

That was the situation when we started North. Everybody felt that it was dangerous to be safe with a physical humourist like O'Connor on the payroll. We hoped that he'd quit playing horse and begin to play ball.

We went so far as to hint that the next rough stuff he put over on the bunch would bring him before the Kangaroo Court and it wouldn't make any difference whether we had any evidence or not. The Kangaroo Court is the last word in physical humour. It's even rougher than taking the Imperial Callithumpian Degree in the Order of the Ornery and Worthless Men of the World.

The last straw fell on us in the home town. Jorgenson came into the dressing room one afternoon with a handful of big square envelopes. There was one for every man on the team.

I opened mine and there was a stiff sheet of cardboard inside of it printed in script. I didn't save mine, but it read something like this:

Mr. Augustus P. Stringer requests the honour of your company at dinner, at the Algonquin Club, 643—Avenue, at seven-thirty on the evening of May the Twelfth, Nineteen Hundred and—. Formal.

Well, there was quite a buzz of excitement over it. "Who is this Mr. Stringer?" asks Uncle Billy. "Any of you boys know him!"

Nobody seemed to, but that wasn't remarkable. All sorts of people give dinners to ballplayers during the playing season. I've seen some winters when a good feed would come in handy, but a ballplayer is only strong with the public between April and October. The rest of the year nobody cares very much whether he eats or not.

"He's probably some young sport who wants to show us a good time and brag about what a whale of a ballplayer he used to be in college," says Pat Dunphy.

"You're wrong!" says Peachy Parsons. "Ten to one you're wrong! I never saw this Mr. Stringer, but I'll bet I've got him pegged to a whisper. In the first place I know about this Algonquin Club. It's the oldest and the most exclusive club in the city. Nothing but rich men belong to it. You can go by there any night and see 'em sitting in the windows, holding their stomachs in their laps. Now this Mr. Stringer is probably a nice old man with a sneaking liking for baseball. He wants to entertain us, but at the same time he's afraid that we're a lot of lowbrows and that we'll show him up before the other club members."

"What makes you think that?" asks Dunphy. "Simple enough. He's got an idea that we don't know what to wear to a banquet, so he tips us off. He puts 'formal' down in one corner."

"What does that mean?"

"It's not usually put on an invitation. It means the old thirteen-and-the-odd. Clawhammer, white tie, silk hat and all the rest of it."

"How about a 'tux'?"

"Absolutely barred. A tuxedo isn't formal."

"That settles it!" says Dunphy "I don't go. If this bird don't want to see me in my street clothes he don't need to see me at all. I never bought one of those beetle-backed coats and I never will!"

"Come now," says Uncle Billy, "don't get excited. I know a place where you can rent an entire outfit for two bucks, shoes and all."

"Oh, well," says Dunphy, "in that case—"

The more we talked about it, the stronger we were taken with the idea. It would be something to say that we'd had dinner at the Algonquin Club. We warned Tom O'Connor that none of his rough comedy would go. He got awfully sore about it. One word led to another and finally he said if we felt that way about it he wouldn't go. We tried to persuade him that it wasn't quite the thing to turn down an invitation, but he wouldn't listen.

You never saw such a hustling round or such a run on the gents' furnishing goods. Everybody was buying white shirts, white ties and silk socks. If we were going to do it at all we felt that it might as well be done right, and of course we wanted to show Mr. Stringer that we knew what was what. Those who didn't own evening clothes hired 'em for the occasion, accordion hats and all. We met a couple of blocks away from the club and marched over in a body like a lot of honourary pall-bearers.

We got by the outer door all right and into the main room where some old gentlemen were sitting round, smoking cigars and reading the newspapers. They seemed kind of annoyed about something and looked at us as if they took us for burglars in disguise, which they probably did. Up comes a flunky in uniform, knee-breeches and mutton-chop whiskers. Uncle Billy did the talking for the bunch.

"Tell Mr. Stringer that we're here," says he. "I—beg your pardon?" says the flunky.

"You don't need to do that," says Uncle Billy. "Just run along and tell Mr. Stringer that his guests are here."

The flunky seemed puzzled for a minute, and then he almost smiled.

"Ah!" says he. "The—Democratic Club is on the opposite corner, sir. Possibly there has been some mistake."

Uncle Billy began to get sore. He flashed his invitation and waved it under the flunky's nose.

"It says here the Algonquin Club. You don't look it, but maybe you can read."

"Oh, yes, sir," says the flunky. He examined the invitation carefully and then he shook his head. "Very, very sorry, sir," says he, "but there is some mistake."

"How can there be any mistake?" roars Uncle Billy. "Where is Mr. Stringer?"

"That is what I do not know, sir," says the flunky. "We have no such member, sir."

Well, that was a knock-out. Even Uncle Billy didn't know what to say to that. The rest of us stood round on one foot and then on the other like a lot of clothing-store dummies. One of the old gentlemen motioned to the flunky, who left us, but not without looking back every few seconds as if he expected us to start something.

"James," pipes up the old gentleman, "perhaps they have been drinking. Have you telephoned for the police?"

"They don't seem to be violent yet, sir," says James. Then he came back to us and explained again that he was very, very sorry, but there must be some mistake. No Mr. Stringer was known at the Algonquin Club.

"This way out, gentlemen," says James.

I think I was the first one that tumbled to it. We were going down the steps when it struck me like a thousand of brick.

"Stringer!" says I. "We've been strung all right.

Tom O'Connor has gone back to the legitimate!" "No wonder he didn't want to come!" says everybody at once.

We stood on the corner under the lamppost and held an indignation meeting, the old gentlemen looking down at us from the windows as if they couldn't make up their minds whether we were dangerous or not. We hadn't decided what we ought to do with Tom when the reporters began to arrive. That cinched it. Every paper had been tipped off by telephone that there was a good josh story at the Algonquin Club, and the funny men had been turned loose on it. Uncle Billy grabbed me by the arm.

"Tip the wink to Dunphy and Parsons and let's get out of this," says he. "I don't often dude myself up and it seems a shame to waste it. We will have dinner at the Casino and frame up a come-back on O'Connor."

I've always said that, in spite of his queer notions about certain things, Uncle Billy is a regular human being. The dinner that he bought us that night proved it, and the idea that he got, along with the coffee, made it even stronger.

"Do you boys know any actresses?" said he. "I mean any that are working in town now?"

"I know Hazel Harrington," says Parsons.

"Ah-hah," says Uncle Billy. "That's the pretty one in *Paris Up to Date*, eh?" Why, the old rascal even had a line on the musical comedy stars! "Is she a good fellow?"

"Best in the world!" says Parsons. "And a strong baseball fan."

"Fine!" says Uncle Billy and he snapped his fingers at a waiter. "Pencil and paper and messenger boy—quick! Now then, Peachy, write this lady a note and say that we will be highly honoured if she will join us here after the show to discuss a matter of grave importance to the Old Guard. Say that you will call in a taxi to get her."

When the note had gone Uncle Billy lighted a fresh cigar and chuckled to himself.

"If she'll go through with it," says he, "I'll guarantee to knock all the funny business out of Tom O'Connor for the rest of his natural life."

Miss Harrington turned up about eleven-thirty, even prettier off the stage than on it, which is going some. She said that she had side-stepped a date with a Pittsburgh millionaire because we were real people. That was a promising start. She ordered a light supper of creamed lobster and champagne and then Uncle Billy began to talk.

He told her that as a manager he was in a bad fix. He said he had a new man on the payroll who was promoting civil war. He explained that unless he was able to tame this fellow the team would be crippled. Miss Harrington said that would be a pity, for she had bet on us to win the pennant. She wanted to know what was the matter. Uncle Billy told her all about Tom O'Connor and his practical jokes. Miss Harrington said it would be a good thing to give him a dose of his own medicine. It was like Uncle Billy to let her think that the idea belonged to her.

"Suppose," says Uncle Billy, "you should get a note from him, asking you to meet him at the stage door some night next week. For the sake of the ball club, would you say 'Yes'?"

"But—what would happen after that?" asked Miss Harrington. "I don't know the man at all and—"

Uncle Billy told her what would happen after that, and as it dawned on the rest of us we nearly rolled out of our chairs. Miss Harrington laughed too.

"It would be terribly funny," said she, "and I suppose it would serve him right; but it might get into the papers and—"

Uncle Billy shook his head.

"My dear young lady," says he, "the only publicity that you get in this town is the publicity that you go after. I am well and favourably known to the police. A lot of 'em get annual passes from me. Captain Murray at the Montmorency Street Station is my pal. He can see a joke without plans and specifications. I promise you that the whole thing will go off like clockwork. We'll suppose that you have attracted the young man's attention during the performance. You would attract any man's attention, my dear."

"I would stand up and bow for that compliment," said Miss Harrington, "but the waiter is looking. Go on."

"We will suppose that you have received a note from him," said Uncle Billy. "He is to meet you at the stage door. . . . One tiny little scream—just one. . . . Would you do that—for the sake of the ball club?"

Miss Harrington giggled.

"If you're sure that you can keep me out of it," said she, "I'll do it for the sake of the joke!"

Uncle Billy was a busy man for a few days, but he found time to state that he didn't believe that Tom O'Connor had anything to do with the Algonquin Club thing. He said it was so clever that Tom couldn't have thought of it, and he said it in the dressing room so loud that everybody heard him. Maybe that was the reason why Tom didn't suspect anything when he was asked to fill out a box party.

Pat Dunphy, Peachy Parsons and some of the rest of us were in on the box party, playing thinking parts mostly. Uncle Billy and Tom O'Connor had the front seats right up against the stage.

Miss Harrington was immense. If she'd had forty rehearsals she couldn't have done it any better. Before she'd been on the stage three minutes Tom was fumbling round for his programme trying to find her name. Pretty soon he began to squirm in his chair.

"By golly, that girl is looking at me all the time!" says he.

"Don't kid yourself!" said Uncle Billy.

"But I tell you she is! There—did you see that?" "Maybe she wants to meet you," says Uncle Billy.

"I've seen her at the ball park a lot of times." "You think she knows who I am?" asks Tom.

"Shouldn't wonder. You're right, Tom. She's after you, that's a fact."

"Oh, rats!" says O'Connor. "Maybe I just think so. No, there it is again! Do you suppose, if I sent my card back—"

"I'm a married man," says Uncle Billy. "I don't suppose anything. But if a girl as pretty as that—"

Tom went out at the end of the first act. I saw him write something on a card and slip it to an usher along with a dollar bill.

When the second act opened Tom was so nervous he couldn't sit still. It was easy to see that he hadn't received any answer to his note and was worrying about it. Pretty soon Miss Harrington came on to sing her song about the moon—they've always got to have a moon song in musical comedy or it doesn't go—and just as the lights went down she looked over toward our box and smiled, the least little bit of a smile, and then she nodded her head. The breath went out of Tom O'Connor in a long sigh.

"Somebody lend me twenty dollars," says he. "I'm going to meet her at the stage door after the show," says Tom, "and she won't think I'm a sport unless I open wine."

Well, he met her all right enough. The whole bunch of us can swear to that because we were across the street, hiding in a doorway. When she came out Tom stepped up, chipper as a canary bird, with his hat in his hand. We couldn't hear what he said, but there was no trouble in hearing Miss Harrington.

"How dare you, sir!" she screams. "Help! Police! Help!"

Two men, who had been loafing round on the edge of the sidewalk, jumped over and grabbed Tom by the arms. He started in to explain matters to 'em, but the men dragged him away down the street and Miss Harrington went in the other direction.

"So far, so good," says Uncle Billy. "Gentlemen, the rest of the comedy will be played out at the Montmorency Street Police Station. Reserved seats are waiting for us. Follow me."

You can say anything you like, but it's a pretty fine thing to be in right with the police. You never know when you may need 'em, and Uncle Billy certainly was an ace at the Montmorency Street Station. We went in by the side door and were shown into a little narrow room with a lot of chairs in it, just like a moving-picture theatre, except that instead of a curtain at the far end there was a tall Japanese screen. What was more, most of the chairs were occupied. Every member of the Old Guard ball club was there, and so was Al Jorgenson and Lije, the rubber.

"Boys," says Uncle Billy, "we are about to have the last act of the thrilling drama entitled The Kidder Kidded, or The Old Guard's Revenge. The first and second acts went off fine. Be as quiet as you can and don't laugh until the blow-off. Not a whisper—not a sound—s-s-sh! They're bringing him in now!"

There was a scuffling of feet and a scraping of chair-legs on the other side of the screen. We couldn't see O'Connor and he couldn't see us, but we could hear every word he said. He was still trying to explain matters.

"But I tell you," says Tom, "I had a date with her." "Yeh," says a gruff voice, "she acted like it! Don't tell us your troubles. Tell 'em to Captain Murray. Here he comes now."

A door opened and closed and another voice cut in: "Well, boys, what luck?"

"We got one, cap," says the gruff party. "Caught him with the goods on—"

"It's all a mistake, sir—captain!" Tom breaks in. "I give you my word of honour as a gentleman—"

"Shut up!" says Captain Murray. "Your word of honour as a gentle-man! That's rich, that is! You keep your trap closed for the present—understand? Now, boys, where did you get him?"

"At the stage door of the Royal Theatre," says the plain-clothes man, who did the talking for the two who made the pinch. "Duffy and me, we saw this bird kind of slinking round, and we remembered that order about bringing in all mashers, so we watched him. A girl came out of the stage door and he braced her. She hollered for help and we grabbed him. Oh, there ain't any question about it, cap; we've got him dead to rights. We don't even need the woman's testimony."

"Good work, boys!" says the captain. "We'll make an example of this guy!"

"Captain," says Torn, "listen to reason! I tell you this girl was flirting with me all through the show—"

"That's what they all say! If she was flirting with you, why did she make a holler when you braced her?"

"I—I don't know," says Tom. "Maybe she didn't recognise me."

"No, I'll bet she didn't!"

"But, captain, I sent her my card and she sent back word—"

"Oh, shut up! What's your name?" Murray shot that one at him quick and Tom took a good long time to answer it.

"Smith," says he at last. "John Smith." That raised a laugh on the other side of the screen.

"Well," says the captain, "unless we can get him identified he can do his bit on the rock pile under the name of Smith as well as any other, eh, boys?"

"Sure thing!" said the plain-clothes men. "The rock pile!" says Tom.

"That's what I said—rock pile! Kind of scares you, don't it? There won't be any bail for you to jump or any fine for you to pay. We've had a lot of complaints about mashers lately and some squeals in the newspapers. You'll be made an example of. Chickens are protected by the game laws of this state, and it's time some of the lady-killers found it out."

Tom began to plead, but he might just as well have kept quiet. They whirled in and gave him the third degree—asked him what he had been pinched for the last time and a whole lot of stuff. We expected he'd tell his name and send for Uncle Billy to get him out, but for some reason or other he fought shy of that. We couldn't understand his play at first, but we knew why soon enough. The door back of the screen opened again.

"Cap'n," says a strange voice, "there's some newspaper men here."

Well, that was all a stall, of course. We didn't let the newspaper men in on it because we wanted them for a whip to hold over Tom's head in the future.

"What do they want?" asks Murray.

"They're after this masher story," says the stranger. "I don't know who tipped it off to 'em, but they've seen the woman and got a statement from her. She says she thinks this fellow is a baseball player."

"I wouldn't care if he was the president of the League!" says the captain. "You know the orders we got to break up mashing and bring 'em in, no matter who they are. Here we've got one of 'em dead to rights; and it's the rock pile for him, you can bet your life on it!"

"And serve him right," says the stranger. "But, cap'n, wouldn't it be a good thing to identify him? These newspapermen say they know all the ballplayers. Shall we have 'em in to give him the once-over?"

"I'll send for 'em in a minute," says Murray.

That was the shot that brought Tom off his perch with a yell.

"Captain," he begs, "anything but that! I'd rather you sent me up for six months—yes, or shot me! If this gets into the papers it'll—! Oh say, if you have any heart at all—please—please—Oh, you don't understand!"

We didn't understand either, but Tom made it plain. I'm not going to write all he said; it made my face burn to sit there and listen to it. It took all the fun out of the joke for me. It seems that this rough kidder—this practical joker who never cared a rap how much he hurt anybody else's feelings—had some pretty tender feelings of his own. He opened up his heart and told that police captain something that he never had told us—told him about the little girl back in the home town who was waiting for him, and how she wouldn't ever be able to hold up her head again if the story got into the papers and he was disgraced.

"It ain't for me, captain," he begs; "it's for her. You wouldn't want her shamed just because I've acted like a fool, would you? Think what it means to the girl, captain! Oh, if there's anything you can do—"

Uncle Billy beat me to it. I was already on my feet when he took two jumps and knocked the screen flat on the floor.

"That's enough!" says Uncle Billy. We had planned to give Tom the horse-laugh when the screen came down, but somehow none of us could laugh just then. If I live to be as old as Hans Wagner I'll never forget the expression on Tom O'Connor's face as he blinked across the room and saw us all sitting there, like an audience in a theatre.

"Tom," says Uncle Billy, "I'm sorry, but this is what always happens with a practical joke. It starts out to be funny, but it gets away from you and then the first thing you know somebody is hurt. You've had a lot of fun with this ball club, my boy, and some of it was pretty rough fun, but—I guess we'll all agree to call it square."

Tom got on his feet, shaking a little and white to the lips. He couldn't seem to find his voice for a minute and he ran his fingers across his mouth before he spoke.

"Is—is this a joke?" says he.

"It started out to be," says Uncle Billy. "I'm sorry."

Tom didn't say another word and he didn't look at any of us. He went out of the room alone and left us there. I wanted to go after him and tell him not to take it so hard; but I thought of the way he had shamed Al Jorgenson, I thought of the girl who wouldn't even speak to Holliday again, I thought of the four kids who went home broken-hearted, all on Tom's account—and I changed my mind. It was a bitter dose, but I decided not to sweeten it any for him.

Tom O'Connor isn't funny any more, and I think he is slowly making up his mind that we're not such a bad outfit after all. To this day the mention of the name of Smith makes him blush, so I guess that in spite of the fact that he's never opened his mouth about it since, he hasn't forgotten what his own stuff feels like.

Pebble Pop

Pebble Pop

Gerald Beaumont

IMMENSELY POPULAR IN HIS DAY, GERALD BEAUMONT (1886–1926) grew up in Northern California, captaining his college baseball team and dabbling in theater before finding his real starring role tapping a typewriter—as sports columnist for the *Oakland Tribune*. From there, he jumped into fiction. Headfirst.

Prolific doesn't begin to cover his output. Beaumont became an unstoppable penner of short stories, the bulk themed around the three arenas he loved best: the racetrack, the boxing ring—he refereed fights in the Bay Area for years—and everything baseball. Their mystiques and characters were ripe for his cinematic style; Hollywood lured him into its orbit, turned him into a screenwriter, and translated dozens of his fables into what were then referred to as B-movies. In 1921, Beaumont published his first story collection, the lighthearted *Hearts and the Diamond*, a series of intertwined baseball tales revolving around a fictional franchise in the Pacific Coast League. The offbeat "Pebble Pop" was the collection's penultimate saga—and in an offbeat way, its glue.

Ten years as ground keeper for the St. Clair ball club had developed in "Pop" Connelly a deep and abiding hatred for pebbles. They interfered with the true course of a baseball; they marred the appearance of his ball park; worse—they compelled him to stoop over and pick them up, and he was fat and rheumatic.

Sometimes Pop Connelly was tempted to quit, but the temptation was not strong. A ground keeper does not figure highly in the estimation of the fans, but when the game is over, after all, it is his ball park, and there is no one to kid him if he wants to hark back twenty years or more, and fool around first base, or go out in right and imagine there's a ball heading for the fence and the bags are full.

When a man has a gold watch charm to prove that he once played in right field and batted in the clean-up role for the old Greenwood and Morans, it is asking a good deal of him to quit the game altogether.

"Yes, sir," he would say: "I remember well. We were playing the Alerts in San Francisco the last day of the season and we had a crowd of eighteen thousand. They had us two to nothing in the ninth when we filled the sacks and I come to bat. Now, 'Demon' Carlisle was pitching, and he—"

That was about as far as Pop Connelly ever got because everybody on the ball club knew the story by heart and always managed to escape, promising to return in a few minutes. Sometimes he would wait, fingering fondly the heavy gold horseshoe with its faint inscription on the back.

But eventually he learned that he was expected to tend to the grounds and let the present generation of ball players do all the talking. Once having reached that conclusion, he became "Pebble Pop," with a determination to have the smoothest infield in the business. Just as he had been a real ball player, so as a ground keeper he sought to be a champion.

If anything further was needed to inspire Pebble Pop to extraordinary interest in the condition of the St. Clair infield, it came when he recommended Jimmy Moran to "Brick" McGovern, and the boy made good at short for the Wolves. Thereafter it was Pebble Pop himself who was out on the diamond every afternoon, picking ground balls out of the dirt, and not the lean, wiry, red-headed youngster of twenty-two whose father had played with Connelly.

From the third row in the right-field bleachers just back of first, where he could see each throw that his protégé made, Connelly watched every game—tensing his muscles when the ball went to short, and leaning forward desperately when Jimmy "laid one down" and tried to beat it out.

Even Brick McGovern, who made a specialty of developing short-stops for the majors, admitted that Pop had "dug up a live one." "Swell pair of hands on that kid," he commented in the dugout. "Gets the ball away from him quick and doesn't have to set himself."

Such praise usually found its way to Connelly's ears, and filled him with an elation equal only to what he experienced when Jimmy Moran said that the St. Clair grounds were better than the new park at Vernon.

Sometimes, after the game, when the outfield was spouting a hundred filmy jets of spray from the concealed sprinkling system, and the copper sun, sinking back of the clubhouse, painted the fountains as the west wind toyed with the mist, and the whole park was a great shimmering emerald, Pebble Pop loitered in the shadow of the fence until the players in their street clothes, came straggling along toward the exit. The greeting between the young shortstop and the old ground keeper seldom varied.

"How's it, Jimmy?"

"Hello, Pop, what's new?"

"Nothing much, Jimmy. Everything all right to-day? Didn't find no pebbles bothering you?"

"Should say not. Got to hand it to you, Pop. That infield is sure a pip. Couldn't be no better."

"Thanks, Jimmy. See you again."

"So long, Pop."

After encouragement like that, Connelly attacked his evening task with fresh energy. But no matter how carefully he rolled and watered the broad expanse of tan soil that separated the green outfield from the diamond itself, it always seemed that the players' cleats, grinding into the top dirt, had brought to light some new menace.

It was his constant fear that some day he would overlook a sun-baked clod of dirt or a small stone that would make a ball bound badly and perhaps cost the Wolves a game.

He liked to imagine, when watching a swift bit of play, that if it had not been for the infield's being so smooth, the player might not have got the ball. But of course this brought an equal measure of responsibility in case the ball did take a bad hop. The possibility that Jimmy Moran might some day be the victim of a false bound was something that destroyed permanently his peace of mind.

And then one day, with a suddenness that left Pebble Pop dazed and crushed, the very thing that he most dreaded actually came to pass. He was in his customary seat in the bleachers. The Wolves were playing Los Angeles, and it was a pitchers' battle between Claude Dugan and "Lefty" Brown, with the score tied up in the sixth. Ellis, a fast man, hit viciously to short and was off like a flash, trying to beat the throw.

Pebble Pop saw O'Donnell at third, hurl himself to the left in a vain effort to intercept the ball, and Jimmy Moran coming in fast behind him to nail it on a natural bound. The next instant there was a cry from the crowd, and the Wolf shortstop reeled blindly with his hands to his face. The ball, rolling slowly toward second, was recovered by Peewee Patterson, who signaled to the umpire to suspend play. From the clubhouse in center field the stubby figure of "Blinker" Burke, the club trainer, hurried forward with his emergency kit.

Connelly tried to rise from his seat but his limbs failed him. He caught the voice of the man next to him.

"Got it right in the eye, didn't he? Must have been buzzing around last night. That's the trouble with them kids."

The power of speech came back to Connelly.

"No, no, no!" he stammered. "It was a bad hop. The ball hit something—oh, my God, it was a bad hop! Couldn't you see it? Let me out!"

He clawed a path to the ground. Blinker Burke was leading Moran away, and Chad Fisher, utility infielder, was already at short, warming up. From the bleachers and grand stand came the subdued ripple of hand-clapping by which baseball fans try to express their sympathy on such occasions.

Hurrying stiffly toward the clubhouse in the wake of the trainer and his charge, the ground keeper's mind revolved dizzily around a single fixed idea: "A bad hop—the ball hit something—a bad hop and it had to be Jimmy! Oh, my God!" He accomplished the three steps leading to the dressing rooms and clung to the doorway.

Moran, sitting on a wicker basket used to hold the uniforms when the team went on the road, was submitting grimly to the ministrations of the trainer. Out of one eye, he spotted the figure in the doorway, and waved a hand assuringly.

"Little bit of hard luck, Pop," he called; "should have had it only I was asleep. Ain't nothing to worry about."

But Pebble Pop saw the blood streaming down the shortstop's cheek and then the eye itself, already closed. He tried twice to say something, and then turned away numbly.

The next afternoon when Senator Frank Lathrop, owner of the Wolves, arrived at his office in the ball park, he found his ground keeper waiting for him. Lathrop was a big, cheerful man, fond of baseball, politics and black cigars. Very little ever troubled him.

"Hello, Pop," he rumbled, "what's wrong now? You look as if the rats had eaten up all the infield canvas."

The ground keeper shook his head.

"I'm quitting you, senator. I'm asking for my release."

Lathrop paused in the act of lighting a cigar.

Had Brick McGovern come to him and asked for a reduction in salary, he could not have been more astonished. Mechanically he opened several letters and stared at them absently. Finally the solution dawned.

"Oh," he said, "oh, I see! Now listen, Pop—you're wrong. Jimmy didn't get hurt through any fault of yours. McGovern told me O'Donnell tipped the ball with his glove, just as it hit the edge of the grass. That's why it bounded badly. Moran says the same thing. As for your quitting, why we couldn't get along without you, so just forget it."

Connelly shook his head stubbornly. "I'd like to believe you, senator, but I can't. All the boys are trying to frame an alibi for me, but there's one thing you and they don't know. The truth is I hounded it last night—my back was hurting me so I could hardly stand. I went home early; get me? I didn't give the infield the attention I should have first time in my life, too. If we lose the pennant account of Jimmy being out of the line-up it's my fault. I don't deserve a job with the Wolves anymore. I'm not fit to work with champions."

Sitting back in his chair with his thumbs in his armpits, and a cigar cocked at a degree indicating deep thought, Senator Lathrop pondered upon this new angle of the game he loved.

Not ten minutes before he had met Blinker Burke out on the sidewalk, and the trainer had solemnly assured him that he—Blinker—would have Moran back in the line-up within ten days, thereby winning the pennant. Now a fat and bald-headed ground keeper assumed personal responsibility for having placed the title in jeopardy.

With a wry smile, Lathrop acknowledged that hitherto he had held positive opinions as to the importance of a club owner who bought the players and paid them their salaries. He wondered whether there was any one from Brick McGovern, pilot of the team, to Paddy, the bat boy, who didn't think the game revolved around him and whether it wasn't just that spirit that made for success. He tapped with his fingers on the flattop desk and considered the man before him. The instincts of the politician came to his rescue.

"Pop," he confided, "I'll tell you what I'm going to do. You're too valuable a man for the club to release outright, and, yet, as a ground keeper, you are subject to discipline the same as any other member of the club. Consider yourself suspended without pay until such time as Moran is back in the line-up. Mind, I don't want you hanging around the park. Go home and get yourself in condition. You've got to have the park in good shape for the finish in October when we win the old flag."

Connelly's faded blue eyes sparkled. The club owner had gauged him adroitly. To be punished and yet held to his job to be fined and suspended like any ball player—that was balm to a wounded soul. Pebble Pop tried to look properly chastened as he nodded and turned his back, but all the way home he walked with head erect and a pink flush on his withered cheeks.

Over and over he repeated to himself: "Got to have the park in good shape for the finish in October, when we win the flag."

That was the first week in August with the Wolves in second place on the heels of the speeding Angels. Following his usual policy, Brick McGovern had eased his club along during the first half of the season and gradually tightened the reins with the passing of July. Now he was driving the team with all the ability and energy for which he was famous. The pitchers were working well, and five of the regulars were hitting better than .280. The injury to Moran was the first serious mishap. If he got back in the line-up in time, Wolf fans were confident that the pennant would fly again in center field.

The team departed for a final swing around the circle. Connelly watched morning and evening papers for the news that would mean his re-instatement. It came at last in the Salt Lake box score, two lines of type bearing this legend:

* Moran........1 0 1 0 0 0 0

* Batted for Slagle in the ninth.

Connelly whooped for joy. "A hit, too," he chuckled; "first time up since he got hurt, and he gets a hit off Berger. 'Atta boy, Jimmy!"

Pebble Pop celebrated his first day back on the job by toiling far into the evening. No lawn was ever more carefully trimmed and manicured; no runner's path was ever better rolled and inspected than that which linked the bases in the St. Clair grounds. He told himself that never again would an aching back keep him from doing his duty; never again would a ball bound badly on Jimmy Moran.

The Wolves came back in the first week of September with just three games separating them from the leaders. Pebble Pop awoke to a new thought—a thought which came to him in the middle of the night and forced him bolt upright in the dark. He was amazed to think that it had never occurred to him before. The Wolves would not finish the season on their home grounds. The schedule called for them to play the Angels in Los Angeles, all of which meant that the crucial series would be fought out on a diamond that he could not supervise. Some other ground keeper who knew nothing about Jimmy Moran being still shy of grounders that hugged the turf, and caring less, would be crushing pebbles into the ground instead of picking them up.

In vain, Connelly tried to comfort himself by recalling Blinker Burke's philosophy that a pebble more or less was as fair for one side as the other. There remained the vivid picture of what had happened once. It might happen again, and this time ruin Moran's career. The thought appalled him. The palms of his hands became moist.

He made up his mind the next morning just where his duty lay and what he would do. Without confiding in anyone, he would go down to Los Angeles for the last week.

Twenty thousand people left the Los Angeles ball park on the evening of Saturday, September thirtieth, with the knowledge that the game on the next day—the last contest of the season—would tell the story. For three successive afternoons the league leadership had changed hands. Sunday would either see McGovern's hard-hitting Wolves retain, the lead and the flag, or be beaten by the Angels in the closest race the Coast League had ever staged.

Long after the last usher and program boy had departed, and a light rain was falling on the apparently deserted grounds, a stout figure squirmed awkwardly from its place of concealment under the right-field bleachers and descended to the diamond.

Pebble Pop had found his self-appointed task more difficult than he had figured. The Los Angeles club was well supplied with ground keepers and he could think of no excuse for intruding on their duties. Also, it had occurred to him that since he was under contract to the Wolves, it was not proper that he should appear to be working for any other club. But the thought that he was doing nothing toward helping the team was unbearable. If he could pick up just one pebble from that infield, it might be the very one that otherwise would cause the downfall of his club.

The plan of secreting himself after the Thursday game had been an inspiration. Helped by a pocket flashlight, that represented a part of his fast-dwindling reserve fund, Pebble Pop worked over the infield, in the dusk, like a well-trained setter on the trail of game. The rain saturated his clothing, the night air enveloped him, the darkness increased, but he stuck obstinately to his patrol. At length, satisfied that when the grounds were given their last treatment in the morning there would be no pebbles to be over-looked, he moved painfully to the top tier of seats in the grandstand and curled up, shivering, until the gates should be opened in the morning.

A special policeman, sauntering through the enclosure at nine o'clock the next morning came upon an old, bald-headed man, whose cheeks were flushed and whose teeth chattered. He could give no clear account of himself, and his coat pockets were filled with pebbles and clods of dirt. He was plainly suffering from exposure and a high fever.

At the City Receiving Hospital, a steward identified the patient by means of letters in his pocket, and promptly telephoned to the hotel where the Wolves were quartered. The message brought Brick McGovern and Jimmy Moran hurrying to the hospital. They listened in amazement to the officer's story and stared at the pile of pebbles on the steward's desk.

Brick McGovern was moved profoundly. "Can you beat that?" he muttered. "The poor old nut! Trying to help us right down to the last day. Wanted to be in on it, too. Well, I'm damned."

Moran felt of the pebbles curiously. "He ain't really bad off, is he?"

The young intern shook his head. "Pneumonia—the right lung is affected, but I guess we got him in time. He seems to be resting easily. Maybe you'd better talk to him."

They tiptoed into a ward where Connelly lay in a white bed, buried under blankets and flanked by hot-water bottles.

"How's it, Pop?" they asked.

He eyed them sheepishly. "All right, I guess. Run down to see you boys win the flag, and I guess I must have made a fool of myself. They ain't"—he looked anxiously at the nurse—"they ain't going to keep me from going to the game this afternoon, are they? You won't let them do that, will you, boys—after old Pop's come all this way?"

They shuffled their feet and looked at one another and then at the intern and nurse. The former shook his head decisively.

"Going to a ball game to-day is out of the question. Your temperature is a hundred and three."

Jimmy Moran had an inspiration. "Listen, Pop," he exclaimed, "you done your bit last night, didn't you? There ain't nothing more you can do for us. Tell you God's honest truth, that infield's been bothering me all week, and now that you've fixed it, don't you see that it ain't necessary for you to be there?"

In the eyes of Brick McGovern there dawned a new respect for his young shortstop. He took the cue.

"You've said it, Jimmy," he affirmed. "Pop's already done everything he could. Now you stay right here, Pop; and play the bed—that's a good one, eh? You play the bed and I'll play the bench, and we'll have some one 'phone you the score by innings. How's that?"

Connelly smiled tremulously. "God bless you, boys. I'll play the bed and pull for luck. Only—just you ask the doc' to get me my horseshoe.

"I want to hold it. Seems like it was only yesterday when I come up there with the bases full and busted that old apple."

The nurse departed and was back in a few minutes with Connelly's watch and heavy gold chain. "Is this it?" she asked. "I don't see any horseshoe."

A strangled cry came from the bed. "It's gone! Somebody's swiped it. My horseshoe's gone; it was hanging right to the chain, Brick—right to the chain, I tell you."

Connelly made a move to climb from the bed, but Brick McGovern held him down.

"Be easy! Nobody's swiped your horseshoe," he hurried, "Jimmy found it near the hotel this morning where you must have dropped it. See, the link is all wore out. Jimmy'll keep it safe for you until we get home."

"You're fooling me; Jimmy hasn't got it—it's been swiped."

Moran helped out: "Sure; I've got it. I put it in the hotel safe so nothing would happen to it. Brick seen me pick it up; didn't you, Brick?" McGovern nodded emphatically.

The sick man sank back upon his pillows. "Forgive me, boys, I believe you—only I wouldn't lose that horseshoe for the world. Maybe when you get as old as me, you'll understand what those kind of things mean. Guess you boys got to be heading for the park pretty soon, eh? Well, Jimmy, mind the hops to-day, and make your throws sure; don't worry none if they hug the ground, cause I sure got every pebble—every last pebble, son!"

"So long, Pop," they chorused; "we'll bring you the pennant tomorrow."

Outside, as they hailed a passing taxi, McGovern turned to the shortstop. "Know what the old man's horseshoe looked like?"

"I think so," Moran reflected, "though I'm not sure about the lettering. Some of the boys ought to remember. We'll hunt up a jeweler first thing after the game. The cop never rolled him for it, because his purse was still on him, and, any-way, the watch and chain is worth more than the horseshoe."

McGovern shrugged. His mind was already at work on the afternoon's game the game that would mean possibly the achievement of his ambition: Four pennants in a row. They alighted at the ballpark and hurried through the players' gate.

Exactly three hours and seven minutes later, the Los Angeles ball park was a swirling bedlam of noise and confusion. The great score board in left field showed the Wolves leading in the last half of the ninth seven to six, but the Angels had the bases full and Bert Jackson, pinch hitter, was at the bat with two gone. The decision rested on the next move.

Jimmy Moran, with every nerve at the snapping point, called to the infield: "Play the nearest bag—the nearest bag for a force."

Obeying McGovern's signals, the infielders moved back into the grass so as to make the circle of defense wider. They crouched there quivering as "Tiny" Goodman, his huge frame taking the full wind-up, shot over a high curve, and the runners got under way.

"Crash!" A streak of white gleamed along the infield as the ball shot past third. The crowd erupted in a volcano of yells which as suddenly was blanketed by a dead calm, for no one could understand the puzzling thing that happened.

Moving at the instant the ball was hit, and racing to the right with apparently no chance to make the play, Jimmy Moran saw the sphere encounter an obstacle. The course of the ball was deflected suddenly upward and within reach of the clutching fingers of his bare hand. Without stopping to set himself he tossed the pill underhand to O'Donnell at third, and out of the corner of one eye saw the umpire's hand go up over the right shoulder. The game was over. The pennant was theirs again.

Pebble Pop guessed the news when the nurse entered the room with the final bulletin.

"We won!" he whooped. "We got it!"

"I don't feel a bit like telling you, either," said the nurse with a laugh, "because I'm an Angel fan. The Wolves did win, seven to six."

"Good gosh almighty," yelled Connelly, "and I'll bet Jimmy pulled the trick. It couldn't have been nobody else."

But no one came to acquaint him with the details, so he tossed restlessly all that night, waiting for the morning newspapers. Early in the morning the nurse brought him the first edition and he turned eagerly to the sporting page. A black headline shrieked at him: "Lucky bound costs Angels the pennant. Fluke play by Wolf shortstop robs Jackson of hit."

The smile froze on his lips. His low moan brought the nurse to his side.

"The first paragraph," he said thickly; "read it to me."

She got as far as the fourth line and then noted that Connelly's eyes were closed and his teeth were chattering.

"There," she exclaimed, "I shouldn't have let you see the papers at all." She swept them all up in her arms, and darkened the room.

"Keep perfectly still and I'll get you some medicine. You must go to sleep."

But Pebble Pop was far from being able to sleep. Fate had played him a cruel trick. The Wolves had won, but not with his aid rather in spite of his meddling interference. The one pebble he had overlooked had brought them the pennant. Unwittingly he had done his best to cheat them of victory, and they must all know it.

He would have to resign, or, simpler still, he would just lie where he was and let the end come.

Early in the afternoon he awoke and concluded that he must be dying, for about his bedside he made out Jimmy Moran, Senator Frank Lathrop, "Tiny" Goodman and several others. He could hear Brick McGovern over by the door arguing indignantly.

"What do you fellers think this is, the dining room? Didn't the doc' say we mustn't excite him?"

And then Bert Slagle gruffly: "Who in hell is going to excite him? I got as much right in there as them pitchers, ain't I?"

Apparently, McGovern gave up in disgust, for the entire team edged into the room and stood around the wall, gazing curiously at the invalid.

Pebble Pop told himself that he did not feel as though he was badly off. In fact, he felt disgustingly better. It was all beyond him.

Senator Lathrop advanced to the bed. "Well, how's the champion?" he inquired. "I thought at first that we had only nine men in the line-up, but I found we had to depend after all on the champion ground keeper of the world!"

Connelly shook his head. "Don't kid me, boys," he begged. "I been reading the papers. The old man tried his best to crab the game for you."

The owner of the four-time pennant winners winked jovially at Brick McGovern. Every one grinned appreciatively.

Connelly flinched. "Go on out and leave me alone. 'Taint fair to come here and laugh at me."

But they only grinned the more. Out of a capacious inside pocket Senator Lathrop produced an envelope.

"It's all right, Pop," he said good-naturedly; "let us have our little fun, and don't get excited. We're all going home on the night train. I've arranged for a drawing-room and a nurse. Meantime here's a little memento of the season." He handed the invalid a check, and Pebble Pop noted that it was for five hundred dollars.

"Part of the bonus offered by the Chamber of Commerce if we won the flag," explained Lathrop. "The boys had a meeting this morning and declared you in on it. And here is a three-year contract which the club is anxious for you to sign as soon as you get back home. It provides for an assistant ground keeper who will be under your direction. Go on, Brick, it's your turn."

McGovern colored. He was not used to that sort of thing, but he saw that the ground keeper's dazed eyes were fixed upon him. "Nothing much to say, Pop," he grumbled; "only I was bulling you yesterday when I told you about Jimmy picking up your horseshoe near the hotel."

"He didn't find it?" Connelly was aghast.

"Oh, yes, he found it all right—but not where I said he did. Kick in, Jimmy; tell Pop where you found it."

Moran fumbled in one pocket and produced a jeweler's box. It was small and bore the marks of the most exclusive shop in Los Angeles.

"After I made that play in the ninth," he said, "I went back to see what made that ball bound like that. I figured if it was a pebble, it was the luckiest pebble in the world, and I was going to keep it. Well, I found it, there in the grass, but I ain't going to keep it."

He spread aside the tissue paper that all might see the gold horseshoe, freshly cleaned and polished, shining in his hand.

"Oh, my God!" gasped Pebble Pop, "you don't mean I lost that on the diamond—that wasn't what the ball hit?" His eyes swept them all incredulously and twenty heads nodded at him solemnly.

"So you see, Pop," said Moran gently, "you see who actually won the pennant for us? Did you look on the back?"

Connelly turned the horseshoe over. "Winner of the championship, 1882," he read glibly, and then his tongue failed him.

"Go on," prompted Brick McGovern—"what else right under that?"

But Pebble Pop could only look at them with flooded eyes, for the freshly engraved legend at the bottom of the horseshoe read: "And the Coast League pennant, 1921."

Pennock's Bad Start

Pennock's Bad Start

Paul Gallico

THERE'S NOTHING OUT OF THE ORDINARY ABOUT THIS *NEW YORK DAILY News* account of a late-season game between the Yankees and the Senators by a recent graduate of both the World War I Army and Columbia University named Paul Gallico (1897–1976). Babe Ruth makes an appearance, as does Tom Zachery, whom the Babe would touch for his venerated sixtieth homer some years down the road. Wally Pipp was the first baseman that Lou Gehrig would soon come in for and never come out again. And then there's Herb Pennock, a Hall of Fame pitcher, who agreed to throw his best stuff at Gallico one day so the writer could experience firsthand how almost impossible it is to catch a first-rate major league curve ball—even when you know that it's coming. You want inside baseball? A writer can't get more inside than that.

Over the next decade and change, Gallico found stardom in the press box. When he finally turned in his credentials in the late thirties, he published a glorious series of essays that he collected between covers, titling the book, appropriately, *Farewell to Sport*. It included an entry called "The Feel," one of the most revered of all sporting dissertations. In addition to trying to catch Pennock, he describes what it was like to play golf with Bobby Jones, go toe to toe with Jack Dempsey, swim against Johnny Weissmuller, dive off an Olympic 10-meter tower, ski the Olympic downhill run in Germany, and run a punt back against an Army football team that showed no mercy. Experiencing—and understanding—what that *felt* like, not just what it looked like, made him, he insisted, a better sportswriter. Before there was a George Plimpton, there was Paul Gallico mapping the route.

His post-sporting life was expansive. Gallico went on to write such novels as the beloved *The Snow Goose*, *The Poseidon Adventure*, *Mrs. 'Arris Goes to Paris*, all of which became successful movies, as was his biography of Gehrig, *Pride of the Yankees*, which migrated to the screen, as well, and for which he received an Oscar nomination.

Judging from the first two minutes of play between the Senators and the Yanks at the Stadium yesterday afternoon, the baseball game had all the earmarks of a Washington holiday and an early shower bath for Herb Pennock. The base blows were coming so fast off Herbie's slants it sounded like firecrackers on an old-fashioned Fourth of July. Evans singled to right. Peckinpaugh hit a triple down the right field foul line. Goslin singled to center. Rice singled to center before Judge popped out and Gharrity hit into a double play. Two runs were over the pan before the fans could even get their pencils sharpened.

Of course, the Yankees won eventually, 4 to 3, but here's the remarkable thing about that first inning: No one got excited over it. No pair of white-suited figures in sweaters were seen heading for the bull pen. Miller Huggins didn't even come out of his trench. Ah, the majesty of a twelve-game lead! Two runs to the bad? Ho, hum! Anybody know what time it is?

Not that there weren't prompt measures instituted to get them back. In the first Witt singled and was forced by Dugan. The Babe sent Joe to third with a long single right, whence he scored on Pipp's forceout of the Babe. And thereafter the main part of this yarn belongs to that same Joe Dugan, with an assist for the Babe. They wouldn't let the game go.

In the third, Dugan doubled, and scored on the Babe's second hit, another double to right. And in the fourth, the redoubtable Dugan tripled down the left field foul line and scored on Pipp's single, the Babe drawing a pass. At this juncture, Zachary, the Washington pitcher, was excused. The Babe scored on Meusel's sacrifice fly.

After the first inning, Pennock was practically invincible.

The Significance of .300

The Significance of .300

Tris Speaker

ONE OF THE GREATEST OUTFIELDERS IN BASEBALL HISTORY, TRIS
Speaker (1888–1958), did about anything a ballplayer could during his
twenty-two years of active duty, largely split in half between the Red Sox
and the Indians. His career mark of 792 doubles has never seriously been
threatened, and though he played his last game in 1928, he still holds
the standard for both assists and double plays made by an outfielder.
His lifetime batting average of .345 ranks ninth of all time. Given his
achievements, it's not surprising that his 1919 dip at the plate—his only
sub-.300 season as a regular—would weigh on him enough to weigh
in on it for *Baseball Magazine* just before the start of the 1920 season.
Though he doesn't mention it, perhaps taking on the double duty of
playing and, for the first time, managing may have had something to do
with his slump. No problem. Speaker would roar back in 1920, hitting
.388 and leading his Indians—on the field and from the dugout—to a
seven-game victory over Brooklyn in the World Series.

A .300 average means more to the baseball public than it does to the
player. For the public has set that arbitrary figure as the standard of good
hitting. And yet it has come to be of considerable importance to the
player also. For in the long run his salary is determined by his reputation,
and that reputation is really what the public thinks of him. So you will
find players who are hitting any where near .300 fighting tooth and nail

to boost their average above that mark, fired by the knowledge that, if they succeed, their names will be inscribed with honorable mention in the records.

All ball players dearly love their hits. But the .300 mark means much more to the player than any other except, of course, the honor of leading the league in batting. And it is a great disappointment to the player when he has hit close to .300 to find himself just shy of that mark in the final season's averages.

Such an experience was mine last season. The records credit me with a mark of .296. Two, or at the most three, extra hits at some time during the season would have boosted my average those necessary four points. Now I am frank to confess it probably made little difference to the Cleveland club whether I hit .296 or whether I hit an even .300. But I had hit for .300 or better ten straight years. And, being human, like the rest of the players, I regretted to see my record marred by one season's failure to hit for the required average, all the more since I came so near that mark.

Still my experience was not so disappointing as that of Napoleon Lajoie, who broke into a long series of brilliant batting seasons by a mark of .299. And I suppose it was less of a blow than the solitary season when Ty Cobb failed to lead the league because I got off to a great start and managed to beat him to the finish. All the same, I wish I had been able to hit for those four extra points.

There are more different opinions about batting, among the public and with the players too, than any other department of baseball. No two players hit in exactly the same way, while there are all kinds of theories in the club house and on the diamond about the proper method of standing at the plate, handling the bat, etc.

There is, however, one radical difference between the player's idea of good hitting and the public's idea. When the player meets the ball fair and drives it out straight and true he knows that he is stinging that ball, even if he is unfortunate enough to drive it right at an outfielder or some one robs him of a hit by a shoe-string catch. On the contrary, when he pops up a little fly and it rolls safe because the infielder wasn't playing for it. He knows that he is one lucky guy. But the public judge a batter mainly if not altogether by the number of balls he drives safe, regardless of how they managed to go safe, and give him little or no credit for meeting the ball and hitting it hard long as it failed to go safe.

In a game of average length I would say that the player who drives two balls straight out across the diamond is hitting in good form. Now he may have days when neither of those two drives goes safe. And, on the other hand, there may be days when both of them go safe as well as one or two others that perhaps didn't deserve to go safe. That is the luck of the game and luck is very partial and uncertain.

Sam Crawford, in one of his good seasons, hit over 100 points better than in the previous season. But he always claimed he was as good one year as he was the other. The difference in his mind was this: In the year when he seemingly failed to hit well, he was driving the ball hard, but the fielders were catching him. The next season his hard drives usually fell safe, as well as some others which perhaps were not hit as hard. Sam claimed, and rightly, that when he hit the ball straight hard he was accomplishing all any batter could do. If the fielders caught his drives that was the luck of the game.

Last season I do not think I was particularly lucky, but the main reason why I fell below .300 was because of my poor start. . . . Every batter has slumps and I am no exception. Sometimes slumps are due to the way a batter stands at the plate. Sometimes they are due to the way he holds his bat. In my own case I have found that I was hitting weakly because I was standing at the plate in such a way that I was off balance. Still, even when I discovered this, I found it difficult to remedy my fault. A lot of slumps are due to worry or over anxiety on the part of the batter. In fact, I believe every slump is made worse by over anxiety. If a batter were perfectly cool and collected he would probably work out of a slump naturally in a few days. But the more anxious he is to overcome his slump the harder it seems for him to hit. No doubt there is a psychological reason for this, but I am not a psychologist. I have observed, however, that for batting to be effective, it has to be done naturally. The less thought and exertion a player puts into his batting the more likely he is to hit freely and naturally.

I do not mean to say that the batter doesn't need to use his head at all times and continually study the pitcher. But I do say that the less the batter's mind is occupied with the details of batting the more likely he is to connect with the ball. And besides, in the long run, luck is a matter of averages. A slump is made worse by hard luck, but there are other times that the player is hitting in great luck and getting away with murder. So, very likely, the luck evens up . . .

I trust my work this season will be an improvement over last year's record so far as batting is concerned. But I can take some satisfaction in the thought that I hit considerably over .300 through the later months and that is the time when base hits count the most. For when the race begins to tighten and you get a whiff of the pennant breeze, you would give more for a batter who could consistently maul the horsehide for even .280 than you would for the fellow who hits .400 in May and slumps around .220 in the month of September.

Did Ty Cobb *Really* Hit .400 in 1922?

Did Ty Cobb *Really* Hit .400 in 1922?

John Kieran

HOW ESSENTIAL WAS IT FOR THE *NEW YORK TIMES* TO POACH THE PRO-
digiously popular name, wit, wisdom, and prose of John Kieran (1892–
1981) back to the pages where his career began? Essential enough for the
Great Gray Lady to bestow upon him something never before bestowed
on a *Times* sportswriter: a byline. And a column to go with it. And not
just any column, a new pillar pronouncing "Sports of the Times"—could
it be more authoritative? (That space would later be passed on to Arthur
Daley, then Red Smith, then Dave Anderson, the first three sports col-
umnists to win Pulitzer Prizes.) For Kieran, this was just the ticket; he'd
have the freedom to let his wild curiosity wander the sporting waterfront.

An acknowledged polymath, Kieran was the son of a college president and a public school teacher; he grew up encouraged to know
everything—and he came close. His mind was so encyclopedic, his curiosity so vast, his recall so quick, his modesty so endearing, and his wit
so irresistibly sharp that while still prowling press boxes for the *Times*,
he became a fixture on the long-running *Information, Please!*, the most
popular quiz show on national radio. Yet it was Kieran's embrace of sports
and the outdoors that propelled him, and it was in that sphere that he let
his talents best serve him. After graduating from Fordham—he played
shortstop and captained the baseball team his senior year—he was pulled
toward a variety of vocations, none with much success. An excellent
golfer growing up, he wondered about a career in the game. But how?
"After giving the matter a little thought," he later recalled, "I decided to
be a newspaperman."

And so he became one.

The *Times* hired him as its golf writer in 1915; seven years later Grantland Rice lured him away to the livelier sports department of the *New York Tribune*. It's there that Kieran's wonderful dive into the brouhaha around Ty Cobb, Ban Johnson, and the error that was scored a hit appeared in December 1922. Kieran's return to the *Times* in 1927 turned the page on the way the *Times* would go on to cover baseball in particular and sports in general. He deemed his position "a cushy billet." It gave him the freedom to write what he wanted, and he expanded his brief to champion his personal zeal for ornithology—he went nowhere without his field glasses—and the natural world overall.

Nevertheless, for Kieran, who entered the writer's wing of the Hall of Fame in 1974, baseball was never far from his typewriter—or his affection. As late as 1939, he still delighted in working out—in full uniform—with big-league clubs during spring training.

According to an Associated Press bulletin from Chicago, President Byron Bancroft Johnson of the American League, speaking ex cathedra and clothed in all his regal robes of office, took occasion to bring to public notice the fact that he personally overruled the official scorer for the New York Yankees in a game played at the Polo Grounds on May 15, in order to present Ty Cobb with a much needed hit to put him in the .400 class for the third time of his gay young career.

We must thrust our maiden modesty aside and, with a bit of shabby-genteel side-scraping and bowing, lay claim to the distinction of being the official scorer in question who is thus thrust ignominiously into exterior darkness.

The reasons for our summary ejection into the wintry night of Johnsonian displeasure are quaint and interesting. Nothing quite so logical has appeared in the public prints or behind the footlights since Constable Dogberry conducted his famous cross-examination in "Much Ado About Nothing," ending with the particularly appropriate words: "Oh, that I had been writ down an ass."

The facts in the case are few but distinctly noticeable above the smoke screen that has been deftly thrown around the whole discussion. On May 15 last the Detroit Tigers were busily engaged in thumping the everlasting daylight out of Squire Sam Jones on the local diamond.

Along about the sixth inning Ty Cobb came to bat, with a runner on second base. Cobb hit a grounder to shortstop, which Everett Scott failed to hold, though he got both hands on it.

It had started to drizzle a bit just prior to this inning, and, in company with two baseball scribes—James Harrison, of *The Times*, and George "Monitor" Dailey, of *The World*—we had slipped back from the press box to a sheltered position in the lower stand just back of the home club dugout.

As soon as Scotty let the ball sift through him, exercising our judgment as official scorer, we called the play an error for the Deacon. Our conferees, Messrs. Dailey and Harrison agreed enthusiastically.

As far as we were concerned the incident was closed. In due course, the official score sheet was filed in the sacred archives of the American League office and we never expected to hear of the matter again.

It so happened that the Associated Press correspondent was unable to discover our whereabouts at the moment when the play was made, and he scored it a hit for Ty Cobb, something he had every right in the world to do if he saw fit.

The only difference was that he was scoring for the A.P. and we had the idea that we were drawing a stipend for filing the official verdict.

The scorer for the Associated Press was Fred Lieb, of the Telegram, a veteran writer and thoroughly reliable judge of hits and errors. But Mr. Lieb has been one of the first to recognize that scoring is entirely a matter of personal judgment in cases of this kind and that the verdict of the official scorer should be accepted as a matter of record.

Up until the time the A.P. correspondent had always accepted the ruling of the official scorers of both clubs, and he would have done so in this case had he been aware of the fact that the play had been charged an error to Scott. In fact, more and more it appears to us that outside of the glorious generosity of Ban Johnson, the thing that gave Ty Cobb his .400 record was the fact that we had no raincoat.

If we had owned such a garment we would have braved the storm with Mr. Lieb, the error would have remained an error and some other official scorer might have the pleasure of incurring the wrath of the eminent czar of the American League . . .

When the official statistician checked up the league records he found that Cobb was one hit short of the quota necessary for entrance into the select .400 class. The discrepancy and an "investigation" instituted. The investigation was just as logical as the ultimate decision.

It was announced from Chicago that "eleven scorers were united against the verdict of the official scorer, who alone ruled it an error. The official scorer first ruled it a hit and then changed his mind."

It must have been a delightful investigation. The searchers after basic truth asked one New York writer who had witnessed the play for an expression of opinion.

We have since been informed by James Crusinberry, sports editor of *The Daily News*: "Daniel" of the *Herald*, Colonel Bulger of *The Evening World* and Harry Schumacher of *The Globe* that they agreed with our decision of the play.

But what boots the vain support of these honest gentlemen? Ban Johnson says it looked like a hit to him from Chicago! A hit it is therefore.

Following out this highly original scheme of deciding plays on the diamond, Johnson should require the American League umpires as the Polo Grounds to call the decision in Fenway Park, Boston, the same afternoon . . .

Was Ty Cobb given a hit because we sat back out of the rain, or because he needed a hit to make the .400 grade. Will the gentleman in Chicago kindly inform a palpitant public and an official scorer, whose whole career has probably been ruined beyond repair, just what other changes he made in American League official records?

"The official score was not 'authenticated,'" says Johnson. We have asked veteran writers just what they meant, and no satisfactory answer has yet come to our ears. We thought the official score was authentic, "per se," as the Latin has it. We know better now.

If we only issued the stipend we draw down from the Paying Colonels for the labor of drawing up those supposedly official score sheets—oh, butcher! baker! candlestick maker! return us those shekels so dishonestly earned and wildly squandered—we would take the magnificent sum to Chicago, we would seek out the kindly hearted Mr. Johnson, we would pour the gold into his lap and say, with tears rolling down our cheeks as big as derbies, "Here, Ban, you take it! You are the world's greatest scorer. We have a tough time sitting in a ball park deciding that a hit is a hit and an error an error but you can sit out here in Chicago and see with your own eyes that an error is a hit on the Polo Grounds of New York."

The Giant Career—and More—
of Wee Willie Keeler

The Giant Career—and More—
of Wee Willie Keeler

Frederick G. Lieb

ALL OF US WHO LOVE BASEBALL HAVE FAVORITE BASEBALL WRITERS, AND I confess that Cooperstown enshrine Fred Lieb (1888–1980) is mine in part (a) because of longevity—he wrote his first piece for *Baseball* magazine in 1909 and his last for the *St. Petersburg Times* a month before his death in 1980, and he covered every World Series game from 1911–1958—in part (b) because when I was a kid he was still writing his elegant columns for *The Sporting News* I was given a subscription to when I was eight, and in part (c) because his memoir, *Baseball As I Have Known It*, which has sat on various shelves of mine since the week it was published in 1978, ranks among the game's holy books. He was born in Philadelphia and became, along with Damon Runyon, Grantland Rice, John Kieran, and Paul Gallico, one of the rocks of New York baseball writing from the teens to the mid-thirties, his byline attached, at various times, to the *New York Press*, the *New York Sun*, the *New York Post*, and the *New York Evening Telegram*, where this affectionate appreciation of the great slapper Willie Keeler appeared in March 1920, a decade after Keeler's retirement. It was Lieb who dubbed Yankee Stadium "the House That Ruth Built."

Lieb was a statistics junkie, not surprising given his role as the American League's official scorer for several years. (His infamous scorebook mishap that boosted Ty Cobb over the magical .400 mark in 1922 is taken to task by Kieran in the previous story.) He also embraced the necessity of keeping the game's history—and historical characters—alive in the present to connect baseball's past to whatever future manifested itself tomorrow. In season and off, he carved out column space for pieces that either extolled the virtues of an old player or compared the accomplishments of two or more via the numbers, those numbers supplied by—and credited so in the statistical box that would accompany the text—his good friend Al Munro Elias, cofounder with his brother Walter of what is today the gold-standard guardian of the baseball's magnificent numerical shebang, the Elias Sports Bureau.

The piece on Keeler's early seasons with the Giants and Orioles was one of those. Though only five-foot-four, Keeler filled a big pair of spikes. His .424 average in 1897 is the best ever recorded by a lefty. His record for singles in a season—206—lasted more than a century until Ichiro Suzuki bested it in 2004. Keeler's record for consecutive two hundred–hit seasons at eight would also stand for more than a century until it, too, was broken, again by Ichiro, whose streak ended at ten in 2010. Keeler's forty-five–game hitting streak of 1896 into 1897 was untouched for more than forty years until Joe DiMaggio's fifty-six consecutive games blew past it in 1941; Keeler still commands second position.

Lieb, too, while approached many times, has rarely been surpassed. A savvy investor in a very touchy time, he was able to buy his freedom from the rigors of daily journalism in 1937 and move to St. Petersburg with his wife. Instead of retiring, though, he just started anew, writing ten baseball books and hammering out weekly columns for the *St. Petersburg Times* and *The Sporting News* into the 1970s.

It was on a Jewish holiday that that famous little son of swat, Willie Keeler, first started to hit them "where they ain't" in the big games. "And I figured it always brought me luck," explained Wee Willie some twenty-seven years later.

Willie, a Brooklyn boy, broke in with the Giants under the management of old Pat Powers on September 30, 1892. The Giants were playing the Phillies on the Polo Grounds.

Keeler still occasionally comes up for air. He was sitting in the Polo Grounds press stand late last season when he recalled reminiscences of his first big league game.

"It seems a long, long time since I started out there," said Willie. "I was only twenty then," and I never was big for my age. I guess I looked like a little peewee alongside of fellows like Rusie, Ewing, Roger Connor and Delahanty. Pat Powers put me on third base, and the Phillies thought I was a pretty good laugh. They thought Pat was playing a joke on them."

However, we see from the files that Keeler, despite his size, made a very favorable impression. A New York daily, in its comment of the game, said: "Keeler made his debut as a Giant, and did remarkably well. He is a fast runner and a good fielder. Manager Powers doubtless has a find in him."

If the Phillies regarded little Keeler as a joke, his work that afternoon didn't prove that he was one. He got one hit, scored a run, stole two bases and handled both of his fielding chances without an error. Perhaps when he stole his bases the Phillies couldn't see him, he was so tiny.

It is amusing to look back and note the two famous lead-off men of the Baltimore Orioles, Keeler and McGraw; both were regarded as baseball jokes when they broke into the majors. Both were so tiny that no one would take them seriously, proving conclusively the old saying that the best goods come in small packages.

Keeler, destined to become one of the game's most remarkable batsmen, started his major league career with a famous array of sluggers. On the Phillies were such noted sluggers us Billy Hamilton, Sam Thompson, Ed Delahanty, Roger Connor and Lave Cross, while among Keeler's fellow players on the Giants were such noted sluggers as Mike Tiernan and Buck Ewing. Yet who among these battling stalwarts would have believed that this Brooklyn midget would hang up batting records that would surpass the great marks of Connor, Hamilton, Thompson and Delahanty?

Keeler also saw two of the game's greatest pitchers in his big league debut. Tim Keefe, the former Giant favorite, was the first big league pitcher that Wee Willie tried his wits against. The speed king of his day, Amos Rusie, was in the box for New York. Though the Quaker biffers made only five hits off Rusie against eleven made by the Giants off Keefe, Amos lost the game by a score of 5 to 4.

Keeler replaced Jim Knowles at third base, and he played eight games with the Giants that fall. Wee Willie proved from the outset that he could hit, as he hit safely in seven straight games before he was stopped in the eighth by Jack Stivetts, of Boston. Through that eighth game he had landed 11 hits in 30 times at bat for an average of .367.

Willie scored five runs for the Giants that fall, and by a freak twist of baseball fate he completed his major league career eighteen years later by scoring five runs for the Giants in the season of 1910.

Keeler, who came to the Giants from the Binghamton team, wasn't permitted to stay long in New York. There was a change in ownership of the New York Nationals in the following winter and John Montgomery Ward succeeded Pat Powers as the Giant manager. Keeler broke his ankle early in the 1893 season, and the Giants, sold him to Brooklyn, his hometown, for $800. The Giants believed he was too small and too light for big league use.

Brooklyn didn't keep him, either. He, too, was considered too light to be of any service in the City of Churches, and Willie's next move was out of the big city entirely—to Baltimore. He joined the Orioles in 1894, the year that Ned Hanlon won his first championship with a team which for batting ability, speed, and cunning never had an equal.

Keeler fitted in with that Oriole bunch like a snug glove. Though he played third base when Pat Powers gave him his first chance in New York, his natural position was the outfield, and in Baltimore Keeler, Kelly and Brody became the most famous outfielders in the game.

Keeler hit .367 in his first year in Baltimore, and he didn't go under that figure until 1901. In 1897 he led the National League hitters with the remarkable average of .424. Keeler is the only batsman who ever lived who has made over 200 hits in eight consecutive seasons, from 1894 to 1901 inclusive. Cobb has collected more than 200 hits seven times, but they were scattered over a ten-year period. Burkett got 200 hits six times and Lajoie five. Hans Wagner only bagged 200 hits twice in his long career.

Keeler remained in Baltimore until Hanlon shifted the mainspring of his Oriole club to Brooklyn, where he won pennants in 1899 and 1900. During the American League war Willie jumped to the New York Yankees, remaining with that club until 1909. On his release from that club, his old Baltimore teammate McGraw signed him to a Giant contract in 1910, enabling Keeler to finish his major league career with the same famous club with which he started. In addition to his batting records, Keeler contributed one of the gems of baseball literature when he gave his recipe for hitting. Asked by a reporter how it was he managed to get so many hits, Willie made the historic remark, "Why, I just hit 'em where they ain't."

The Capper

The Capper

Jeff Silverman

Permit this indulgence if you will. I'm choosing to end with one of my own, a piece I wrote for *The New York Times* in 1997, because of the specific connection it makes. Baseball has such a fascinating way of linking past to future and fathers to their sons and daughters, generation by generation, generation *to* generation. It comes mostly through the stories we tell. My father and I shared little beyond the love for the game he instilled in me. He once told me that his greatest wish for me was that I could have witnessed the spectacle of Babe Ruth rounding the bases. Of course, I couldn't. But the link also comes around in more unexpected ways. Take, for instance, a baseball cap . . .

The summer that I turned twelve my father promised to take me to Cooperstown. For a couple of baseball fanatics like us, a hadj to the Hall was an essential pilgrimage. The game had already begun to define our relationship; it tied us together as nothing else ever would.

Four years earlier, in 1958, he took me to Old Timers Day at Yankee Stadium, and when we left, I not only had the memory of my first trip to a major league game; I had the autographs of Ty Cobb, Roger Hornsby, and Joe DiMaggio too. My father, who was born only a few years after the century began, had seen them all play. His stories about them were the stories I grew up on.

In 1961, we went to our first World Series game together—Whitey Ford two-hit the Reds that afternoon—and my father actually caught a foul ball, instantly achieving paternal apotheosis. The next year, just before the arrival of the Cooperstown promise, we were in the stands to watch the Mets play their first game at the Polo Grounds. For nearly the next two decades, until I moved to Los Angeles, the World Series, when it was played in New York, and the Mets' opening day became family traditions for us, signposts along our mutual journey and a significant part of our history.

Still, we never did make it to Cooperstown that summer nor for that matter, any summer after that. From our home on Long Island, it wouldn't have been that long a trip, but summer after summer, year after year, something always seemed to get in the way. Sometimes they were his things; sometimes they were mine. Sometimes they were big things—he didn't drive a car, for starters; or the entire year I spent in Europe after college. Sometimes they were forgettably small. The point is, we could always find *something*—my father at first, me later on—to stand in the way of the journey.

Not that we didn't continue to plan for it. As I grew older and moved West, the subject had a way of filling entire phone conversations. But after the first few failed efforts, I think my father and I both knew that our trip to Cooperstown would never happen. It was our illusion, the beacon on the distant horizon that was comfortably—and comfortingly—always there. When we had nothing else to talk about, which was most of the time, our trip to Cooperstown could fill the silence.

It's funny, but sometimes it's the journeys we *don't* take that ultimately matter most to us. We are haunted by their potential. They are perfect in the way our minds can complete their uncertainty. The car never runs out of gas; there's always room at the inn; the food arrives hot; and you never lose your wallet, take a wrong turn, or get fleeced trying to bring home some memorabilia. The days are invigorating and the nights, restful. There are no lines at the door—ever. Nor are there any disappointments, hurt feelings, or regrets. Because we never go, there don't have to be any.

I have made thousands of these journeys in my imagination over time, and most were terrific fun, gauzy in a dreamlike sort of way. I've dog-sledded through Alaska in midwinter, basked in the warm solitude of my own Pacific island, broken the bank at Monte Carlo, danced the night in a Paris disco, played the Old Course at St. Andrews, and stuffed myself with lobster on the coast of Maine. I've fished the Snake River with my college roommate, trekked New Guinea with an ex-girlfriend, caught Koufax in his prime, joined Hemingway on safari, and proposed to my fiancée through the mists on the Scottish moors.

But the trip not taken to Cooperstown is different. It's more symbolic than any fantasy. Year after year, it grows bigger and more significant— less for what it could be than for what it never would be; a wistfulness slips in between every annual ring. The more it recedes from reality, the more we're left with disappointment, hurt feelings, and regret as its sad souvenirs. What if? What if? But deep in the chambers of our hearts, we know the answer to that; there's a reason we're not taking the trip, and maybe—just maybe—it's for the better.

Once in 1987, Cooperstown felt like a possibility again. My father was turning eighty-two, and I decided to surprise him with a couple of tickets to Opening Day at Shea. I'd flown in from Los Angeles the day before but didn't reveal my gift until the morning. When I showed him the tickets, he seemed instantly younger. Over the course of nine innings—the last we'd ever spend at a ballpark together—my father, a reticent fellow by any definition, was amazingly abrim with stories. When I mentioned that I'd just moved to third base in my weekly ball game, he responded that the hot corner was the most underrepresented position in the Hall of Fame.

Then, unexpectedly, he said the magic words: "You know, while you're here, we should go to Cooperstown."

My heart hopped. This was tender territory.

He said he wanted to pay his respects—not to Ruth, not to Gehrig, not to DiMaggio, not to Mantle—to his boyhood idol, Home Run Baker.

Baker—real name Frank—had been the third baseman for the old Philadelphia Athletics before signing with the Yankees. (Grantland Rice extols his heroics in an earlier chapter.) Just the thought of him opened a long-closed window on my father's past.

The year was 1916. My father had just turned eleven, and his father, a sternly religious tailor from Russia, had no use for games and not much more for my father, the youngest of seven. The family lived in Lower Manhattan; the Polo Grounds, where both the Giants and Yankees played on 155th Street, might as well have been in Utah.

Still, my father worshipped Baker, and on the day his champion was about to make his Yankee debut, my father was resolved to make his, too, even if it meant going to the game—his first major league game—alone. He left for school that morning but never got there. He took the train to the ballpark, snuck under the turnstile—he was always short—and found a seat in the second deck up the third base line, ideal for Baker watching. He remembered how good, on a pre-dynastic team of forgotten shadows, a star of Home Run's stature looked in his new Yankee cap.

Of course, we didn't get to Cooperstown and never talked about going again. When my father died in August 1993—I'm convinced the 1993 Mets contributed to his passing as much as old age and a tired heart—I resolved to complete the journey on my own, face the regret squarely, and forever cross this trip not taken off of my personal cosmic to-do list.

Four days after his funeral, I rented a car and made the drive. I took at least two wrong turns, was greeted by a misplaced hotel reservation, couldn't find a parking space, and waited in line to get into the Hall, which was so crowded I could barely move. My father, who couldn't stand inconvenience, would have been griping at all of this, I thought, and I could feel the tension that would have flowed between us. It had all been much better when the itinerary remained safely locked in our heads.

Still, there were moments. I felt an obvious melancholy staring into the bronze image of Baker on the plaque in the Hall that my father wanted to see and found myself thinking about all the other things we should have done but never did. About an hour later, wandering through the Hall's museum section—I marveled at Ty Cobb's spikes and smiled at the recollection of shaking the hand of the old grump on my first visit to Yankee Stadium—an item in another exhibition case stopped me cold. I felt myself shaking. I was staring at the cap Home Run Baker had worn as a Yankee in 1916, the one he looked so very good under the day my father saw him play on his first trip to the ballpark. The cap was frayed, like our relationship had been, but it had somehow survived, a secular icon filled with personal significance, its loose ends tying a father to his son and salvaging the threads of an unfinished journey.

My father, I know, would have hated the trip. But I suspect seeing that old cap again would have defrayed all the bothers.